THE COMPLETE
GERMAN SHEPHERD DOG

Ch. Bar v. Weiherturchen, the "Bear" dog, one of the all-time great winners of the breed with a record unsurpassed by any living German Shepherd Dog— 12 Bests in Show, 46 Group Firsts, and 107 Bests of Breed. Owned by Barbara and John Schermerhorn, and shown by Denise Kodner.

THE COMPLETE

German Shepherd Dog

by
MILO DENLINGER
ANNE F. PARAMOURE
GERDA M. UMLAUFF

NEW EDITION

Revised with the assistance of
JANE G. BENNETT
Editor, German Shepherd Dog Review

1971—Fourth Printing
HOWELL BOOK HOUSE INC.
845 THIRD AVENUE
NEW YORK, N.Y. 10022

An Appreciation

In this, the Fourth Edition of THE COMPLETE GERMAN SHEPHERD DOG, you will find much that is new—the new American Kennel Club standard approved in 1968, over a hundred added pictures of the most famous German Shepherd Dogs in the 70-year history of the breed, pedigrees of influential lines in America, and considerable updating of the text. For their help in the obtaining of these pictures, we are indebted to many, but most especially to Mrs. Jane G. Bennett and Mr. and Mrs. James A. Cole.

We hope that the book thus better serves a breed that has itself served mankind so well.

—THE PUBLISHERS

Canadian Grand Victor, Am. and Can. Ch. Ulk Wikingerblut, SchH III, A.D., CACIB, R.O.M. (1956–1968), pictured with the fruits of his sensational winning. One of the great Shepherd showmen of all time with an overall record (in U.S. and Canada) of 128 Bests of Breed, 50 Group Firsts and 28 Bests in Show. During his show career, Ulk travelled over 200,000 air miles, and competed in 38 states, always handled by his co-owner, Mary Roberts. He stands as the highest Register of Merit sire of all time with 2,069 R.O.M. points, replacing his sire Troll. Ulk sired 46 champions including a U.S. Grand Victrix, and 9 Best in Show winners. He was owned by Ralph S. and Mary Roberts.

Contents

Depicted in work native to the breed is Int. Ch. Asta v.d. Kaltenweide, SchH, German Siegerin for 1922, 1923, and 1924, and American Grand Victrix for 1926.

1

Character of the German Shepherd Dog

by Jane G. Bennett
Editor, German Shepherd Dog Review

> *"The German Shepherd Dog should possess firmness of nerves, attentiveness, imperturbable nature, watchfulness, loyalty and incorruptibility, in addition to courage, fighting spirit, and aggressiveness when required. These traits make him outstanding as a Working Dog in general, and in particular as a Watch Dog, Guide Dog, Protection Dog, Tracking Dog."*
> —Quoted from the standard of the Deutsches Schäferhunde.

A working dog is one belonging to a breed that is physically and mentally capable of carrying out particular duties. Included in the classification of working dogs are many breeds that are no longer required to perform the functions for which they were intended. The German Shepherd Dog, however, since it was first developed, has continued to serve mankind in many capacities.

Sincere, dedicated breeders—particularly in Germany—have maintained and improved upon the structure of the agile, handy, trotting dog used for herding, and have developed the mental characteristics necessary for stability and trainability. Seventy years of selection, weeding out the dull, the vicious, and the timid, has resulted in a breed of superb intelligence.

German Shepherd Dogs serve in nearly every country of the world, and the breed has become synonymous with intelligence. Unfortunately, we find outside of Germany that many breeders place too little emphasis on what is in the head. Their obsession with beauty leaves some breeders only handsome conformation specimens with "feathers in their heads". Empty-headedness is sad enough, but timidity or viciousness are even worse.

A German Shepherd Dog should be self-confident, poised, eager, alert, and willing to make friends—unless it has been specially trained not to do so. It should *never* be timid, nervous, tail-tucking, looking for spooks in the air, or aggressive without provocation.

Which category does your dog fall into? If the first, you have a good start. If the latter, you have our sympathy, and you should look for a good veterinarian to painlessly dispose of him. A dog with bad temperament is a nuisance and a hazard. When there are so many attractive German Shepherd Dogs available, don't settle for a condition that can only bring trouble and heartache. Recent studies by the United States Health Department have placed dog bites in the millions each year. A shy dog is just as prone to bite as a vicious one, so don't harbor either.

Assuming that you have a dog of acceptable temperament and wish to enjoy his companionship to the utmost, the best investment you can make is to attend an obedience training school. If there is none in your area, then purchase a good book on the subject and at least give your dog the basic training needed to make a good citizen of him. Remember always that the German Shepherd Dog is a family dog, not a kennel dog. He craves and thrives on human companionship, and is willing to learn whatever you offer in training.

The companionship and devotion of a handsome, intelligent, well-trained German Shepherd Dog will bring rewards that are unique in dogdom. Once you have owned a good one, no dog of another breed can supplant him.

Ch. Fels v.d. Rottumbrucke of Dornwald, current all-breed Best in Show winner, pictured in 1968 in Central Park, with the New York skyline behind him. Fels, an import, is owned by Mr. and Mrs. James A. Cole.

11

THE DIAGRAM OF RELATIONSHIP (*from* BUFFON'S "NATURAL HISTORY")

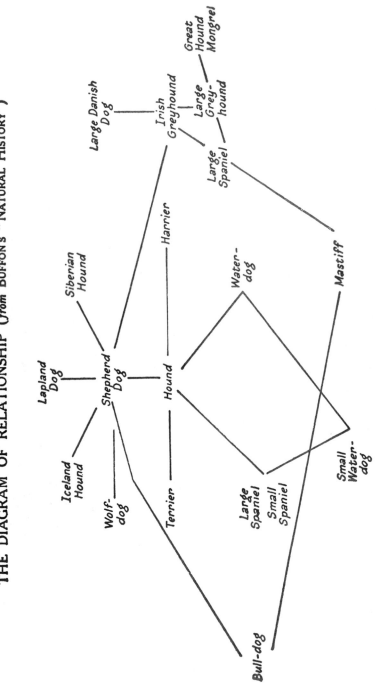

Wolf (Canis Lupus). From a photograph by O. Anschutz, Berlin. Until 1930, the German Shepherd Dog was known as the Alsatian Wolfdog in England. This, coupled with the breed's similarity in coloring and appearance, has led to a belief by some that the Shepherd is descended from the wolf. Actually whatever common ancestry they share would go back to the prehistoric Tomarctus of 15 million years ago. It is more likely that the breed became known to some as a *wolfdog* because as a shepherd in earlier times, he protected man and his sheep flocks from the ravaging of the wolves.

Head of a wolf.

Head of a modern German Shepherd Dog.

14

Wolf, from Poland.

German Shepherd Dog of today.

Captain Max von Stephanitz
"Father of the German Shepherd Dog"

2

Origin and Early History
in Germany

THE German Shepherd Dog is a comparative newcomer to the dog shows of America. To understand this it is necessary to know briefly something about the history of the breed in Germany, the country of its birth.

The shepherds of Germany had used dogs with their flocks time out of mind, but they were dogs of no specific breed and type. In various parts of the country there was some tendency toward empiric uniformity, but it was not marked. In the flat plains of the north a small, fast dog sufficed; in the mountains south, a larger, more substantial dog (probably derived from the same stock as the Rottweiler) was needed. Long dogs, tall dogs, short dogs, low dogs, prick-eared dogs, lop-eared dogs, any kind of dog that would do the work were lumped as shepherd dogs.

Even such soundness as these nondescripts possessed was a fortuitous thing. Unsound dogs, as a lot, were unable to do as much work as a herdsman as sound dogs. Some unsound dogs—cowhocked, or loose shouldered, or soft backed, or bandy legged—

17

worked admirably despite their deformities, and were bred from. Looks counted for nothing at all; the sole criterion was the dog's ability to perform its tasks.

It was late in the nineteenth century that anything whatever was done about developing uniformity and beauty in this heterogeneous congeries of shepherd's dogs. The world was already beginning to grow smaller; communications were faster and easier; no longer did a pocket in the mountains protect men or dogs from outside influences. This movement to combine the dogs of the various parts of the country into a definite breed with a definite type was sporadic and half-hearted, but it was deliberately undertaken to improve the methods of herding sheep.

It led to the formation of the Verein fur Deutsche Schaferhunde SV., which was established in April of 1899 during the Karlsruhe Exhibition. The moving spirits in the organization were Herr Artur Meyer and Rittmeister (cavalry captain) Max von Stephanitz, who was the first president. Stephanitz was an opinionated disciplinarian. However, we cannot but admire the old man's enthusiasm and talents for organization. In a few short years the Verein, absolutely dominated by Stephanitz, through careful selection and in-breeding, had molded the amorphous mass of herding dogs in Germany into the uniform, beautiful, sapient and useful breed we know as the German Shepherd Dog.

Stephanitz was adamant in his demands of utility and intelligence in the breed. In its utility and intelligence, according to him, lay a dog's beauty, and it had no beauty aside from those qualities. The standard was and is designed to describe the kind of dog fittest for herd service; and von Stephanitz saw to it that no German should ever entertain any other ideal for the breed. Any added beauty for beauty's sake was considered by Stephanitz and his followers as beside the point. Of any attribute a dog might possess, Stephanitz's only question was whether it might aid or hinder the dog in his work.

While it retarded the acceptance of the breed in other countries for many years, it was not a disservice to the German Shepherd Dog. This intense concern with fundamentals enabled the breeders to construct their canine work machine just so much more rapidly. Aesthetics, Stephanitz did not concern himself about. Efficiency, efficiency, always efficiency. Having developed an efficient

18

An early type of shepherd dog

machine, Stephanitz later tolerated, however grudgingly, some effort to develop show beauty in the dogs, but he insisted until the end that efficiency should take precedence over mere beauty.

Because the true old-time work of our dogs, service with the flocks, became impossible for the overwhelming majority owing to the tremendous spread of the breed, since opportunities for work with the flocks were lacking, this true Mentor of the breed concluded to open up other fields of work. As transition he introduced during the early years training contests in which the dogs were tested for obedience and activity. From these, important divisions of work developed very early. Herr von Stephanitz pleaded for the use of dogs by the police and other authorities. At first his efforts were opposed and laughed at. But he kept at it unflaggingly, and eventually succeeded in getting various authorities to introduce the use of dogs for police service. When we view the wide use of dogs in service duty today, not only in Germany but throughout the world, we must newly admire the achievement of von Stephanitz. The younger fanciers now take it for granted, but we older fanciers remember well enough the difficult negotiations and struggles that had to be carried on in behalf of the service dog. Because of his

19

Hektor v. Linksrhein, renamed Horand von Grafrath-
SZ-1, the first registered German Shepherd Dog.

Roland v. Starkenburg, SZ-1537, Grand Champion of 1906 and 1907. Virtually
all German Shepherd Dog pedigrees in America today stem from Roland.
He was a grandson of Hektor von Schwaben on his sire's side, and a grandson of Hektor's son, Beowulf, on his dam's side.

20

pioneer work in this field, the Captain—along with other honors—must be regarded as Father of the dog service system.

It was clearly proper that the largest specialty club should also be called to play an authoritative role in the general affairs of dogdom. But, as so frequently happens in life to those whose labor has achieved great success, it was attacked and vilified. Envy and malice played their part here also in rendering the task of Herr von Stephanitz more difficult. But in his case his opponents had caught the wrong man; and while in defense he often struck hard it was not by any chance out of personal vindictiveness but only to further the success of the point of view in which he believed. Here also he won the victory. In the Deutschen Kartell für Hundewesen, of which the SV was among the charter members, Herr von Stephanitz had a decisive influence. His executive ability also bore fruit here. And in the Reichsrerband für das Deutsche Hundewesen he was a valued collaborator whose word carried weight.

There were essentially three strains utilized in the founding of the breed: the Thuringia Strain, the Wurttemburg Strain and the Krone Strain. It is vain at this time to go into the various early dogs and how they were produced. The strains have since become so muddled and mixed up through crossing and recrossing that it is impossible to detect the attributes of any particular one or particular strain of these earlier dogs in the dogs we have today. It serves no purpose here to trace the ancestry of the breed to its earliest exponents, although it is interesting to consider how profound an influence, through inbreedings, a few individuals had upon the breed. Emerging from these early dogs we find a group of dominant dogs, which includes Horand von Grafrath (otherwise known as Hektor von Linksrhein), Dewett Barbarosso, Hektor von Schwaben, Beowulf, Roland von Starkenburg, and Graf Eberhard von Hohen Esp. These dogs are found in the pedigrees of the earlier American dogs. When it is considered how intensely inbred these early dogs were, it is easy to understand their profound influence upon their breed.

Many American pedigrees in particular trace to Roland von Starkenburg, especially through his son Hettle Uckermark, although Roland was himself a son of Hektor von Schwaben, who was by Horand von Grafrath, and was out of a daughter of Beowulf, also by Hektor von Schwaben, the first to attain the status of Sieger.

21

There is a temptation, which must be resisted, to go on and tell something about the famous early German dogs that never came to America and the distinct strains formed by them; especially about the Kriminalpolizei, the Boll, and the exquisite Riedekenburgs, about Horst von Boll, the most bred-to dog of his time; about Tell and Yung Tell von Kriminalpolizei; and most of all about Flora Berkemeyer, foundress of the Riedekenburg Strain, to which we are indebted for the class and beauty of our present-day dogs. Flora was something of a mutation toward the beautiful. Her progeny and their progeny have contributed more than all other members of the breed that delicacy and grace and beauty and sensitiveness that has made the breed acceptable as show dogs and which has made the breed popular outside Germany.

The Verein fur Deutsche Schaferhunde became big business, with more than fifty thousand members and over six hundred branches. It was the largest and best organized association of breeders pertaining to a single breed in the entire world. It kept and published a stud book of the breed and published its semi-monthly Gazette, which was sent to all its members. It held its "Sieger Show," at which the top German Shepherd Dogs—one male and one bitch—were named.

The Verein assumed jurisdiction over breeding and breeding practices, undertook to declare what dogs were fit to breed from and what dogs were unfit, and went so far as to dictate what dogs should be bred to what bitches and to forbid the rearing of more than a stated number of puppies from each litter. It forbade the breeding of bitches before a stated age, and set a maximum age at which a dog could be employed at stud. It was parental in its attitude toward breeders, authoritarian, doctrinal and dictatorial. Verein laws were immutable and inflexible. It was typically German, with its hierarchy of authority, which was not to be gainsaid nor questioned.

The breeders became mere automata to carry out the mandates of the Verein, which they accepted uncritically. In the breed's beginning this concerted action was valuable; it was largely responsible for the rapidity with which a vast number of amorphous dogs were transformed into a uniform breed.

American breeders took seriously the dicta of the Verein, and sought to accept its authority. German "authorities" were invited

Hektor von Schwaben, SZ-13, HGH, Grand Champion 1900 and 1901. Son of Horand v. Grafrath, the Adam of the breed.

Beowulf, SZ-10.

Flora Berkemeyer, founder of the Riedekenburg strain. Her progeny, and their progeny in turn, have contributed more than all others to the grace and beauty that the German Shepherd Dog displays in the rings today.

Hettel Uckermark, SZ–3897, HGH,
German Grand Champion, 1909.

to America to judge and to make "surveys" of the dogs. American breeders hung on to the words of these judges as if they had been chiseled on stone and handed down from Sinai. "Chiseled" was right.

Von Stephanitz wrote an ostensibly learned book, which was translated into English and published in 1923 under the title "The German Shepherd Dog in Word and Picture," and was widely circulated. It was an impressive tome of more than 700 pages and purported to tell all. It was in fact a congeries of valid information and misinformation, outmoded scientific theories, and personal and racial prejudices. It was verbose and turgid as only a German book can be. It is only natural that von Stephanitz should have written about the breed in Germany and under German conditions, but many Americans sought to apply it to American conditions. The book to the critical reader, especially in retrospect, embodies Nazism in microcosm long before Nazism was ever heard of under such a name.

Despite the aging author's good nature and heavy humor, the book was distasteful to many American readers and in the long run did the breed much harm. To Americans *their dogs are but a means to an end, not an end in themselves.* Americans are individualists and do not succumb to authoritarianism. They have no wish to be dictated to; they want to do things in their own way.

This brief German background has been necessary in order to understand the role the German Shepherd Dog has played on the American scene. We may now come to the breed as it has actually appeared on American soil.

Memorial tablet at tomb of Captain von Stephanitz.

25

A memorable picture of two of the all-time German Shepherd Dog greats in competition—at left, Ch. Pfeffer v. Bern, handled by Ernest Loeb, and right, Ch. Odin v. Busecker-Schloss, handled by Sidney F. Heckert, Jr. When Odin and Pfeffer were shown against each other at the German Sieger show in 1937, Pfeffer won. (Pfeffer had already been exported to America the year before, but was brought back to Germany for this Sieger show by owner John Gans. He is the only dog to win Sieger and Grand Victor honors in the same year.) However, in two later confrontations in America, Odin was placed over Pfeffer each time, and was to finish his career undefeated in the breed in this country. The two half brothers (both were sired by Dachs v. Bern) complimented each other in physical attributes, and the famous Long-Worth winning strain was founded on a combination of the blood of these two dogs together with that of the 1936 Sieger, Ch. Arras a.d. Stadt-Velbert. Pfeffer and Odin are pictured again on page 49, and Arras is pictured on page 51.

3

Development of the Breed in America

THE first recorded reference to a German Shepherd Dog in America was when Mira of Dalmore (never registered), property of the Dalmore Kennels of H. A. Dalrymple, of Port Allegheny, Pennsylvania, was exhibited. She was first, open class, at Newcastle, and first, open, Philadelphia. These awards were probably in the Miscellaneous Classes at those shows, for we find the same bitch appearing and winning the Miscellaneous Class at New York in 1907, entered as a Belgium (sic) Sheepdog.

The bitch's real name was Mira von Offingen, imported by Otto H. Gross in 1906, along with two others. How she came to be shown in Dalrymple's name is not known. However, Gross brought her over, and, as nobody in America appeared to be interested in the breed, he eventually took her back to Germany. Her picture indicates a somewhat doggy bitch with very large ears, great bone, and generally of good type.

Mira of Dalmore was never registered in the American Kennel Club Studbook, and probably went neglected and unappreciated.

Nina Dexter, pioneer German Shepherd Dog
breeder in the West, with Ch. Gilda v. Doernhoft
and Ernani v. Graustein.

She was bred from the very best blood of the era, being by Beowulf
out of Hella von Schwaben, sister to Hector von Schwaben. She
was whelped July 12, 1905, and was bred by one P. Stetter.

She was again exhibited in the Miscellaneous Class at New York
in 1908, this time entered as a German Sheepdog. In this class she
had competition within her own breed, another German Sheepdog, know simply as Queen, being exhibited by Adolph Vogt, who
won first in her class, defeating Mira. This Queen was, in all probability, Queen of Switzerland (115006), of largely Krone blood,
the first German Sheepdog to be registered in the Studbook of the
American Kennel Club.

The classification of Mira of Dalmore as a Belgian Sheepdog in the New York show in 1907 is not strange. There appears to have been little distinction between the Belgian and the German Shepherd Dogs at that time in America. As late as 1912 the two breeds were lumped together in some show classifications, although they were kept separate in the studbook. This made little difference since they were exhibited in Miscellaneous Classes.

The year 1912 is noteworthy in the annals of the German Shepherd Dog, since it is the year in which Benjamin H. Throop, of Scranton, Pennsylvania, and Miss Anne Tracy, of Highland Falls-on-Hudson, New York, each registered their first dogs of the breed. These two ardent fanciers are all but forgotten and unknown to the current generation of fanciers of the German Shepherd Dog, but they were the moving spirits in the organization of the German Shepherd Dog Club of America in 1913. There were twenty-six charter members, of which Mrs. C. Halstead Yates was named president; F. Empkin, vice-president; and Benjamin H. Throop, secretary.

The breed was Miss Tracy's premier interest and she was indefatigable in her propagation of the faith in it. She owned one of the first two champions of record in America, Luchs (or Lux), 161964; the other being Herta von Ehrangrund, 163047, property of the Winterview Kennels of L. I. De Winter of Suttenburg, New Jersey, for many years a prominent exhibitor at eastern shows and ardent supporter of the club and of the breed. These championships were made in the same year (1913) and it is impossible to know which takes precedence over the other.

Championships made prior to 1917 mean little in any event, since a show's rating was determined by the entire number of dogs of all breeds exhibited, and a single exhibit received the same number of points as the most numerous breed in the show. Many champions in obscure breeds were made without any competition whatever. Moreover, the judging was, to put the matter mildly, "spotty" until well into the twenties. Few judges knew the standard and what it meant, and they were sadly reluctant to learn. Many of the judges were British or at least Anglophile and scornful of anything of German origin. They gave their prizes to dogs as square as possible and as big as possible. One well-known judge, who is still alive and now an expert on the breed, as late as 1917, went on record in a printed critique as having set a dog back in his class because of his length. Show awards, looked at in a most objective way, were preposterous.

The German Shepherd Dog Club of America staged its first specialty show, at Greenwich, Connecticut, June 11, 1915, with forty dogs benched and four points toward championship. Miss Tracy was the judge, as she was to be the judge of the show of the same club in New York City on November 16 of the following year, when ninety-six dogs were benched. The point rating had been revised and the show carried only four points again, despite the more than doubled entry.

The foremost stud dog of the period was Nero Affolter, property of Mr. Throop's Elmview Kennels. Nero was a tremendous, square, common kind of dog, who won at some shows and went away down in the prize list at others. It was doubtless his size that made him such a favorite. He had little else to recommend him, and his blood, despite his quondam popularity, has been weeded well out of American strains.

The first truly great dog to come to America was Champion Apollo von Hunenstein, 182499, imported by Elmview in 1914. He was whelped February 20, 1912, had become the Austrian and Belgian champion of the year 1913, French and German champion of the year 1914. He easily won his American championship, but was neglected in the stud in favor of Nero Affolter, his kennel mate. He had been mated in Germany before shipment to the greatest of all brood bitches up to that time, Flora Berkemeyer, and was sire of her most successful litter, which included Dorte, Diethelm, Danko, Drusus, and Dulo von Riedeckenburg; and so his merits as a stud dog were not unknown.

Apollo was different from the dogs that had previously come to America, distinctly of the correct and modern type, a long dog of tremendous quality and refinement. He was before his time and failed of appreciation by the American fanciers until it was too late to avail themselves of his services. We can only speculate what a blood foundation he might have laid, if only he had been utilized.

Upon the untimely death of Mr. Throop, about 1923, Apollo passed into the safe keeping of the Joselle Kennels of Peter A. B. Widener of Elkins Park, Pennsylvania, where he was given the best of care until his death. His mounted body went to the Peabody Museum of Yale University, where it may now be seen. Mr. Widener did not undervalue Apollo so much as he overvalued Dolf von Dustenbrook, the German Sieger of 1920, a grandson of Apollo through Dorte von Riedeckenburg. We shall hear more of Widener and Dolf anon.

The Oak Ridge Kennels of Thomas Fortune Ryan came into the picture in 1913, with Oak Ridge Alarich von der Alpenluft, and a host of other dogs. Alarich was a significant dog for his day, but only for his day which was short. The Ryan interest in the breed was even shorter, and his best dogs soon passed to Mr. and Mrs. Halsted Yates. Yates was at the time superintendent of the Ryan Oak Ridge estate. Subsequently Alarich became the property of Mrs. Alvin Untermeyer, who was later to be an important factor in Shepherd Dogs on the West Coast.

It was at about that period that John Gans' Hoheluft Kennels entered the lists, with dogs that were not good enough. He was later to be heard from with some of the greatest German Shepherd Dogs that have ever lived and was active until 1951.

Early in 1917 America intervened in the World War, and all things of German origin suddenly became tabu. Even before the entry of this country into the War, sympathy for the British cause had injured the interests of German breeds of dogs; but after America's entrance into the war, the German Shepherd Dog shared the obloquy of the Dachshund, Beethoven's symphonies, Wagner's operas, Goethe's poetry, Frankfurter sausages, sauerkraut, and hamburger steak.

The official name of the breed, allotted to it by the American Kennel Club, had been the German Sheepdog, although the member club that sponsored the breed was known as the German Shepherd Dog Club of America. In an effort to save the breed from the vengeance of the super-patriots, the American Kennel Club changed its official name to Shepherd Dog, without any reference to its German origin, just as it changed the name of the Dachshund to Badger Dog. The change did little to allay the furor. Nobody was fooled. The sponsoring club was even prevailed upon to drop "German" from its name.

The prejudice against things German abated with the signing of the armistice in 1918. Nobody any longer held the country of its origin against the German Shepherd Dog. American soldiers returned from Europe with incredible tales of the intelligence, beauty, usefulness and wisdom of the dogs that they had seen. Strongheart and Rin-Tin-Tin were starred in the silent pictures. Everybody wanted, and almost everybody had, a German Shepherd Dog. However, it was not until 1931 that the word "German" was restored to the name of the club that sponsored the breed and to the breed itself. The word "shepherd" was retained in the name; it did not revert to German Sheepdog, but became the German Shepherd Dog, as it should have been from the beginning. The breed is one of but five that have the word *dog* in their names.

Fortunately, in the more recent conflict the animosity of Americans was reasonably confined to the German Government, to Hitler, and Nazism. Beethoven's music was not forbidden, and German breeds of dogs did not have to suffer for German behavior. Dachshunds flourished, Boxers grew popular, and German Shepherd Dogs were frankly German. The American mind had grown more mature and did not surrender itself to the racial hysteria that had animated it in the former struggle.

With all the vain effort in America to deny the breed its German birthright, the nomenclature situation in Britain was even worse. There was an equal upsurge of interest in the breed in Britain, where it was first known as the Alsatian Wolfdog. The breed was not Alsatian in its origin, and there is nothing wolf-like about it. The "wolfdog" part of the name was recognized to interfere with its popularity, and was soon discarded. However, the breed is to this day known in Britain as the Alsatian, a misnomer as great as that of the Great Dane, which is not a Danish dog but a German.

The German Shepherd Dog pot was on the fire and was getting pretty hot. Everybody wanted a Shepherd (or Police Dog as it was erroneously called), but only the very rich for the most part could afford one. In the fall of 1920, Peter A. B. Widener II imported Dolf von Dustrenbrook, 289407, to whose name Widener prefixed his kennel name of Joselle. Dolf, whelped April 16, 1918, was by Lucks von Uckermark out of Dorte von Riedeckenburg, a member of Flora Berkemeyer's litter by Apollo von Hunenstein. Dolf had been Sieger (Grand Champion) of Germany for the year 1919, and Grand Champion of Austria 1920. He was a sensation in America, defeating every German Shepherd Dog he ever met, and was many

International Champion Dolf von Durstenbrook, P.H. German
Sieger for 1919 and U.S. Grand Victor, 1923. Owned by
Peter A. B. Widener's Joselle Kennels.

Int. Ch. Hamilton Erich v. Grafenwerth, PH, German Sieger 1920 and U.S.
Grand Champion 1922. An immortal sire. Imported by Hamilton Farms in
1921, and acquired in his later years by Giralda Farms.

times best dog of all breeds in the show. Widener is alleged to have paid $10,000 for Dolf and a bitch known as Joselle's Debora von Weimar, an unheard of price at the time.

The Joselle Kennels at Elkins Park, Pennsylvania, besides Dolf and Apollo von Hunenstein, housed some notable bitches, the greatest of the breed. Dolf was not the success at stud that his record in the show ring might have warranted us to expect.

But he was in competition in the stud with Hamilton Erich von Grafenworth, 323540, which was imported early in 1921, and was owned by the Hamilton Farms Kennels of J. C. Brady, at Gladstone, New Jersey. He was some three months younger than Dolf, having been whelped July 7, 1918. He was by Alex von Westfalenheim out of Bianca von Riedeckenburg, who was by Hettle Uckermark out of Flora Berkemeyer. Erich had been Sieger of Germany for 1920, and was the dog of his time. He had a tremendous show career in America. But more than a mere show dog, here was a stud. The largest part of the fine dogs to come from Germany for years claimed Erich as sire or grandsire. He was utilized in America as his merits deserved, but he was the sire of the largest part of the best dogs that were bred on this side of the ocean. Erich had everything, and transmitted it to his get. He was utterly invaluable.

Along with Erich at Hamilton Farms was the noteworthy bitch Hamilton Anni vom Humboltspark, Siegerin of Germany for two successive years, 1919 and 1920, besides being the Holland female champion for 1919. Hamilton Farms housed many lesser lights, but these two were tops.

Erich and Anni had been brought to America for Hamilton Farms by Otto Gross. Subsequently, Erich was sold to Mrs. M. Hartley Dodge's Giralda Farms, and spent his last years there at Madison, New Jersey.

Then early in 1922 the Hoheluft Kennels of John Gans, of Staten Island, New York, in cooperation with the Rexden-Belcarza Kennels, a partnership of which Reginald M. Cleveland was the leading spirit, brought to America Gerri von Oberklamm, 326000. Gerri had been Grand Champion of Austria, but had missed out on the German Siegership because he was not gun-sure. He was somewhat older than the others, having been whelped August 31, 1917. He was by Arnim von Riedeckenburg, a member of Flora Berkemeyer's litter by Kuno Edelweiss, her first. Gerri's dam was

Ch. Hamilton Anni v. Humboldtpark, Siegerin for 1919 and 1920. Imported by Hamilton Farms.

Alice vom Karlspring, by Billo von Riedeckenburg, from Flora's Hettle Uckermark litter. Thus Gerri was a grandson of Flora on the one side and a great-grandson on the other.

He was a superb dog, of great size, impressive, refined, sensitive, and beautiful. Above all was his ability to move. How that dog could move! It was a joy to watch him cover ground. Like clockwork.

Gerri had been extensively bred from in Germany before his exportation, and he was widely, if not always judiciously, used in America. There was somewhere in his germ-plasm a shy streak, for a good many of his progeny were over-sensitive. He also tended to transmit a good many soft ears. Despite these failings, he was a stud dog par excellence. His progeny as a lot were notably sound and moved magnificently. Gerri chafed at kennel life, and subsequently was sold to Mrs. Elliott Dexter, in whose California home he ruled as the kingpin, regained his spirits, and did the western fancy a vast good.

The fourth of the quartette of great dogs was Cito Bergerslust, 350000, who was born December 28, 1920, was Sieger of Germany for 1922, and was purchased by John Gans late the same year. Cito was a son of Gerri and resembled his sire in many respects, especially in his ability to cover ground. His dam was Goda von Munsdorf, by Alex Westfalenheim out of a daughter of Billo von Riedeckenburg, giving him three crosses of Flora Berkemeyer. Cito was the top dog in America for several years, was bred to extensively, but not so much as his merits warranted.

Dolf, Erich, and Gerri had all been whelped during the War. It is to be remembered that Germany was not devastated, not even invaded, in the First World War, as it was in the Second, but it will ever remain a mystery how the Germans succeeded in turning out these supreme dogs, in addition to others only slightly inferior to them, and many magnificent bitches, in the hurly-burly of a war that was depleting the country's entire economy.

It is even more of a mystery that the Germans should have sold such paragons. In the early twenties inflation was at its height in Germany. One American dollar was worth millions of marks. A few thousand American dollars meant luxury and independence. The buyers were all men of great wealth.

A notable thing about these dogs is that the three older ones were

Int. Grand Champion Gerri von Oberklamm, P.H., Imported to
America by John Gans.

Ch. Cito Bergerslust, SchH, German Sieger 1922 and 1923, U.S.
Grand Victor 1924 and 1925. Imported to America by John Gans.

all grand-progeny of Flora Berkemeyer, and the fourth was the product of three crosses of Flora's blood. Most of the great bitches that came over in the same era and the only slightly inferior dogs were bred along the same lines—Flora Berkemeyer, usually combined with Uckermark blood, particularly with Alex Westfalenheim. Flora is an instance of a bitch (which as compared with a dog is capable of producing only a limited number of progeny) influencing a whole breed for its betterment. It is she and she alone that explains the vast output of fine German dogs in the era referred to.

In the summer of 1921, Bruno Hoffman of the Protection Kennels, White Plains, New York, imported Etzel von Oeringen, 285737, a dog that was to become famous as a motion picture star under the name of Strongheart. During his motion picture career Etzel was the property of Jane Murfin, an actor and writer, and Larry Trimble, who trained the dog for pictures. Etzel had been whelped in Germany, October 1, 1917, and had been completely trained for police service. It was Trimble's job to untrain the dog of his police regimentation, and retrain him for the pictures. The success of the new star was instantaneous and sensational. Everybody wanted a dog just like him, and believed that just any German Shepherd Dog would exhibit feats of sagacity like those of Strongheart in the pictures. He was a good dog without being a great dog, a handsome, upstanding animal, but lacking in the essentials of German Shepherd Dog type. The acting was of course three-fourths Trimble and one-fourth dog. However, the advent of Strongheart gave a greater impetus to the popularity of the breed than any other single event to that time.

Etzel von Oeringen (Strongheart) was a son of Nores von der Kriminalpoletzi, 318118, a dog born March 15, 1915, and sire of some notable but over-rated Shepherds, such as Grimm von der Mainkur, Deborah von Weimar, Dora von Rheinwald, and the 1921 German Grand Champion Harras von der Juch, as well as Strongheart. Nores was a Boll bred dog, without a trace of Flora Berkemeyer. He was not too long, not too well angulated in the shoulder, and the last section of his tail was missing, a hereditary fault seen in many offspring of Nores.

Nonetheless, he was touted as a great sire, and in the summer of 1921 Lawrence H. Armour, Lake Forest, Illinois, imported Nores

Strongheart (Etzel von Oeringen) .

The original Rin Tin Tin.

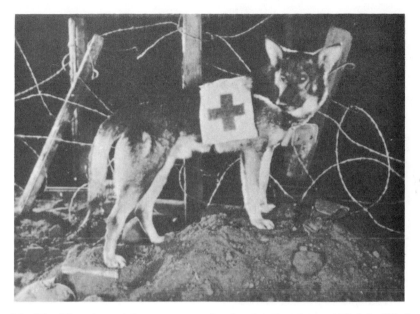

Rin Tin Tin, pictured here as a casualty dog locating the wounded in "Find Your Man," became the most famous of canine movie stars. In all, he made 19 films, and their success is credited with keeping Warner Brothers studios afloat in hard times. One of the writers most frequently employed on his stories was Darryl F. Zanuck, then in his twenties. The basic idea of most of the pictures was to involve "Rinty" in as many human dilemmas as possible. For example, in one he had to choose whether to save his canine lady-friend or the heroine. "Rinty" died in 1932, passing away (according to legend) in the lap of his devoted admirer, Jean Harlow.

Miss Marie J. Leary, pioneer German Shepherd Dog breeder (Cosalta Kennels) with Ch. Armin v. Salon, SchH III, American Tracking degree.

to head his Green Bay Kennels. Everybody wanted a brother to Strongheart, and Nores was much bred to for that reason as well as for his reputation as the sire of winners. He was not a success in the stud in America, however, and is introduced here not because of his significance in the breed but because he was so much used and talked about. Most of his progeny were upright in shoulder, and a percentage of them were short of tail and were a dead loss. The Nores influence is now happily weeded from the breed and we hear no more of him.

Lee Duncan brought back from France after the War a puppy that was to become famous as Rin-Tin-Tin. This dog could not be registered, since he had but one generation of pedigree. He was bred by a Captain Bryant, was whelped January 15, 1919, by "Fritz" out of "Betty." It is said that his dam was captured in the trenches. While he was in training, he was exhibited a few times, but took third in classes of three, and was not a show dog at all. However, under the able and loving tutelage of Duncan, Rin-Tin-Tin became more famous than any show dog has ever been. He developed into a motion picture star of the first magnitude, reinforced and bettered the record Strongheart had made in the pictures. His popularity added to the already well-established popularity of the breed.

In 1923 Miss Marie Leary established her Cosalta Kennels at Greenwich, Connecticut, and exhibited a dog known as Hector, which she had imported from France. The dog as an individual had no significance of his own, but he was the first Cosalta. Little was it dreamed at the time that Miss Leary was establishing what was to become one of the major kennels for the breed in the world. She turned out champion after champion, largely home bred, and continued to breed excellent dogs in great numbers until 1961.

Miss Leary's success was the more remarkable in that her dogs were largely American-bred and that they won despite an obvious judicial preference for imported dogs. There were American bred dogs in abundance, but for their very top awards judges have turned largely to dogs of German origin. The glamor of importation seems to have played a considerable part in this, and it is not to be gainsaid that in the twenties the general run of American-breds were not as good as the foremost of the German dogs. Buying the greatest dogs that Germany could produce, the Ameri-

1946 Grand Victrix in both U.S. and Canada, Ch. Leda v. Liebestraum, R.O.M. Being shown here by breeder-owner, Grant E. Mann, to win under Mrs. M. Hartley Dodge.

Ch. Giralda's Iso v. Doernerhof, SchH, wh. 1922. A prepotent black who contributed strongly to the breed.

Ch. Dewet v.d. Starrenburg, SchH, wh. 1932, a son of German Sieger Odin v. Stolzenfels. Dewet, a Best in Show winner, figures prominently in many top pedigrees. Owned by Giralda Farms.

1925 German Sieger, Ch. Klodo von Boxberg, son of Ch. Erich v. Grafenwerth, an important sire. Owned by William Goldbecker.

cans appear not to have known how best to utilize them. To this rule Miss Leary was a notable exception. She took advantage of the great imported stallions to breed her bitches to them, and consistently produced dogs of a high order.

The same year of 1923 brought to the shows for the first time dogs from the Giralda Farms Kennels of Mrs. M. Hartley Dodge of Madison, New Jersey. Mrs. Dodge's beginnings were made with high class stock, to be sure. However, the Lady of Giralda was soon to be in the very forefront of exhibitors, with such magnificent bitches as the 1926 Siegerin of Germany, Arna aus der Ehrenzelle, the Siegerin of Austria, Pia von Haus Schutting, and Giralda's Teuthilde von Hagenschiess. The first of the truly noteworthy stud dogs at Giralda was Iso von Doernerhof, but he was to be followed by many of the greatest dogs in the world.

Mrs. Dodge is a daughter of the late William Rockefeller, one of the founders of the American Kennel Club. Her tremendous fortune has enabled her to acquire the dogs of her choice, which has been very judicious, and to provide a large number of dogs with accommodations and care such as dogs seldom receive. Mrs. Dodge did not exhibit dogs as extensively as some other kennels. She cared less about show records than about the possession of a magnificent lot of dogs. Her ardent love of dogs and interest in their betterment prompted her in 1927 to establish the great Morris and Essex Dog Show, which was held annually on the polo field of her Giralda Farms estate. It was the largest outdoor dog show in the world, and set a record for the most entries at an American show (5,002 entries in behalf of 4,456 different dogs in 1939) that still stands.

In late 1926 the Maraldene Kennels of Hamden, Connecticut, imported the German Sieger Klodo von Boxberg, 551052, which subsequently went to a Mr. Kane in Chicago. Klodo a comparatively small dog, without any exaggeration of type, would hardly be noticed except by the German Shepherd Dog expert. He was one of those plain and undistinguished dogs, but so superbly constructed that there was little fault to find with him. One of the notable things about him was that he was a son of Erich von Grafenworth, and had been whelped August 20, 1921.

In 1929, the Mardex Kennels imported Utz von Haus Schutting, 707401, whelped March 12, 1926, another German Sieger and son

1929 Sieger, Utz v. Haus Schutting, Z Pr, son of Sieger Klodo v. Boxberg, great-grandsire of both Ch. Pfeffer V. Bern and Ch. Odin v. Busecker-Schloss. Utz was owned by Dexter Hewitt, Mardex Kennels.

of Klodo von Boxberg. He was out of a bitch by Falco von Indetal, another son of Erich from a daughter of Billo von Riedeckenburg. Utz had another cross of Flora Berkemeyer on his dam's side through Diethelm von Riedeckenburg. Utz was a small dog of exceptional excellence, and his Erich blood was to tell in a host of superb progeny.

The German Shepherd Dog had had its day of glory. All through the twenties the domestic production was unable to supply the market for puppies, despite that the breed is very prolific. The Germans recognized a good thing when they saw it and dumped on the American market all kinds of nondescript dogs. People liked to talk about their importations. The fortunate few and discriminating obtained the best the Germans were able to turn out, but hoi polloi assumed that just any dog imported from Germany was a good one. Many were their disillusions.

The demand was satiated. Big dogs were a burden. The cost of their food was considerable. The depression set in and buyers were few. Puppies went begging. Entries in the breed in the dog shows slackened off. All this was deemed to be harmful to the breed, but it turned out to be salutary. It purged the fancy of its triflers. True lovers of German Shepherd Dogs stuck with the breed, but they were on their own. There were few importations. If we were to have good dogs, Americans would have to breed them.

There are two particularly notable exceptions to that statement, however. In the summer of 1936 John Gans imported Sieger Pfeffer von Bern, A-87262, whelped June 20, 1934. He was by Dachs von Bern, a grandson of Utz von Haus Schutting, and his dam was also by a Utz dog. We see how the Erich blood has carried on. Pfeffer just about revolutionized the breed in America. Champion after champion issued from his loins, many of them of such excellence as to stultify the best the Germans ever bred, with the exception of the great four, Dolf, Erich, Gerri and Cito. Pfeffer von Bern sired literally hundreds of champions and winning dogs. The most famous and certainly one of the best of the Pfeffer get was Nox of Ruthland, A-350676, whelped May 16, 1939, bred and exhibited by the Ruthland Kennels, of Scarsdale, New York. Nox in his turn has carried on the line with sons and grandsons and great-grandsons of the highest excellence.

The other noteworthy importation was Odin vom Busecher

48

The immortal Ch. Pfeffer v. Bern, 1937 Sieger, and Grand Victor 1937 and 1938. Owned by John Gans.

The immortal Ch. Odin v. Busecker-Schloss. Owned by Sidney F. Heckert, Jr.

Schloss, A-262642, whelped April 23, 1934, and imported in the fall of 1938 by Mr. and Mrs. Sidney F. Heckert, Jr., of the Villa Marina Kennels at Santa Barbara, California. This was a ten-strike. The dog was extensively exhibited and rather consistently swept all before him. Again is the Erich blood in evidence, since Odin was a half brother to Pfeffer von Bern, being also by Dachs von Bern, a grandson of Utz, whereas the dam of Odin was a grand-daughter of Klodo von Boxberg.

Odin was especially notable for his strength of back and transmission of power. He was a magnificent mover, especially at a rapid trot. Western breeders utilized him extensively with the most excellent results, and many of the wisest breeders of the eastern seaboard sent their best bitches to his court.

To choose among the best get of Odin is not easy, since he was so consistently excellent as a sire. Worthy of mention, however are Tasso of Villa Marina, owned by the Heckerts, bred by Lee Duncan (owner of Rin-Tin-Tin); Boris of San Miguel, bred and owned by the Rancho San Miguel Kennels of the Misses Michler and Brundred, of Chula Vista, California; and Nocturne of Gretta-marc, owned by Mrs. Arthur Schwind of Sherman Oaks, California.

This survey is so brief that it is impossible in it to touch upon, even to name, the hundreds of great breeders and thousands of great dogs we have in America today. The German Shepherd Dog is a breed that does not lend itself readily to mass production, and most of its sponsors confine themselves to work with half a dozen bitches and a dog or two. Most breeders find that by concentrating attention and care upon a few dogs they obtain better results than in raising German Shepherds on a wholesale scale. Few are concerned with the commercial possibilities of the breed. For the most part, German Shepherd breeders are men and women affluent, if not rich. They love and admire the breed for its own worthy sake and do not attempt to commercialize upon it.

Ch. Odin von Busecker-Schloss winning one of the two Group Firsts he scored at America's largest outdoor show, the Morris and Essex fixture held at Mrs. M. Hartley Dodge's estate for many years.

1936 German Sieger, Arras a.d. Stadt-Velbert, ZPr, a force behind many American pedigrees of today. By Eng. Ch. Luchs of Ceara ex Siegerin Stella v. Haus Schutting, Arras was imported to America by Maurice Rose.

Ch. Hero von Aichtal of Giralda, owned by Giralda Farms.

Ch. Armin von Wolfsturm of Giralda, a German import.

Ch. Pixie of Giralda, a Best in Show winner of the '50's.

Ch. Giralda's Gelmar, a Best in Show winner of the '50's.

1968 Grand Victrix, Valtara's Image, owned by Al Engelmann.

4

The German Shepherd Dog
in America Today

by Jane G. Bennett

IN the pages that follow you will find pedigrees of a number of outstanding German Shepherd Dogs of recent years. Many of them are pictured in the book.

These pedigrees provide but a sampling of those that have proven a great influence on the breed. However, it will be recognized that certain kennels have made a particularly lasting impression upon the breed. The contributions of Hoheluft, Giralda, Edgetowne, Benlore, Lahngold, San Miguel, Cosalta, Rocky Reach, Long-Worth, Liebestraum, Grafmar and Dornwald remain especially noteworthy.

Present day kennels do not have as intense a dominance as did these strains. Perhaps it is due to the great influx of imported dogs. We find certain individual dogs credited with breed influence rather than bloodlines of particular kennels. Ease of transporting bitches to top stud dogs has broadened the breed base so that one dog's qualities are no longer confined to a small area. Too, there are many, many small kennels producing far-above-average dogs, and fewer enormous kennel operations. This trend is good for the breed since German Shepherd Dogs flourish best in a family situation.

There are dedicated breeders too numerous to mention, and to attempt to single out certain ones deserving of credit for outstanding accomplishment would be quite a task. The development is too widespread.

As we move now into the Seventies, there is a greater effort to breed more uniformly to type. Exchange of ideas, travel to distant shows and meeting with other breeders, the various projects of the German Shepherd Dog Club of America, Inc. (i.e., the National Futurity Sweepstakes), the increase of regional clubs with their educational programs—all increase knowledge of breed goals.

The end of World War II brought a flood of imported dogs from Germany, but after the first rush American breeders became more selective in their use of these dogs. New blood has erased the American-bred bloodlines in many areas, but intelligent use of dogs resulting from the best efforts of German breeders can be most advantageous. The names of Bill vom Kleistweg, Troll vom Richterbach, Ulk Wikingerblut, Greif von Elfenhain, Bernd von Kallengarten, Klodo Eremitenklause, Condor vom Stoerstrudel, Harry vom Donakai, Axel von Poldihaus, Raps Piastendam, and Cent von Funf Giebeln identify imports whose influence will be felt for many years to come. A marked breed improvement has already been noted from the use of these dogs with the vast number of excellent American-bred bitches.

There is still much to be done in this country to bring the breed to its zenith. Uniformity of type remains a goal to strive for. Temperament in many lines is far from admirable. Properly-angled shoulders are the exception. Teeth faults have happily diminished. Side gaits are better than average, but action coming and going needs improvement.

Much study, and proper attention to breeding partners, can correct a great deal in several generations. So, newcomers, beware of hit-or-miss breeding; having a litter of puppies is hard work, so make the project worthwhile. If your bitch is a healthy, typey German Shepherd Dog, breed her to the best male available. If she is not, have her spayed rather than clutter the dog population with more mediocre to less-than-average specimens.

Three males of the famous Arbywood "F" litter of six champions—
Ch. Fels, Ch. Fortune, and Ch. Field Marshal, C.D. Owned by Mr. and
Mrs. Ronald Woodard.

*The pedigrees appearing on Pages
58 to 89 represent a sampling—
but a choice sampling—of
dominant American bloodlines.*

```
                  Nestor v Wiegerfelsen SchH III MH I
             Immo v Hasenfang SchH III
              Doerte v Hasenfang SchH I
     Axel vd Deininghauserheide SchH III DPH FH
             Gnom v Kalsmuntter SchH III
          Helma v Hildegardsheim SchH III
             Tita vd Starrenburg SchH II
   Ch. Troll v Richterbach SchH III FH ROM
             Claudius v Hain SchH II
         Fels v Vogtlandshof SchH III
             Baerbel v Haus Trippe SchH I
   Lende v Richterbach SchH III
             Lex Preussenblut SchH III FH
         Rosel v Osnabrueckerland SchH I
             Maja v Osnabrueckerland SchH II
ARBYWOOD "F" LITTER
             Nestor v Goldborn SchH II
         Ajax v Stieg-Anger SchH III
             Cora vd Wolfslust
   Ch. Cito vd Herrmannschleuse
             Pirol vd Buchenhohe SchH II
         Hanna v Equord SchH II
             Uda v Maschtor SchH I
   Frigga of Silver Lane ROM
             Ch. Pfeffer v Bern
         Ch. Dex of Parrylin UD
             Ch. Ada of Ruthland
   Ch. Jewel of Judex
             Baron of Chicagoland
         Judith of Blassmor
             Allie of Chicagoland
```

Jewel of Judex, grand-dam of the Arbywood "F" litter of six champions.
Owned by Clarence Alexander.

Frigga of Silverlane, dam of the famous Arbywood "F" litter.

Ch. Lord vom Zenntal, SchH II. Although used but little while at stud in the United States, Lord proved dominant for correct shoulder. He was later sold to Japan.

```
                    Arko v Lenzfried HGH ZPr
            Artus v Wilmstor PH
                    Hilde vd Suhler Schweiz ZPr
        Bar v Oliverforst Sch H II
                    Odin v Busecker-Schloss PH
            Ruma v Hans Schuetting SchH II MH
                    Perla v Hooptal ZPr
CH. LORD v ZENNTAL SchH II
                    Bodo vd Brahmenau ZPr
            Gerbod vd Brahmenau SchH
                    Ruth v Stolzenfels ZPr
        Dora vd Drei Galgen SchH II
                    Etu vd Fuerstensalmburg SchH
            Anita v Hengster SchH
                    Alma Zum Goldenen Apfel SchH
```

```
                Kuno v Al Bobenberg
            Arno vd Bildhauerglide SchH II
                Cilly v Haus Theby
        Cito v Coburger Land SchH II
                Kosak v Holzheimer Eichwald
            Ossy v Schafergrub SchH I
                Centa v Schafergrub
    Arras v Adam-Riesezwinger SchH III FH
                Super vd Buchenhohe
            Ulf im Strudel SchH II
                Xira im Strudel
        Ella ad Eremitenklause SchH I
                Cralo v Haunstetten
            Jlla v Haunstetten SchH III FH
                Lisl v Haunstetten
KLODO aus der EREMITENKLAUSE SchH III ROM
                Claudius v Hain
            Benno v Herbeder Schlob SchH III
                Barbel vd Crengeldanzburg
    Iwo v Johanneshauch SchH I
                Ch. Lord v Zenntal
            Jlse v Sieghaus SchH II
                Burga vd Marienbruecke
        Halla ad Eremitenklause SchH III FH
                Siggo v Corneliushof
            Arno vd Pfaffenau SchH III
                Dora v Haus Stephan
    Freia ad Eremitenklause SchH I
                Craulo v Haunstetten
            Jlla v Haunstetten SchH III FH
                Lisl v Haunstetten
```

Ch. Gwynllan's Jeffrey of Browvale, R.O.M., owned by Gwynllan Kennels.

```
                Sg Dachs v Bern
          Sg Pfeffer v Bern
                Sgn Clara v Bern
      Ch. Vetter of Dornwald
                Gwynllan's Ch. Vetter v Haus Schutting
          Ch. Fritzie of Gwynllan
                Gwynllan's Mira Westfalenstolz
CH. GWYNLLAN'S JEFFREY OF BROWVALE, ROM
                Sg Dachs v Bern
          Sg Pfeffer v Bern
                Sgn Clara v Bern
      Ch. Tempest of Ruthland
                Int. Ch. Ferdl vd Secretainerie
          Ch. Carol of Ruthland
                Devise v Haus Schutting
```

Ch. Merrilea's Vetter of Dornwald, C.D., a son of Pfeffer and a noted winner and sire in his own right, owned by Mr. and Mrs. James A. Cole.

A trio of Dornwald champions—
Vetter, C.D.; Haakon and Heathcliff.

63

Ch. Lido von Johanneshauch, owned by Yorkdom Kennels.

```
                       Baldur v Befreiungsplatz
             Kosak v Holzheimer Eichwald
                       Ria v Holzheimer Eichwald
          Arry v Eilsbrunn
                       Voss vd Starrenburg
             Kudrun vd Natternburg
                       Kuniza vd Natternburg
CH. LIDO v JOHANNESHAUCH
                       Bar v Oliverforst
             Lord v Zenntal
                       Dora vd drei Galgen
          Ise v Sieghaus
                       Ingo v Plastendamm
             Burga vd Marienbrucke
                       Madl v Schafergrub
```

1962 Grand Victor, Ch. Yorkdom's Pak, owned by Mrs. Polly Katz and Ted Yonemoto.

```
                Kosak v Holzheimer Eichwald SchH I
           Arry v Eilsbrunn SchH III
                Kudrun vd Natternburg SchH III
      Ch. Lido v Johannesbauch
                Ch. Lord v Zenntal SchH II
           Ilse v Sieghaus SchH II
                Burga vd Marienbrucke SchH I
1962 GRAND VICTOR -
CH. YORKDOM'S PAK
                Rolf v Osnabruecker Land SchH II
           Caser v Haus Amlung SchH III FH
                Bianka Preussenblut SchH I
      Jutta v Colonia Agrippina
                Cuno vd Kroschburg SchH I
           Asta vd Bisheiligangrotte SchH II
                Bella v Nassauhugel SchH I
```

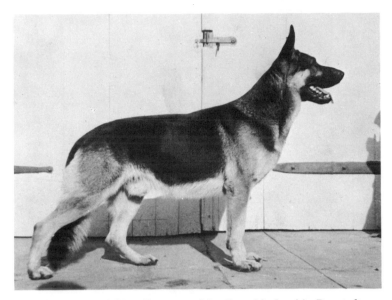

Ch. Hussar of Maur-Ray, owned by Jean MacLatchie Borgstedt, Penllyn Kennels.

```
            Ch. & Sg. Pfeffer v Bern, G.V.'37,'38
        Ch. Nox of Ruthland, G.V.'41,'44
            Carol of Ruthland
    Ch. Viking v Hoheluft
            Ch. & Sg. Pfeffer v Bern, G.V.'37,'38
        Ch. Lady of Ruthland, G.V.'40
            Ch. Frigga v Kannerbackerland, G.V.'36
CH. HUSSAR of MAUR-RAY
            Ch. & Sg. Pfeffer v Bern, G.V. '37,'38
        Ch. Noble of Ruthland,G.V.'42
            Carol of Ruthland
    Ch. Leda of Ireton
            Ch. Brando v Heidelbeerberg
        Donna of Ireton
            Rita of Ireton
```

1953 Grand Victor, Ch. Alert of Mi-Noah's, R.O.M., owned by Noah Bloomer, Mi-Noah's Kennels.

```
            Ch. Arno of San Miguel CDX
        Ch. San Miguel's Ilo of Rocky Reach UD
            Ch. Franza of Rocky Reach CD
    Ch. San Miguel's Baron of Arbor UD
            Ch. Colonel v Haus Hodes CDX
        Afra of Pangamore
            Ch. Christel v Scholarskamp SchH
1953 GRAND VICTOR -
CH. ALERT OF MI-NOAH'S
            Ch. Odin v Busecker-Schloss PH
        Alert of Long-Worth
            Orla v Liebestraum
    Mi-Noah's Ophelia of Long-Worth
            Sgr GV Ch. Pfeffer v Bern Zpr
        Ch. Long-Worth's Ophelia of Greenfair
            Ch. Lucie vd Drei-Kronen
```

67

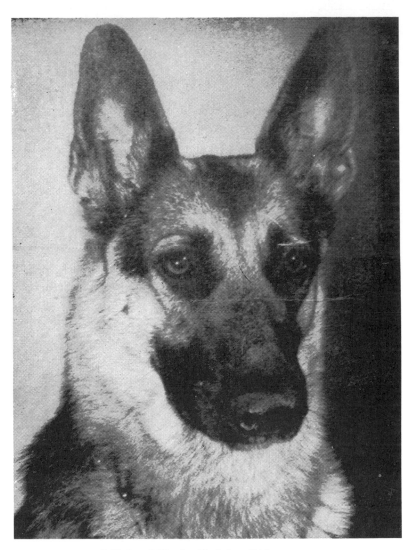

1947 Grand Victrix, Ch. Jola v. Liebestraum,
owned by Liebestraum Kennels.

Ch. Garry of Benlore (1940–1948), credited as sire of 60 champions in the U.S. and Canada. His progeny included two Grand Victrixes, Leda v. Liebestraum and Jola v. Liebestraum. Owned by Mr. and Mrs. George F. Bennett.

```
                    Ch. Odin v Busecker-Schloss PH
              Falko of Benlore
                    Ch. Erna of Benlore
        Ch. Garry of Benlore
                    Eburt of Benlore
              Ardis of Mergenhaus
                    Quip of Garastanna
1947 GRAND VICTRIX -
CH. JOLA v LIEBESTRAUM
                    Ch. Rex v Liebestraum II
              Int. Ch. Orex v Liebestraum
                    Orla v Liebestraum
        Zaida v Liebestraum
                    Norbert of Briarnole
              Delilah v Liebestraum
                    Lameg v Larro
```

```
                    Ch. Pfeffer v Bern ROM
               Ch. Marlo v Hoheluft ROM
               Cita of Shereston
          Ch. Derry of Long-Worth ROM
                    Ch. Garry of Benlore ROM
               Ch. Nyx of Long-Worth ROM
               Elga v Saliba
     Ch. Vol of Long-Worth ROM
               Dachs v Bern
          Ch. Pfeffer v Bern ROM
          Clara v Bern
     Ch. Ophelia of Greenfair ROM
               Dolch v Bern
          Ch. Lucie v Drei-Kronen
          Dagmara v Drei-Kronen

CH. JOLLY ARNO OF EDGETOWNE, C.D.X., ROM
                    Ch. Pfeffer v Bern ROM
               Ch. Marlo v Hoheluft ROM
               Cita of Shereston
          Ch. Derry of Long-Worth ROM
                    Ch. Garry of Benlore ROM
               Ch. Nyx of Long-Worth ROM
               Elga v Saliba
     Ch. Orpha of Edgetowne, Hon.ROM
                    Ch. Arno of San Miguel ROM
               Ch. San Miguel's Ilo of Rocky Reach ROM
               Ch. Franza of Rocky Reach ROM
          Bonita of Gretana
                    Ch. Pfeffer v Bern ROM
               Tatja v Hoheluft
                    Ch. Traute v Bern
```

70

Ch. Jolly Arno of Edgetowne, C.D.X., R.O.M.,
owned by Rocky Reach Kennels.

Ch. Karah v. Kuperhof, R.O.M., by Ch. Jolly Arno of Edgetowne,
C.D.X., R.O.M. ex Ch. Oricka of Rocky Reach, C.D., R.O.M. Owned
by Margaret Pooley, Rocky Reach Kennels.

71

Ch. Bismark v. Graustein, one of the Graustein "B" litter that has been so influential on the West Coast. Owned by Court E. and Cale Cowley.

Ch. Ulla of Rocky Reach II, owned by Court and Cale Cowley.

Ch. Nordraak of Matterhorn, owned by Helen and Harry Polonitza. A tremendous breeding influence on the West Coast. Nordraak was by Ch. Jory of Edgetowne, ex Charm of Dornwald II, whose pedigrees appear on the following two pages.

```
                    Ch. Vol of Long-Worth
        Ch. Jory of Edgetowne
                    Orpha of Edgetowne
    Ch. Nordraak of Matterhorn
                    Ch. Dorn of Dornwald
        Charm of Dornwald
                    Ch. Sappho of Dornwald
GRAUSTEIN "B" LITTER
                    Ch. Vol of Long-Worth
        Ch. Jolly Arno of Edgetowne
                    Ch. Orpha of Edgetowne
    Ch. Ulla of Rocky Reach
                    Ch. Baron of Rocky Reach
        Ch. Moritza of Rocky Reach
                    Riva of Rocky Reach
```

73

```
                    Ch. Pfeffer v Bern ROM
             Ch. Marlo v Hoheluft ROM
             Cita of Shereston
      Ch. Derry of Long-Worth ROM
                    Ch. Garry of Benlore ROM
             Ch. Nyx of Long-Worth ROM
             Elga v Saliba
   Ch. Vol of Long-Worth ROM
                    Dachs v Bern
             Ch. Pfeffer v Bern ROM
             Clara v Bern
      Ch. Ophelia of Greenfair ROM
                    Dolch v Bern
             Ch. Lucie v Drei-Kronen
             Dagmara v Drei-Kronen
Ch. Jory of Edgetowne ROM
                    Ch. Pfeffer v Bern ROM
             Ch. Marlo v Hoheluft ROM
             Cita of Shereston
      Ch. Derry of Long-Worth ROM
                    Ch. Garry of Benlore ROM
             Ch. Nyx of Long-Worth ROM
             Elgo v Saliba
   Ch. Orpha of Edgetowne Hon ROM
                    Ch. Arno of San Miguel ROM
             Ch. San Miguel's Illo of Rocky Reach ROM
             Ch. Franza of Rocky Reach ROM
      Bonita of Gretana
                    Ch. Pfeffer v Bern ROM
             Tatja v Hoheluft
                    Ch. Traute v Bern
```

74

```
                Ch. Burt of Garastana
        Ch. Peter of Garastana
                Ch. Asta vd Sonnenbild
     Ch. Star v Grafmar
                Ch. Golf v Hooptal
         Una of Bar-Orch
         Klodo v Bar-Orch
  Ch. Dorn of Dornwald
                Harras v Maraldene
         Ch. Klodo of Stone ·Home
         Kobrun v Bar-Orch
     Merrilea's Sally of Dornwald
                Ch. Utz v Haus Schuetting
         Sally Cita of Mardex
         Cita v Wiefdorf
Charm of Dornwald II
                Luchs of Ceora
         Ch. Arras ad Stadt-Velbert
         Stella v Haus Schuetting
     Ch. Conde del Llano Estacado
                Ch. Pfeffer v Bern ROM
         Ch. Hella of Dornwald
         Klodette v Bar-Orch
  Ch. Sappho of Dornwald Hon ROM
                Harras v Maraldene
         Ch. Klodo of Stone Home
         Kobrun v Bar-Orch
     Ch. Eroica of Dornwald ROM
                Ch. Arras ad Stadt-Velbert
         Stella v Saliba
         Mitzie v Saliba
```

Ch. Sappho of Dornwald, R.O.M., owned by Mr. and Mrs. James A. Cole, Dornwald Kennels. Sappho was grand-dam of Ch. Nordraak of Matterhorn.

Sarise of Cosalta, a typical Cosalta bitch out of an Ace daughter.

Immo v Hasenfang SchH III
Axel vd Deininghauserheide SchH III DPH FH
Helma v Hildegardsheim SchH III
Ch. Troll v Richterbach SchH III FH ROM
Fels v Vogtlandshof SchH III
Lende v Richterbach SchH III
Rosel v Osnabrueckerland SchH III
CH. ULK WIKINGERBLUT SchH III A.D. ROM
Drusus zu den Sieben-Faulen SchH III
Ch. Amor v Haus Hoheide SchH III
Christel v Fredeholz SchH II
Natja Wikingerblut SchH II
Rolf v Osnabrueckerland SchH III FH
Moni v Stuveschacht SchH I
Quote v Stuveschacht SchH I

Ch. Vox Wikingerblut, R.O.M., Best in Show winner. Vox's eight champion progeny includes five from one litter, two of which are Best in Show winners. Dam of the litter was Ch. Val-Koa's Kellee, a Best in Show daughter of Ulk. Owned by Ralph S. and Mary Roberts.

```
                    Ch. Pfeffer v Bern
            Pfeffer v Saliba
                    Katie Utz Coblentz
        Pfeffer v Karinhof
                    Ch. Dewett vd Starrenburg
            Elfe v Irmendorf
                    Debora v Irmendorf
    Erich of Bar-Orch
                    Ziggy v Bar-Orch
            Jiggs v Bar-Orch
                    Flodo v Bar-Orch
        Tippie v Bar-Orch
                    Neeko v Bar-Orch
            Vilma v Bar-Orch
                    Rinty v Bar-Orch
CH. COSALTA'S ACE OF WYLIEWOOD, C.D., R.O.M.
                    Sieger Erich v Glockenbrinck
            Ch. Bodo v Siekerfeld
                    Irma v Meerestern
        Ch. Giralda's Denis, C.D.
                    Ch. Chlodo v Gubinnenhort
            Giralda's Zaida
                    Giralda's Now Then
    Anne of Nelgerstan
                    Ch. Dewett vd Starrenburg
            Ch. Giralda's Falko, C.D.
                    Ch. Dora of Shereston
        Frenda of Shereston
                    Ch. Pfeffer v Bern
            Abigail II of Shereston
                    Megan of Shereston
```

Ch. Cosalta's Ace of Wyliewood, C.D.X., R.O.M., an important breeding influence in the East. Owned by Marie J. Leary.

Four generations of San Miguel champions with obedience degrees. From left to right: Ch. Arno of San Miguel, C.D.X.; Arno's son, Ch. San Miguel's Ilo of Rocky Reach, C.D.X.; Ilo's son, Ch. San Miguel's Baron of Afbor, C.D.; and Baron's son, Ch. San Miguel's Kip of Rocky Reach, C.D.

```
                    Ch. Chlodulf v Pelztierhof P.H.Zpr Sch H
           Ch. Arno of San Miguel CDX
           Ch. Ramona of Cosalta
    Ch. San Miguel's Ilo of Rocky Reach, UD
           Ch. Odin v Busecker-Schloss P.H.
           Ch. Franza of Rocky Reach CD
           Davida of Rocky Reach
CH. SAN MIGUEL'S CHULA OF AFBOR CD
           Tillar v Haus Hodes
           Ch. Colonel v Haus Hodes
           Blackie v Berge
    Afra of Pangamor
           Dux v Haus Schutting
           Ch. Christel v Scholerskamp SchH
           Elsa Drei Eicheln
```

80

Ch. Franza of Rocky Reach, owned by Margaret Pooley.

```
                    Edi a.d. Leineweberhofe P.H. SchH
           Ch. Chlodulf v Pelztierhof PH Zpr SchH
                    Bella vd Lohruggehohe SchH
       Ch. Arno of San Miguel CDX
                    Derek of Cosalta
            Ch. Ramona of Cosalta
                    Ch. Sheila of Cosalta
CH. OREX OF ROCKY REACH CD
                    Ch. Alex Friedrichsruhe
            Burschl v Stroheim
                    Nazi Fortunate Fields
       Ch. Rock Burr v Schwabenland
                    Ch. Geier v Blasienberg
            Hedwig v Schwabenland
                    Lore v Schaeferheim
```

Ch. San Miguel's Imp of Rocky Reach, U.D., owned by Margaret Pooley.

Ch. Lass of Seamair, C.D.X., owned by Rocky Reach Kennels.

```
                    Ch. Burt of Garastana
              Ch. Peter of Garastana
                    Ch. Asta vd Sonnenbild
         Ch. Cito v Grafmar
                 Billo v Grafmar
              Velva v Grafmar
                 Grafmar's Alto of Merrilea
      Ch. Baron of Rocky Reach
                    Ch. Arno of San Miguel ROM
              Ch. San Miguel's Imp of Rocky Reach ROM
                 Ch. Franza of Rocky Reach ROM
         Ch. Lass of Seamair
                    Ch. Odin v Busecker Schloss ROM
              Ch. Autumn of Seamair ROM
                 Ch. Thora v Liebestraum
CII. MORITZA OF ROCKY REACH ROM
                    Ch. Nox of Glenmor
              Ch. Cotswold of Cosalta
                 Loraine of Cosalta
         San Miguel's Lar of Rocky Reach
                    Ch. Alex v Friedrichsruhe
              Davida of Rocky Reach
                 Pert and Saucy of Rocky Reach
      Riva of Rocky Reach
                    Ch. Chlodulf v Pelztierhof ROM
              Ch. Arno of San Miguel ROM
                 Ch. Ramona of Cosalta
         Ch. San Miguel's Iva of Rocky Reach
                    Ch. Odin v Busecker Schloss ROM
              Ch. Franza of Rocky Reach ROM
                 Davida of Rocky Reach
```

Ch. Bernd vom Kallengarten, an important influence for good in the breed.
Owned by Ernest Loeb.

```
                    Immo v Hassenfang
             Axel vd Deininghauserheide
                  Helma v Hildegardsheim
         Watzer v Bad Melle
                  Rolf v Osnabrueckerland
             Imme v Bad Melle
                  Betty v Haus Herberhold
CH. BERND v KALLENGARTEN ROM
                  Iran vd Buchenhohe
             Kuno v Jungfernsprung
                  Bella v Haus Weinberg
         Carin vd Rassweilermuhle
                  Lesko aus Kattenstroth
             Cora vd Silverweide
                  Bioka vd Silverweide
```

84

1959 Grand Victor, Ch. Red Rock's Gino, C.D., R.O.M. Owned by
Nether-Lair Kennels.

```
                    Ch. Vol of Long-Worth ROM
            Ch. Jolly Arno of Edgetowne Cdx ROM
                    Ch. Orpha of Edgetowne ROM
        Ch. Edenvale's Nikki CD Hon ROM
                    Ch. Marlo v Hoheluft ROM
            Lois of Edgetowne
                    Donna of Edgetowne
1959 GRAND VICTOR -
CH. RED ROCK'S GINO CD ROM
                    GV Ch. Valiant of Draham CD
            Ch. Keenland of Grafmar UDT
                    Donna v Grafmar UDT
        Kay of Ayron
                    GV Ch. Nox of Ruthland
            Nikki of Browvale
                    Ch. Vicki v Hoheluft
```

```
                    Baldur v Befreiungsplatz
              Arry vd Gassenquelle
                    Claudia v Marquardstein
        Grimm vd Fahrmuhle
                    Udo v Langerkamp
              Fella vd Fahrmuhle
                    Helma v Orlastrand
    Ch. Atlas v Elfenhain
                    Lex Preussenblut
              Rolf v Osnabrueckerland
                    Maja v Osnabrueckerland
        Lexa v Osnabrueckerland
                    Racker v Osnabrueckerland
              Vena v Osnabrueckerland
                    Blanka Portunastol
CH. HESSIAN'S BALDUR, R.O.M.
                    Baldur v Befreiungsplatz
              Pirol vd Buchenhohne
                    Carmen vd Buchenhohne
        Ch. Quell v Fredeholz, R.O.M.
                    Faust v Busecker-Schloss
              Nixie v Fredeholz
                    Festa v Fredeholz
    Ch. Kern Delta's Exakta, R.O.M.
                    Ch. Baron of Afbor, R.O.M.
              G.V. Ch. Alert of Mi-Noah's, R.O.M.
                    Ophelia of Long-Worth
        Ch. Gale of Stevens Rancho, R.O.M.
                    Ch. York of San Miguel
              Ch. Storm of Stevens Rancho
                    W.N.W.'s Pogie Bait
```

Ch. Hessian's Baldur, R.O.M. Select 1963.
Owned by Art and Helen Hess.

1964 Canadian Grand Victor, Am. & Can. Ch. Hessian's Caribe.

1963 Grand Victrix (U.S.), Ch. Hessian's Vogue, R.O.M.
Bred and owned by Helen Hess.

```
                Immo v Hassenfang
           Axel vd Deininghauserheide
               Helma v Vogtlandshof
      G.V. Ch. Troll v Richterbach, ROM
               Fels v. Vogtlandshof
           Lende v Richterbach
               Rosel v Osnabrueckerland
   Ch. Kurt v Bid-Scono
               Utz vd Schwbenheimat
           Arno v Beerbach
               Katja v Leihenfeld
       Bella vd Wagnersgruben
               Hussan v Sanriterstift
           Cita v Tauenwalde
               Tilla vd Katenburg
1963 GRAND VICTRIX -
CH. HESSIAN'S VOGUE, R.O.M.
               Ch. San Miguel's Ilo of Rocky Reach,ROM
           Ch. Baron of Afbor, ROM
               Afra of Pangamor
      G.V. Ch. Alert of Mi-Noah's, ROM
               Alert of Long-Worth
           Ophelia of Long-Worth
               Ophelia of Greenfair, ROM
       Hessian's Quella, ROM
               Pirol vd Buchenhohne
           Ch. Quell v. Fredeholz, ROM
               Nixie v Fredeholz
   Ch. Kern Delta's Exakta, ROM
               G.V. Ch. Alert of Mi-Noah's, ROM
           Ch. Gale of Stevens Rancho, ROM
               Ch. Storm of Stevens Rancho
```

89

1957 U.S. Grand Victor, 1956 Holland Grand Victor, Ch. Troll vom Richter-bach, SchH III, F.H., R.O.M., a sire of tremendous impact upon the breed. Owned by Irving Appelbaum. Troll is pictured with the world-famous Von Stephanitz trophy (at left), awarded to the Best of Breed and Best of Opposite Sex at the annual specialty of the German Shepherd Dog Club of America.

5

The Grand Victors
and Grand Victrixes-U.S.A.

Note: The title "Grand Victor" is bestowed upon the male winning Best of Breed or Best of Opposite Sex at the annual Specialty Show of the German Shepherd Dog Club of America, and the title "Grand Victrix" is given to the bitch winning Best of Breed or Best of Opposite Sex. In early years, until 1925, the winners were called "Grand Champion."

No awards were made in 1932 because the judge (brought over from Germany for the show) felt that there was neither a dog or bitch that was worthy of the title. Again in 1936, a judge from Germany felt that there was no male worthy of the "Grand Victor" designation, but did select a Grand Victrix.

Because a date could not be agreed upon with the American Kennel Club, there was no Specialty Show in 1964, and hence no awards for that year.

1939 Grand Victor, Ch. Hugo of Cosalta, C.D., owned by Marie J. Leary.

1942 Grand Victor, Ch. Noble of Ruthland, a Ch. Pfeffer v. Bern son.
Owned by Henry J. Daube.

GRAND VICTORS

1918   Komet v. Hoheluft
1919   Appollo v. Huenenstein
1920   Rex Buckel
1921   Grimm v. d. Mainkur, PH
1922   Erich v. Grafenwerth, PH
1923   Dolf v. Duesternbrook, PH
1924   Cito Bergerslust, SchH
1925   Cito Bergerslust, SchH
1926   Donar v. Overstolzen, SchH
1927   Arko v. Sadowaberg, SchH
1928   Arko v. Sadowaberg, SchH
1929   Arko v. Sadowaberg, SchH
1930   Bimbo v. Stolzenfels
1931   Arko v. Sadowaberg, SchH
1932   Not Awarded
1933   Golf v. Hooptal
1934   Erekind of Shereston
1935   Nox of Glenmar
1936   Not awarded
1937   Pfeffer v. Bern, ZPrMH
1938   Pfeffer v. Bern, ZPrMH
1939   Hugo of Cosalta, C.D.
1940   Cotswold of Cosalta, C.D.
1941   Nox of Ruthland
1942   Noble of Ruthland
1943   Major of Northmere
1944   Nox of Ruthland
1945   Adam of Veralda
1946   Dex of Talladega, C.D.
1947   Dorian v. Beckgold
1948   Valiant of Draham, C.D.
1949   Kirk of San Miguel
1950   Kirk of San Miguel
1951   Jory of Edgetowne, C.D.
1952   Ingo Wunschelrute
1953   Alert of Mi-Noah's
1954   Brando v. Aichtal

1955 Rasant v. Holzheimer Eichwald
1956 Bill v. Kliestweg
1957 Troll v. Richterbach, SchH III
1958 Yasko v. Zenntal, SchH III
1959 Red Rocks Gino, C.D.
1960 Axel v. d. Poldihaus
1961 Lido v. Mellerland
1962 Yorkdom's Pak
1963 Condor v. Stoerstrudel
1964 No Competition
1965 Brix v. d. Grafenkrone, SchH III
1966 Yoncalla's Mike
1967 Lance of Fran-Jo
1968 Yoncalla's Mike
1969 Arno v.d. Kurpfalzhalle

1948 Grand Victor, Int. Ch. Valiant of Draham, C.D.,
owned by David McCahill.

1947 Grand Victor, Ch. Dorian von Beckgold,
bred and owned by William Goldbecker.

1955 Grand Victor, Ch. Rasant vom Holzheimer Eichwald, SchH II, owned
by Frank S. Kupfer.

95

1951 Grand Victor, Ch. Jory of Edgetowne, C.D., a very important influence on today's bloodlines (see pedigree, p. 74). Owned by Mrs. Betty Ford.

1954 Grand Victor, Ch. Brando vom Aichtal, owned by Mrs. Marion McDermott, Sarego Kennels.

1960 Grand Victor, Axel v.d. Poldihaus, owned by Otto Meier.

1963 Grand Victor, Ch. Condor vom Stoerstrudel, R.O.M., owned by T. L. Bennett and Fred Becker, Jr. Handled by Lamar Kunz.

97

1952 Grand Victor, Ch. Ingo Wunschelrute, owned by
Mrs. Margrit V. Fischer.

1961 Grand Victor, Ch. Lido v. Mellerland, owned by Ernest Loeb and
Neil Geltzeiler.

1965 Grand Victor, Brix v.d. Grafenkrone, SchH III.

1961 Grand Victrix Nanhall's Donna shown in win at Wolverine Specialty under judge Lloyd C. Brackett (of Long-Worth Kennels fame). Handler, T. Hall Keyes III.

1952 Grand Victrix, Ch. Afra von Heilholtkamp. With kennelmate Ch. Ingo Wunschelrute winning Grand Victor the same year, Afra's win meant a sweep for owner, Mrs. Margrit Fischer.

1955 Grand Victrix, Ch. Solo Nina of Rushagen, C.D., owned by Mr. and Mrs. Harvey Arnold.

GRAND VICTRIXES

1918	Lotte v. Edelweiss
1919	Vanhall's Herta
1920	Boda v. d. Fuerstenburg
1921	Dora v. Rehinwald
1922	Debora v. Weimar
1923	Boda v. d. Fuerstenburg
1924	Irma v. Doernerhof, SchH
1925	Irma v. Doernerhof, SchH
1926	Asta v. d. Kaltenweide, SchH
1927	Inky of Willowgate
1928	Erich's Merceda of Shereston
1929	Katja v. Blaisenberg, ZPr
1930	Christel v. Stimmberg, PH
1931	Gisa v. Koenigsbruch
1932	Not Awarded
1933	Dora of Shereston
1934	Dora of Shereston
1935	Nanka v. Schwyn
1936	Frigga v. Kannenbaeckerland
1937	Perchta v. Bern
1938	Giralda's Geisha
1939	Thora v. Bern of Giralda
1940	Lady of Ruthland
1941	Hexe of Rotundina
1942	Bella v. Haus Hagen
1943	Bella v. Haus Hagen
1944	Frigga v. Hoheluft
1945	Olga of Ruthland
1946	Leda v. Leibestraum
1947	Jola v. Leibestraum
1948	Duchess of Browvale
1949	Doris v. Votlandshof
1950	Yola of Long-Worth
1951	Tawnee v. Leibestraum
1952	Afra v. Heilholtkamp
1953	Ulla of San Miguel
1954	Jem of Penllyn

1955   Solo Nina of Rushagen
1956   Kobeil's Barda
1957   Jeff-Lynne's Bella
1958   Tan-Zar Desiree
1959   Alice v. d. Guten Fee, SchH I
1960   Robin of Kingscroft
1961   Nanhall's Donna
1962   Bonnie Bergere of Ken-Rose
1963   Hessian's Vogue
1964   No Competition
1965   Marsa's Velvet of Malabar
1966   Hanarob's Touche
1967   Hanarob's Touche
1968   Valtara's Image
1969   DeCloudt's Heidi

Beginning in 1968, the German Shepherd Dog Club of America established a designation to honor the dog achieving the highest combined score in Obedience each year. If the winner is a male, he will be called OBEDIENCE VICTOR and if it is a female, the title will be OBEDIENCE VICTRIX. In the inaugural year, Heidi von Zook, U.D.T., owned-trained-handled by Ron Roberts, became the first OBEDIENCE VICTRIX.

1944 Grand Victrix, Ch. Frigga v. Hoheluft, owned by Bernard Daku.

1962 Grand Victrix, Ch. Bonnie Bergere of Ken-Rose, C.D., R.O.M., dam of the 1961 Grand Victrix, Ch. Nanhalls Donna. Owned by Nanhall Kennels and W. P. Sanders.

1961 Grand Victrix, Ch. Nanhalls Donna (at 17 months). Owned by Nanhall Kennels and W. P. Sanders.

1946 Grand Victrix Ch. Leda v. Liebestraum.

1957 Grand Victrix, Ch. Jeff-Lynne's Bella, owned by Mr. and Mrs. Robert O'Donnell.

1948 Grand Victrix, Ch. Duchess of Browvale,
owned by Mr. and Mrs. Gus Schindler.

1951 Grand Victrix, Ch. Tawnee v. Liebestraum, owned by Grant Mann.

Grand Victor 1949 and 1950, Ch. Kirk of San Miguel, owned by Marie J. Leary.

Official Breed Standard
of the German Shepherd Dog

Submitted by the German Shepherd Dog Club of America, and approved by the American Kennel Club, April 9, 1968.

General Appearance—The first impression of a good German Shepherd Dog is that of a strong, agile, well-muscled animal, alert and full of life. It is well balanced, with harmonious development of the forequarter and hindquarter. The dog is longer than tall, deep-bodied, and presents an outline of smooth curves rather than angles. It looks substantial and not spindly, giving the impression, both at rest and in motion, of muscular fitness and nimbleness without any look of clumsiness or soft living. The ideal dog is stamped with a look of quality and nobility—difficult to define, but unmistakable when present. Secondary sex characteristics are strongly marked, and every animal gives a definite impression of masculinity or femininity, according to its sex.

Character—The breed has a distinct personality marked by direct and fearless, but not hostile, expression, self-confidence and a certain aloofness that does not lend itself to immediate and indiscriminate friendships. The dog must be approachable, quietly standing its ground and showing confidence and willingness to meet overtures without itself making them. It is poised, but when the occasion demands, eager and alert; both fit and willing to serve in its capacity as companion, watchdog, blind leader, herding dog, or guardian, whichever the circumstances may demand. The dog must not be timid, shrinking behind its master or handler; it should not be nervous, looking about or upward with anxious expression or showing nervous reactions, such as tucking of tail, to strange sounds or sights. Lack of confidence under any surroundings is not typical of good character. Any of the above deficiencies in character which indicate shyness must be penalized as very serious faults. It must be possible for the judge to observe the teeth and to determine that both testicles are descended. Any dog that attempts to bite the judge must be disqualified. The ideal dog is a working animal with an incorruptible character combined with body and gait suitable for the arduous work that constitutes its primary purpose.

Head—The head is noble, cleanly chiseled, strong without coarseness, but above all not fine, and in proportion to the body. The head of the male is distinctively masculine, and that of the bitch distinctly feminine. The muzzle is long and strong with the lips firmly fitted, and its topline is parallel to the topline of the skull. Seen from the front, the forehead is only moderately arched, and the skull slopes into the long, wedge-shaped muzzle without abrupt stop. Jaws are strongly developed. *Ears*—Ears are moderately pointed, in proportion to the skull, open toward the front, and carried erect when at attention, the ideal carriage being one in which the center lines of the ears, viewed from the front, are parallel to each other and perpendicular to the ground. A dog with cropped or hanging ears must be disqualified. *Eyes*—Of medium size, almond shaped, set a little obliquely and not protruding. The color is as dark as possible. The expression keen, intelligent and composed. *Teeth*—42 in number—20 upper and 22 lower—are strongly developed and meet in a scissors bite in which part of the inner surface of the upper incisors meet and engage part of the outer surface of the lower incisors. An overshot jaw or a level bite is undesirable. An undershot jaw is a disqualifying fault. Complete dentition is to be preferred. Any missing teeth other than first premolars is a serious fault.

Neck—The neck is strong and muscular, clean-cut and relatively long, proportionate in size to the head and without loose folds of skin. When the dog is at attention or excited, the head is raised and the neck carried high; otherwise typical carriage of the head is forward rather than up and but little higher than the top of the shoulders, particularly in motion.

Forequarters—The shoulder blades are long and obliquely angled, laid on flat and not placed forward. The upper arm joins the shoulder blade at about a right angle. Both the upper arm and the shoulder blade are well muscled. The forelegs, viewed from all sides, are straight and the bone oval rather than round. The pasterns are strong and springy and angulated at approximately a 25-degree angle from the vertical.

Feet—The feet are short, compact, with toes well arched, pads thick and firm, nails short and dark. The dewclaws, if any, should be removed from the hind legs. Dewclaws on the forelegs may be removed, but are normally left on.

Proportion—The German Shepherd Dog is longer than tall, with the most desirable proportion as 10 to 8½. The desired height for males at the top of the highest point of the shoulder blade is 24 to 26 inches; and for bitches, 22 to 24 inches. The length is measured from the point of the prosternum or breast bone to the rear edge of the pelvis, the ischial tuberosity.

Body—The whole structure of the body gives an impression of depth and solidity without bulkiness. *Chest*—Commencing at the prosternum, it is well filled and carried well down between the legs. It is deep and capacious, never shallow, with ample room for lungs and heart, carried well forward, with the prosternum showing ahead of the shoulder in profile. *Ribs*—Well sprung and long, neither barrel-shaped nor too flat, and carried down to a sternum which reaches to the elbows. Correct ribbing allows the elbows to move

109

back freely when the dog is at a trot. Too round causes interference and throws the elbows out; too flat or short causes pinched elbows. Ribbing is carried well back so that the loin is relatively short. *Abdomen*—Firmly held and not paunchy. The bottom line is only moderately tucked up in the loin.

Topline—Withers—The withers are higher than and sloping into the level back. *Back*—The back is straight, very strongly developed without sag or roach, and relatively short. The desirable long proportion is not derived from a long back, but from over-all length with relation to height, which is achieved by length of forequarter and length of withers and hindquarter, viewed from the side. *Loin*—Viewed from the top, broad and strong. Undue length between the last rib and the thigh, when viewed from the side, is undesirable. *Croup*—Long and gradually sloping. *Tail*—Bushy, with the last vertebra extended at least to the hock joint. It is set smoothly into the croup and low rather than high. At rest, the tail hangs in a slight curve like a saber. A slight hook—sometimes carried to one side—is faulty only to the extent that it mars general appearance. When the dog is excited or in motion, the curve is accentuated and the tail raised, but it should never be curled forward beyond a vertical line. Tails too short, or with clumpy ends due to ankylosis, are serious faults. A dog with a docked tail must be disqualified.

Hindquarters—The whole assembly of the thigh, viewed from the side, is broad, with both upper and lower thigh well muscled, forming as nearly as possible a right angle. The upper thigh bone parallels the shoulder blade while the lower thigh bone parallels the upper arm. The metatarsus (the unit between the hock joint and the foot) is short, strong and tightly articulated.

Gait—A German Shepherd Dog is a trotting dog, and its structure has been developed to meet the requirements of its work. *General Impression*—The gait is outreaching, elastic, seemingly without effort, smooth and rhythmic, covering the maximum amount of ground with the minimum number of steps. At a walk it covers a great deal of ground, with long stride of both hind legs and forelegs. At a trot the dog covers still more ground with even longer stride, and moves powerfully but easily, with co-ordination and balance so that the gait appears to be the steady motion of a well-lubricated machine. The feet travel close to the ground on both forward reach and backward push. In order to achieve ideal movement of this kind, there must be good muscular development and ligamentation. The hindquarters deliver, through the back, a powerful forward thrust which slightly lifts the whole animal and drives the body forward. Reaching far under, and passing the imprint left by the front foot, the hind foot takes hold of the ground; then hock, stifle and upper thigh come into play and sweep back, the stroke of the hind leg finishing with the foot still close to the ground in a smooth follow-through. The over-reach of the hindquarter usually necessitates one hind foot passing outside and the other hind foot passing inside the track of the forefeet, and such action is not faulty unless the locomotion is crabwise with the dog's body sideways out of the normal straight line.

Transmission—The typical smooth, flowing gait is maintained with great strength and firmness of back. The whole effort of the hindquarter is transmitted to the forequarter through the loin, back and withers. At full trot, the back must remain firm and level without sway, roll, whip or roach. Unlevel topline with withers lower than the hip is a fault. To compensate for the forward motion imparted by the hindquarters, the shoulder should open to its full extent. The forelegs should reach out close to the ground in a long stride in harmony with that of the hindquarters. The dog does not track on widely separated parallel lines, but brings the feet inward toward the middle line of the body when trotting in order to maintain balance. The feet track closely but do not strike or cross over. Viewed from the front, the front legs function from the shoulder joint to the pad in a straight line. Viewed from the rear, the hind legs function from the hip joint to the pad in a straight line. Faults of gait, whether from front, rear or side, are to be considered very serious faults.

111

Color—The German Shepherd Dog varies in color, and most colors are permissible. Strong rich colors are preferred. Nose black. Pale, washed-out colors and blues or livers are serious faults. A white dog or a dog with a nose that is not predominantly black, must be disqualified.

Coat—The ideal dog has a double coat of medium length. The outer coat should be as dense as possible, hair straight, harsh and lying close to the body. A slightly wavy outer coat, often of wiry texture, is permissible. The head, including the inner ear and fore-face, and the legs and paws are covered with short. hair, and the neck with longer and thicker hair. The rear of the forelegs and hind legs has somewhat longer hair extending to the pastern and hock, respectively. Faults in coat include soft, silky, too long outer coat, woolly, curly, and open coat.

DISQUALIFICATIONS

Cropped or hanging ears.

Undershot jaw.

Docked tail.

White dogs.

Dogs with noses not predominantly black.

Any dog that attempts to bite the judge.

Ch. Nyx of Long-Worth and three of the famous six-champion "D" litter, Ch. Drum, Ch. Derry, and Ch. Dennis—all of Long-Worth.

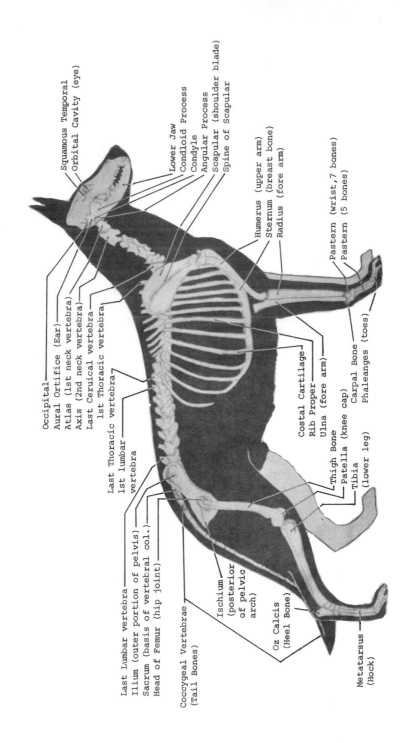

Occipital
Aural Ortifice (Ear)
Atlas (1st neck vertebra)
Axis (2nd neck vertebra)
Last Cervical vertebra
1st Thoracic vertebra

Squamous Temporal
Orbital Cavity (eye)

Lower Jaw
Condloid Process
Condyle
Angular Process
Scapular (shoulder blade)
Spine of Scapular

Humerus (upper arm)
Sternum (breast bone)
Radius (fore arm)

Pastern (wrist,7 bones)
Pastern (5 bones)

Last Thoracic vertebra
1st lumbar
vertebra

Costal Cartilage
Rib Proper
Ulna (fore arm)

Phaleanges (toes)

Last Lumbar vertebra
Ilium (outer portion of pelvis)
Sacrum (basis of vertebral col.)
Head of Femur (hip joint)

Coccygeal Vertebrae
(Tail Bones)

Ischium
(posterior
of pelvic
arch)

Thigh Bone
Patella (knee cap)
Carpal Bone
Tibia
(lower leg)

Oz Calcis
(Heel Bone)

Metatarsus
(Hock)

7

Blueprint of the
German Shepherd Dog

THE affection of the owner for his German Shepherd Dog is seldom predicated upon its comparative excellence as a show dog. Character, temperament, responsiveness, intelligence, and the ability to perform the services for which he is trained and used is to the owner more important than the conformation to a physical ideal. How many of us would not prefer to possess another Rin-Tin-Tin, a dog without any of the qualifications of a great show dog, than to have the greatest champion that ever lived?

The difficulty of developing the personalities and temperaments of a large number of dogs at the same time makes the breeding of German Shepherd Dogs in wholesale numbers an insuperable task. Other breeds may be reared in the kennels, duly fed and cared for, and left to themselves. The mentality of the German Shepherd Dog is so highly organized that he stagnates or becomes neurotic without human companionship which he craves.

Much of the shyness and the sharpness and other undesirable temperaments observed in the breed are not inherited but are conditioned by neglect, indifference, ill treatment, or some avoidable or unavoidable mental trauma that the dog has suffered. Of course some German Shepherd Dogs are more alert and receptive to the regimen of training than others, but almost any young German Shepherd Dog can be developed into an agreeable and responsive companion and many of them can be taught to perform routine duties. A few can be developed into super dogs with what appears to be a strong faculty to reason like a human being.

However much the mental attributes of the German Shepherd Dog may overweigh his physical appearance, the ability to exercise his mental faculties depends at least in part upon his physique. The joy of possessing an intelligent dog is doubly enhanced by having that intelligence encased in a beautiful, sound, and symmetrical body. Even if a leggy, square dog could function as well as one of correct proportions, the rightly-constructed animal is an added joy to watch. The economy of effort in the well-made dog is a never ceasing source of satisfaction.

Why A Standard of Perfection?

It is to be admitted that correct construction in the German Shepherd Dog is a convention. But it is much more than a convention. It is not merely arbitrary. There is a reason behind every specification which the standard lays down.

The standard, however, merely establishes the specifications; it does not explain them. The standards of dog breeds are established by the specialty clubs (subject to the approval of the American Kennel Club) and are intended to describe dogs most fitted to perform the tasks for which the respective breeds are to be used. They are guides to perfection in the breed.

However, the most expertly written standard, while fully comprehensible to persons trained in the application of standards to living animals, may be mere jargon to the amateur or novice owner of a dog.

It is the function of the standard to describe the breed as briefly as possible. It describes an ideal. There is no room or place in it for an elucidation of the reasons behind that ideal, and, even in the statement of the ideal, it is not always as specific as it might be. It is the product of many minds, which require compromise. There

Hussan v. Haus Kilmark, U.D.T., an immortal among American Obedience winners. Bred in Germany in 1951, Hussan's winning included 15 perfect scores, and 65 firsts. Owned by famous trainer Winifred G. Strickland.

The German Shepherd Dog has been the eminent breed in Obedience. A compilation of Obedience titles by breeds for the years 1965 through 1968, as reported in "Chips"—the national Obedience magazine, shows the German Shepherd Dog well out in front with a cumulative score of 4,224 CD's, 959 CDX's, 328 UD's, and 137 T's. In contrast, next highest ranking breeds were Poodles with 3,139 CD's, Shelties with 1,294 CD's, and Dobes with 690 CD's.

117

are conflicting interests and varied opinions among the framers of the standard, to conciliate which it is sometimes necessary to remain vague.

This is not an unmixed curse of standards, since some degree of uncertainty in their terms leaves a leeway for growth and development of the breeds they describe, leaves some play for the personal equation and experimentation of the breeders, saves the breeds from too cast iron a mould. Breeds change, subtly and gradually. They have an evolution. Desirable attributes are added, undesirable attributes eliminated—but all must be done within the standard. Too hide-bound a standard would forestall such evolution.

Moreover, standards do not describe faults in detail. *They are concerned with perfection, setting forth what a perfect dog shall be—not what he shall not be.* The economy of space precludes argument within the standard.

This is not so say however, that there is no room for argument outside the standard. Everybody who seeks to apply it has a slightly different concept about its meaning. Otherwise, judges would not vary as they do in making awards. Even when they do not differ about the meaning of the standard's terms, there is no absolute consensus about the comparative importance of the respective parts of the dog.

While the standard is designed to define and describe the perfect German Shepherd Dog, perfection does not exist. There is no perfect dog. Even among the greatest champions, perfection is merely approximated. A dog is not discredited and disqualified by a few or many minor deviations from the standard description. In judging the breed, the judge is not seeking a perfect dog; he is but choosing the best ones in the classes that come before him.

However, in evaluating one's own stock for breeding, each individual *should* be judged against the standard.

It is not surprising then that with so flexible a standard, judicial opinions should vary somewhat. What is more amazing is that judges should concur so much and so often as they do. While in the dog shows a dog may win on one day under one judge and be defeated the following day against the same competition under another judge, it is usually to be found the same group of dogs gravitate to the tops of the classes and a less excellent group are left out of the awards in both shows. The order in which the good

118

Am. & Can. Ch. Zarek v. Liebestraum, R.O.M., bred and owned by Mr. and
Mrs. Grant Mann.

Ch. Bursch vom Sylvenstein, owned by Liebestraum Kennels.

dogs are placed may vary, but there is little difference in judicial opinion about what is excellent and what is mediocre.

It is sometimes possible to find out in advance of a show what idiosyncrasies or prejudices a judge may hold and to show a dog under a judge predisposed to like his type or to withhold from the show another type that the judge does not like. For instance, although there is no valid preference between a gray dog and a black-and-tan, certain judges exercise a prejudice for or against certain colors. To exhibit a gray dog under a judge who habitually gives his prizes to a black-and-tan without regard to the fundamental merits of the exhibits is to court defeat.

Some judges simply refuse to give prizes to dogs with missing pre-molars (a minor fault) and will place a definitely inferior animal over another, no matter how good, with a gap in its mouth. Others may penalize a light eye to the same extent. It is hazardous to expose a dog to the tender mercies of a judge who is over-emphatic in his penalties for the particular fault the dog may possess.

Thus we see why there is nothing final about the position a dog may take in the award list of a single show. This is the reason for the rules which require a dog to win in a series of shows to obtain the title of champion. Otherwise, one show would settle everything. The position of a dog in the prize list of a single show is no final criterion of his merits or the lack of them.

Judges are reluctant, if they are not too tired after a day's work, to give an owner of a dog an opinion about it more than is contained in the dog's position in the awards. They wish not to add the insult of criticism of the dog to the injury of having placed it low in the prize list. They seek to avoid argument and above all wish not to be misquoted, which they frequently are.

It therefore behooves the owner to evaluate his own dog, unless he wishes to take the dog to a series of shows to ascertain the truth about it. Most owners do not want to take their dog even to one show to have the dog disparaged or ridiculed. An owner may not necessarily expect to win, but he wants to know before he exhibits the dog that it is worthy of being exhibited. He can make his own survey. While he may not be able to determine from such a survey whether or not the dog can achieve a championship, being unaware of the competition the dog may encounter, he can determine whether it is or is not worthy to be exhibited at all.

No professional handler has been more identified with the top German Shepherd Dogs in America over the last three decades than has Ernest Loeb. Mr. Loeb is pictured here with Ch. Quell von Fredeholz, SchH III, important German-import winner and sire, owned by the late all-breed judge, Anton Korbel.

Ch. Cito v. Haus Tippersruh, U.D.T., a distinguished post-war German import, Best in Show winner, and sire of many champions. Owned by Mr. and Mrs. Michel Kay.

Ch. Enno v. Spilledam, a Ch. Troll v. Richterbach son, owned by Harold Marcus.

In the early twenties, following upon the movie success of "Strongheart" and "Rin-Tin-Tin," the country went "police dog" mad. Mediocre and even positively bad dogs were bred from to supply a market that would absorb at high prices any puppy that had four legs, prick ears, and a tail. The German breeders exported to America at high prices all the near-mongrels they could lay hands upon. There was a German Shepherd Dog craze, like the tulip craze in Holland or the Belgian Hare craze of the early part of the century. Anything that could pretend to be a German Shepherd Dog was treasured, valued, and like as not exhibited. Long, short, high, low, sound or crippled, anything that even resembled a German Shepherd was accepted as a "police dog."

The craze was so great that the reaction to it was equally violent. From such an influx of mediocrity the good dogs of the breed were bound to suffer. It had been a mark of distinction to own a German Shepherd Dog. The breed has large litters and it multiplied itself rapidly. Prices fell. The bottom had dropped out. The breed was out of favor and out of fashion. It was not to be wondered at that such enthusiasm could not last.

However, a group of persistent and discriminating fanciers stuck to the breed through thick and thin. While the Germans were shipping to America all the trash they could produce, astute American buyers were acquiring the very best and greatest of the German output, which the German monetary inflation enabled them to do. Breeding steadily and carefully from these truly great German dogs, the persistent exponents of the breed have succeeded in purging it of its inferior blood and in developing strains that breed true for desirable attributes. The results are that we now possess better individual dogs and a breed of higher average excellence than ever before in the breed's history. This has resulted in an recrudescence in public interest in the breed, not as a craze or fad but as a serious and persistent interest.

The German Shepherd Dog is now becoming numerous, and the average excellence of the specimens exhibited is incomparably better than ever before. The greatest imported dogs of the breed's earlier days would be unable to hold their own with the best of the American-bred dogs of today, and dogs that could at one time have obtained championships would today receive little recognition in minor classes.

123

Accordingly, it is necessary in looking at a dog to seek for a high state of excellence. Mediocrity will not suffice. To be good at all, a present day dog must be very good.

Let us take your dog out on the lawn or in the park and have a look at him. The German Shepherd Dog requires space. He does not look his best in cramped or constricted quarters. The rings allotted to the judging of Shepherds in most all-breed dog shows are not spacious enough to enable the judges to see the exhibits to best advantage. What is needed is an open space at least a hundred feet long, and more can be utilized. Type can be examined in comparatively small space, but even for that purpose it is necessary to stand away from the dog in order to see him whole, as well as to stand close enough to handle him and examine the individual parts. But gait is the test of structure, a statement that we shall have occasion to repeat, and space is required to examine the dog's action.

Indeed, the gait of a German Shepherd Dog is as important as the gait of a horse, and the largest part of our survey leads up to our examination of the dog for action. The gait can be largely predicated from the dog's make and shape, but it must be confirmed.

When early German authorities came to America to judge and to vent their fads and fancies, which they did to accord with the dogs they or other German fanciers had to sell, they were very emphatic in their insistence upon a powerful drive in their winning dogs. They were more lenient in regard to soundness and trueness of movement than were American judges. A dog might be cow-hocked or out at the elbow, he might be scrawny, insignificant, or yellow eyed, but to satisfy these Germans he had to cover a short distance with asserted vigor and reserve of power. (Few German judges have adjucated in shows in America in recent years, but those who have seem to prefer much the same dogs as our better judges.)

This lessened emphasis upon a powerful drive by some judges, has been less due to negligence on the part of American judges or to their indifference as to the requirements of the breed than it has resulted from a lack of space in which to judge the dogs. It is impossible to evaluate the power and drive with which a dog moves in the cramped rings available in an indoors all-breed dog

Ch. Ricella's Frigga, one of the all-time top winning bitches, with 2 all-breed Bests in Show, 7 Specialty Bests in Show and 43 Bests of Breed to her credit. Select at 1965 and 1966 National Specialties. Bred and owned by Dr. C. R. Peluso and handled by Denise Kodner.

Canadian Grand Victor, Am. and Can. Ch. Chimney Sweep of Long-Worth, C.D., R.O.M., one of the nation's top show dogs of the early '50s, and sire of many champions. Owned by Virginia McCoy.

1966 and 1968 Grand Victor, Ch. Yoncalla's Mike,
owned by Bob and Linda Freeney.

1967 Grand Victor, Ch. Lance of Fran-Jo, R.O.M.,
owned by Joan and Francis Ford.

126

show. Therefore a powerful drive in a dog is of but little moment if our purpose is merely to win prizes with our dog; it is, however, of major importance in our search for perfection as such.

We shall return to consideration of gait after we have considered the structure of the dog and the application of the standard.

Type

The word "type" is erroneously used by many dog-show ring-siders and would-be authorities. The word has been mis-used so often that it has left many novices confused, and they in turn pass on the misinformation.

Are *you* confused? You need not be. Just keep in mind that a typey German Shepherd Dog is one that displays conformation, sex characteristics, expression and temperament considered desirable and representative of the breed.

There cannot be more than one type within our breed. There can be only variations of the type required, and we should all avoid them, and strive to breed as closely to the ideal standard type as possible. All breeders should aim to approximate the desirable type, and all judges must (or should) prefer only the standard type. The choice in the ring should attempt to bring to the fore those animals that vary least from the ideal.

Of course the condition of the animal has much to do with determining its merits. In any event the dog should be clean, thoroughly well-fed on a balanced diet, free from intestinal parasites, clear-eyed, with teeth free from slime, dirt or tartar, and with skin free from lesions, whether produced by injury or disease. He should have been brought with judicious exercise to a high state of physical vigor and firmness of muscle. His nails should be shortened enough to give compactness to the feet, but not to injure the quick.

The state of the coat is not material for the purposes of this examination, since it is a temporary matter and subject to shedding in any event. Allowance can be made for the dog's ability to grow a coat, and even the tearing out of the undercoat, whether by accident or design, does not affect the animal's fundamental excellence. Of course the absence of undercoat may possibly affect the position of the dog in the official prize list of a dog show, but in such an unofficial survey as we are making, his known ability to grow a coat is more important than his actual possession of an underjacket.

The expert handling of the dog may also be discounted. Anybody who can lead and pose the dog for us will suffice. It is the function of the professional dog handler to present the dog to the judge in the most favorable light, to emphasize its favorable attributes and to conceal its faults. The German Shepherd Dog is so forthright an animal that even the cleverest handler is unable to deceive a good judge. There is nothing to trim, nothing to conceal, nothing to fake. Moreover, in this survey we wish to arrive at a true evaluation of the dog for *our own* satisfaction. We are not seeking to have ourselves deceived. An amateur handler is for our purposes even better than the expert, somebody who will follow our instructions about the dog's pose and about moving him.

The slip chain collar is conventional for the breed, and does not so interrupt the sweep of the eye over the whole dog as does a leather collar. The lead should be of leather, at least a yard in length (and it can be longer), strong enough to control the dog in any emergency but light enough not to be cumbersome.

Size

The size of the German Shepherd Dog is, within limits, not of great importance. The standard defines the ideal height, established by taking a perpendicular line from the top of the shoulder blade to the ground with the coat parted or so pushed down that the measurement will show only the actual height of the frame or structure of the dog, as 24 to 26 inches for dogs, and between 22 and 24 inches for bitches. A dog of standard size is sometimes criticized by the uninformed, and to some degree by the informed, as being too small. The public taste is for a larger dog, and judicial opinion frequently tends to favor dogs and bitches that are oversized according to the standard.

Clumsiness and an excess of bone are faults, whether they be found in dogs of regulation height or in dogs with an excess of height as set down in the standard. They are faults in themselves, without reference to the size of the dog that manifests them.

The Maur-ray Kennels has been established as premier breeder of the black German Shepherd Dog in America. Seen here are four consecutive generations of homebred black champion bitches. Above, owner Maureen Yentzen is pictured with Ch. Gerda of Maur-ray, finished in 1951; Gerda's daughter, Ch. Marlene of Maur-ray, finished in 1953; and Marlene's daughter, Ch. Wilma of Maur-ray, finished in 1955. At left is Wilma's daughter, Ch. Arla of Maur-ray, finished in 1959.

129

Nobility.

The Head

The description of the head given us in the standard is adequate for the purposes. The structure of the head is within limits a comparatively minor part of the German Shepherd Dog. Less than in most other breeds may the head be said to be the index.

There is no scale of points in the standard, and it must remain an idiosyncrasy of the individual judge just what allotment he is to make for head structure in his analysis of the entire dog. Von Stephanitz in his unofficial scale of points allots five points in his scale of 100 to head, in which he includes mouth, eyes, and ears. This is preposterously insufficient, since with such calculation it would be possible for a dog with a good body and gait to win despite a clublike head, yellow eye, overshot mouth, and lopped ears. On the other hand, some exquisite heads, perfect mouths, dark eyes, and superb ears are attached to and followed by intolerable bodies and running gear. For the dog to pass inspection at all the head must be characteristic, although a dog may be a good one with a head structure that is far from perfect. We can only say that body, legs and feet are of considerably greater import than mere beauty of head.

The head of the Shepherd is by no means fine drawn, but it has the "quality" that marks nobility. Let us dispose at once of the tradition that the width of a dog's head has anything at all to do with his intelligence, else the Bulldog would be the most intelligent of dogs and the Terrier the most stupid. The brainpan of the dog is comparatively small, and the animal's intelligence has nothing whatever to do with the size of the brain, but rather with the amount or number of its convolutions. There is no need to fear that in the refinement of head of the German Shepherd Dog we are courting stupidity.

The muzzle should be well carried out. If it has the depth and power required, there is little reason to fear that it can be too long. This statement is made despite the caution of Von Stephanitz and other German authorities. This muzzle is wedge-shaped. The stop is small, a mere demarcation between the top-skull and the top line of the muzzle, which should be parallel to the top surface of the skull, neither down-faced nor dish-faced.

Miss Joan R. Michler and Miss Lois Brundred,
owners of San Miguel Kennels.

Teeth

The formation of the teeth becomes important: first, because the teeth are employed in the dog's work and, secondly, because the structure of the mouth and teeth is heritable. The scissors bite is described in the standard, with the inner surface of the upper incisors meeting and engaging the outer surface of the lower incisors. There is a valid reason for this type of bite. The erosion of the incisors with the pinchers bite (one in which the edges of the teeth meet directly) is much greater than with the scissors formation. A three- or four-year-old dog with a pinchers bite will display incisors worn well nigh to the gums, while a sound scissors mouth may last as long as the dog.

The undershot mouth (one in which the lower teeth protrude beyond the upper teeth) is seldom to be found in the German Shepherd. When it is observed, the animal is to be disqualified. Its opposite number, the overshot mouth is much more prevalent. While the over-elongation of the jaw is not to be feared for its own sake, the overshot jaw which accompanies it must be penalized, for, with the tight, "dry" lips of the breed, it gives the face a chinless-wonder aspect, makes of the dog a canine Andy Gump.

Some judges make a fetish of counting the four pre-molars to be found on each side of each jaw, and to such judges one such missing tooth condemns the whole dog. The German judges in one era introduced the counting of these teeth as a fad and some of their American sycophants have adhered to it. However, having any teeth missing other than first pre-molars, is a serious fault.

The canine teeth or fangs of some herding dogs, especially those from the south part of Germany, have been filed down to prevent damage to the sheep in the dog's control of them. This is not to be penalized, and will rarely be found in American bred dogs.

The so-called "distemper mouth" has been the object of considerable controversy as to whether it should be subject to penalty. By the term "distemper mouth" is meant chipped, worn, and discolored teeth, which are presumed to be due to depletion of calcium in the system resultant from distemper or other diseases which manifest themselves with high or prolonged fevers. The fact is that it may be a symptom of earlier richitis. While it may not in itself be inheritable, the predisposition to it appears to be. The standard makes no mention of distemper mouth. The teeth of the distemper mouth are not strong, which justifies a penalty for the condition if one chooses to impose it. It is more prevalent in German breeds than in most others, and may be due to the swill with which the Germans generally feed their dogs. Whether to penalize or to overlook the condition is a matter which each judge must de-

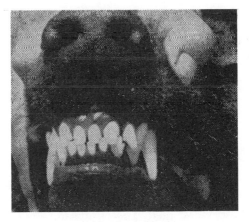

A scissors bite.

133

cide for himself. In our survey of our dog, we must assume that that distemper mouth is liable to penalty under many judges, although there will be others who will pass over it as not worthy of cognizance.

Ears

There is little to add to the description of the ears as given in the standard, except that in "discarding" cropped or hanging ears we also discard the whole dog that carries them.

Nothing adds to the nobility and animation of a German Shepherd Dog more than well-placed and carried ears. He talks with them. Weak or lopped ears are a perennial problem in the breed. Erect-eared parents frequently produce progeny with soft ears, although one parent with soft ears mated to another with correct ears may produce puppies with erect ears. The statement in the standard that "dogs with cropped or hanging ears must be disqualified," helps to eliminate from breeding stock the hereditary fault of soft ears.

Small, pointed, stingy ears are more certain of erection than larger ones, but they are harmful to the expression. The ideal ear is generous in size without being disproportionately large, although it would be a captious critic who would penalize a dog for excessive ear size, provided that the ears were erect and active. Puppies with large ears, however, as a rule do not raise their ears as early as those with smaller ears, and just possibly will never raise them at all. An absolutely upright ear set directly on the top of the head makes the skull appear narrow and gives the dog a slightly "foreign" expression. Such ears are likely not to spread correctly and to "nick inward" if not to fall toward the center of the head, due to a weakness of the erectile muscles.

Eyes

The description of the eyes in the German Shepherd Dog standard is unfortunate in not being more definitive. The best eyes are somewhat more than medium in size, only slightly ovoid or almond shaped. The expression should indeed be lively, composed, and intelligent. Dignity and a possible aloofness is acceptable, but any show of animosity is contra indicated. The most desirable eye is wide-spaced and generous. Narrowly spaced eyes give the animal stingy and querulous outlook, which is not characteristic of the breed.

While yellow eyes do not affect a dog's working ability, they spoil the appearance of an exhibition dog. Short of dead blackness and the absence of color differentiation between pupil and iris, the eye can hardly be too dark, and even that dead blackness is to be preferred to any of the shades of lemon. Contrary to the standard, light eyes are no more frequently found in light colored dogs of this breed than in black or black-and-tan dogs and are equally objectionable in all colors.

The German Shepherd Dog is the most normally made and the least freakish of all the breeds of dogs and has fewer merely arbitrary qualifications that have nothing at all to do with its functions and purpose. The German Shepherd Dog is a unit and no part of it is to be overweighed or be considered separately from any other part. The structure of the parts behind the head determines the structure of the head. It will be found that a lean, scrawny, narrow chested dog without substance is prone to carry an overly fine and elongated head, and a clumsy, cloddy dog with too much bone for its size is prone to carry a coarse, chunky, short head. Neither sort of dog is desirable. We want the maximum of agility plus an adequacy of power, which is obtainable without compromise.

We may now leave the head and consider the structure behind it.

One of the most important factors concerning the German Shepherd Dog is the proportion of his length over all (not his length of back) to his height at the withers. His trotting gait depends upon this. The tall dog or one approaching squareness is intolerable.

It is all but impossible to make accurate measurements, but the approximate ratio of 10 units of length to 9 units of height is acceptable, 10 to 8½ is even better, or even 10 to 8 is acceptable. These measurements must be made by the eye, from the very front of the pro-sternum to the back of the buttocks and from the top of the shoulder blade to the ground. Allowance must be made for the length of the hair, which should not be included. That the dog shall be longer than high is of the utmost importance.

It is possible for a German Shepherd Dog to be so short of leg

135

as to present a Dachshund-like appearance, but it is quite unlikely that the length in proportion to the height will be found too great. A dog with great depth of brisket appears lower on the leg than one that is too shallow, but unless the dog immediately appears deformed, short legs and long body remains a virtue.

The Neck

The German Shepherd Dog's neck reaches from its body to its head, a considerable distance—more than it appears in its ruff of hair. A dog with an upright shoulder will certainly have an inadequate length of neck. The base of the neck extends in a diagonal line along the shoulder blade from the forechest to the withers, and should be deep and thick as well as long. The depth of the neck as well as the thickness of the hair makes the neck appear shorter than it really is. It is in proportion to the head it is called upon to manipulate.

A slightly crested neck is an evidence of power, whereas an ewe-neck is a sign of weakness.

The neck should be free from dewlap or throatiness, a fault seldom found in the German Shepherd Dog. The carriage of the head as it is described in the standard is not to be accepted too seriously. The German Shepherd Dog is a confident, high-headed dog. He has the carriage of head to be expected in any noble dog. It is true that in a fast trot he lowers his head for the sake of balance, but it would be a strange and depressed dog whose "head is carried but little higher than the top of his shoulders" except in excitement, as the standard declares. Dogs with inadequate length or strength of neck are prone to slump, as is one with too coarse or heavy a head. But the normal head carriage is high and alert.

The Body

It is the body of the dog, rather than its back, that should be long. The back is comparatively short. The dog is not a pack animal and does not have to support weight upon its back, which nevertheless must be very firm for the transmission of energy from the hindquarters to the forehand, as will be discussed later.

Distinction must be made between the length of the body and

STRUCTURAL FAULTS

Note: *Dotted lines indicate faults in structure,*
solid lines indicate the correct profile.

Overbuilt.

Short-bodied.

the length of the back. The body extends from the point of the shoulders to the rear of the buttocks, whereas the back extends only from the withers to the pelvic bones. The back is but the bridge to carry the power developed in the powerful hindquarters to the square shoulder formation. The forequarters develop no power of their own and merely serve as points of suspension to prevent the dog from falling forward on his face. Such being the case, the emphasis upon the correct shoulder and forehand may seem to be misplaced. However, a dog's step can be no longer than is permitted by the angle of the scapula or shoulder blade and the humerus or bone of the upper arm. This must be great enough to permit the front end of the dog to keep up with the hindquarters, which in the best dogs is approximately a right angle.

There is little point in having a powerful and well-angulated hindquarters to propel the animal without a forequarter with a sufficient angle of shoulder to absorb the stride.

The back should be absolutely straight, level, and unroached from the pelvic bone to the shoulder blade. The ideal, although so far as known it has never been practically attained, is a back upon which a glass brimful of water could rest without spilling with the dog at a straightaway trot. It is not implied that such a test shall be made; it is liable to be disappointing.

Any tendency of the back to sag or sway results in a loss of transmitted power and must be heavily penalized. A carp back or roached back, while not so reprehensible as an equal degree of sag, which is its opposite fault, denotes a constriction in the muscles of the loin which, to the extent of the roach, tends to destroy the dog's liberty. It results in a shortness of stride in the hindquarters and a greater expenditure of energy in covering ground.

While the dog overall should be long, and the back should be comparatively short, this does not mean as short as possible. While a short back is more efficient for a dog moving in a direct line, it does not admit of sinuosity, flexibility, and lithesomeness in quick turning, weaving, rising and stooping, for which the work of the German Shepherd Dog calls.

In depth of body, the chest should extend at least to the elbow of a fully matured dog. It may well be even deeper than that. No allowance is to be made for coat in such measurement. The German Shepherd Dog does not reach full maturity until it is two

Carp back.

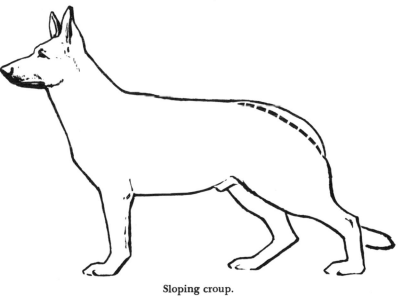

Sloping croup.

139

years, sometimes two and a half years old, and no final judgment of the depth of body can be reached before that approximate age.

The chest should be capacious with ample room for heart and lungs. This must be achieved by a wide spring of rib at the junction of rib and with the spine, followed by an abrupt drop of the rib. This leaves the sides of the dog flat. Such a formation offers a maximum of capacity with the least impediment to the action. A barrel-like rib, while it may be spectacular, does not provide the capacity that it seems to hold, causes a dog to wobble from side to side in his action, and interferes with the play of his elbows.

Thoracic capacity is also achieved by the extension of the ribs horizontally. The chest should be long as possible as well as deep. This means, not that the German Shepherd Dog has more ribs than other dogs, but that the individual ribs are wider and wider spaced along the spine.

The loin is heavy and of moderate length. It must be long enough for flexibility and short enough for strength. This is achieved by depth of loin. There is a minimum of tuck up of belly, although there is no paunch-like flabbiness. The great girth of loin is the result of solid, hard muscle. It is impossible to disguise too great a tuck up with fat pulling the belly down. That becomes a double fault. It is better to accept somewhat too much tuck up than to fill it in with soft flabbiness.

The croup of the German Shepherd Dog is exceedingly long, but not steep. It forms a gradual slope from the pelvic bones to the set-on of tail. It will be found in dogs with a level croup that their tendency is to carry their tails in the air—a terrier-like formation. Dogs with too abrupt a croup are hampered in their stride, appear short of body, and lack balance.

The croup leads into the tail, which is a mere continuation of the spine. The ideal length is that the tail itself, not merely the hair on it, shall reach to the point of the hock. Additional length, however, is not to be penalized. Greater difficulty is found in tails too short than in those too long; if noticeably too short, symmetry and balance of the entire animal are affected. Tails with clumpy ends due to ankylosis are serious faults. A dog with a docked tail must be disqualified.

When the dog is in repose, the tail should hang almost straight down, but with a slight saber curve to prevent an appearance of

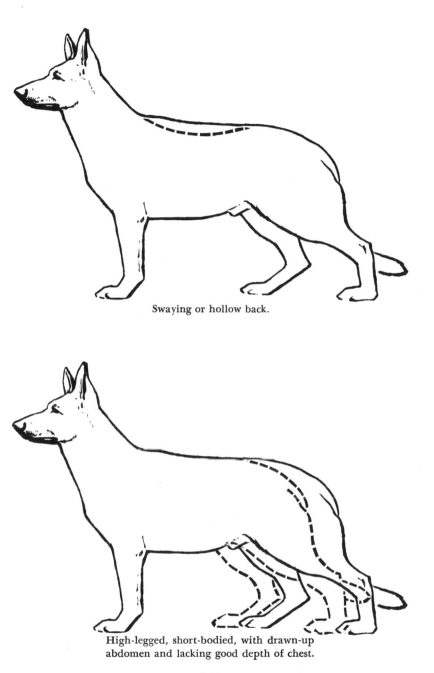

Swaying or hollow back.

High-legged, short-bodied, with drawn-up
abdomen and lacking good depth of chest.

deadness. Twists or curls or kinks in the tail are, to put it mildly, undesirable.

In extreme animation or excitement a dog is likely to raise his tail, which is all right, but the tail should never rise so high as the vertical, much less turn over the dog's back. There is little likelihood of this occurring in a dog with a correctly formed croup.

The tail serves the dog as a rudder and is a practical part of its anatomy and affects the gait. Short tails are inadequate for the purpose, and a tail with a kink serves the dog only down to the point where the kink begins. Beyond that point the tail is dead weight and a hindrance to the steering.

The German Shepherd Dog tail is never whiplike or fragile, and it is not sharply pointed. It forms a good handful and is a powerful instrument in the balancing and guiding of the dog in the making of quick turns.

The Front

The German Shepherd Dog is an animal of extreme angulations both of the forehand and of the hindquarters, and it is largely by its angulation that the merits of a dog are evaluated. The angulation of the shoulder (that is the junction of the upper arm with the shoulder blade), as we have said, should be as nearly a right angle as possible, with the dog standing firmly and normally on the floor. Such an angle permits him the maximum opening of the forehand and the longest possible step. With a shoulder of such angulation is to be found a magnificent forechest with great depth of neck. There is no padding or bunchiness of shoulder muscles to be found with such a formation. The shoulder blade is extremely long, and of approximately equal length with the upper arm. The longer the better, and, with adequate angulation, the greater the forechest. It is this forechest that, in part, increases the length of the entire dog over its height.

From the upper arm the forearm drops straight to the pastern joint, turning neither in nor out. If it turns inward to make the dog appear pigeon-toed, it will be found that the dog is "out at elbow," the attachment of the shoulder blades to the body is not firm, and the dog will wobble in its action. Turning of the feet outward results from either of two faulty formations. The fault may be in too tight a shoulder, forcing the elbow close to the body, and the whole leg may be twisted outward, which usually is associated with a narrow, pigeon-breasted chest. Or the outward turn of the feet may result from a twist of the pastern joint, an effort of the organism to compensate for too narrow a chest and a consequently insecure stance. This latter formation is called "Frenching," from its resemblance to the position attributed to French dancing masters. This term, which is in general usage, was introduced by the Germans in their efforts to disparage anything French, but it serves its purpose.

The pastern is moderately long and almost straight. There is in it a minute give which saves the leg, as seen from the side, from being absolutely straight. This give in the pastern joint absorbs some of the shock in a rapid or prolonged trot. But it must be very slight. It is better that it shall not occur at all than that it shall be pronounced. Too much of it, especially if accompanied with insufficient bone formation, is a source of weakness and lack of endurance. The absolutely straight, terrier-like front gives a stilty and awkward appearance to a dog, but in a choice between it and a broken down pastern, the straight front is to be chosen. A knuckled over pastern, and semblance of double joints is highly reprehensible and subject to severe penalty.

The straight front is usually found with cat-like feet, the weak pastern with hare-like feet. Correct German Shepherd Dog feet are neither cat-like nor hare-like, but midway between them in their length. A cat foot serves well enough for a dog traveling straight forward, but it is likely to burn in making a quick turn. What is more important than the mere length of the foot is its well knuckled compactness and depth of pad. Nails should be heavy and thick. Long thin nails are usually found on a thin, weak foot. Nails can, of course, be shortened, but a dog with good feet will with plenty of exercise keep his nails worn down sufficiently that they require little cutting back.

Looked at from the front, the legs are entirely straight and parallel one to the other. The front is neither wide nor narrow. A wide front impairs the dog's speed and agility, whereas a narrow front does not provide a stance to support the dog with the greatest ease.

The bone of the German Shepherd Dog is ample, without being

143

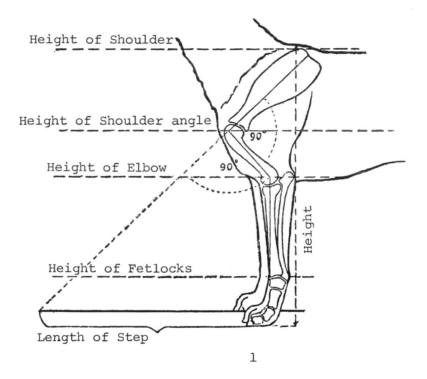

Height of Shoulder

Height of Shoulder angle

90°

Height of Elbow

90°

Height

Height of Fetlocks

Length of Step

1

BREAST AND FORELEGS

1. Good formation of prosternum and lower sternum. Neck powerfully set, high long withers, strong bones, and good leverage for the forelimbs. Plenty of play for the shoulder, which makes a good long pace and advance possible.

144

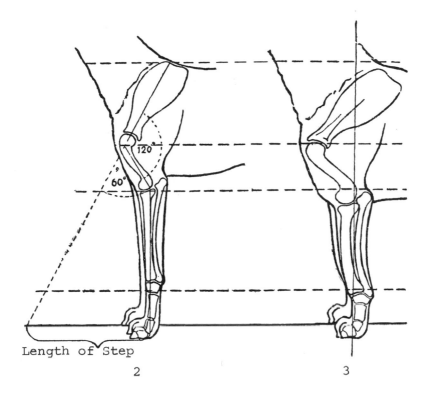

Length of Step

2   3

2. Faulty prosternum. Depth of breast too narrow, thin neck, low withers, bones too long and too thin, faulty angles and accordingly faulty leverage for the limbs. Little play for the shoulder, and consequently a short pace and advance. Fetlocks long and too steep. Stork-like build with poor gait. Deceptively appears to be good because of the long bones.

3. Faulty. Compressed formation of breast and neck, large bones, shoulders somewhat advanced. Bent radius and ulna with distended joints (the result of weakness in the bones). Fetlocks oversteep and short. Build of a thick-set dog with bound rolling gait.

145

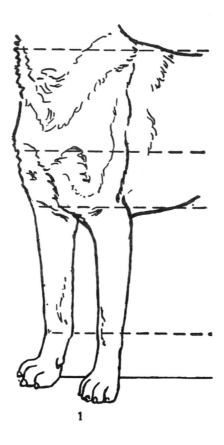

BREAST AND FORELEGS

1. Good formation of breast and forelegs.

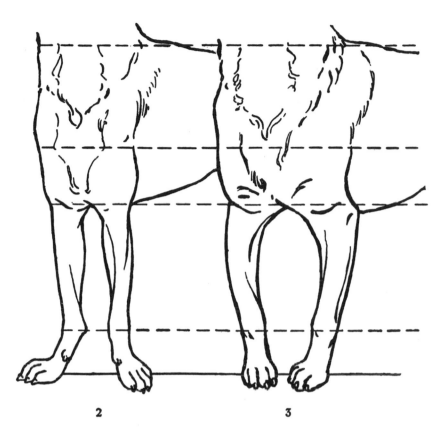

2   3

2. Faulty. Small breast without depth, faulty prosternum,
   drawn out or loosely-knit body, drawn-in elbows, weak
   fetlocks, stand like that of a dancing master.

3. Faulty. Broad, barrel-shaped breast, distended or turned-
   out elbows, bent lower arm, knees too wide apart giving
   a bad stand on the ground and the toes.

147

massive. A dog with frail, fragile, inadequate bone will be unable to stand the gaff of persistent, hard work. On the other hand, too much bone, or soft and spongy bone, makes for lumbering clumsiness. Where choice must be made between too much bone and too little, too much is to be preferred. A dog is seldom criticized for his possession of a superfluity of bone. The formation of the bone of the lower arm is the usual criterion of the bone structure of the whole dog: if it is adequate, that of the rest of the dog may be depended upon to suffice.

The Rear

The hindquarters are formed with long bones, the thigh bone being at an approximate right angle with the hip bone, with the dog standing normally, and the stifle bones at right angle to the thigh bone. The hock drops vertically from the hock joint. Such a formation gives the dog the maximum of leverage and propulsive power. This is of supreme· importance.

The dog should be permitted to stand normally during its examination. The efforts on the part of some exhibitors to stretch the hindquarters and to place the feet, or one of them, as far back as is possible deceives nobody except the veriest novice. In the show ring it is not unusual to see dogs stretched all out of shape until the rear of the dog looks like a pair of props and the front legs are thrown off the perpendicular in the dog's effort to compensate for the extreme stretching of the hindquarters and to keep his balance. A correctly-made dog can be posed with the lead to exhibit his extreme angulation; it does not require the stretching out of the dog by hand with the admonition to him to hold his pose. Many judges rightly resent this artificial posing of the dog, and, in the effort to examine the dog in his normal position, ask that the handler break the pose by moving the dog by a step or two. Some handlers are so persistent in their efforts to distort the natural position that they immediately set about stretching their dog artificially again and the judge is compelled to break the pose again and again. Some handlers will persist in this artificial stretching of their dogs in the face of specific instructions from the judge that the dogs shall be permitted to pose themselves naturally.

The exact angles of the various bones are impossible to state

148

since they depend upon the position assumed by the hindquarters. The estimated ideal of 90 degrees each at pelvis and stifle joints is for an ideal dog with a normal stance with a vertical line from the ischium tuberosity to the horizontal floor passing through the foot immediately in front of the hock. By stretching the dog's quarters, while it gives an optical illusion of greater length, the angulation is made less acute rather than more acute.

This bony structure should be as large and substantial as possible and the bones should be extremely long. To manipulate these vast levers the muscles must be long and powerful and their attachments must be strong. The hams are immense, both in depth and thickness.

Such a formation enables the animal to take a long, flexible stride, the power of which is transferred to the spine and carried by it to the forequarters. The shoulder joint must be acute enough to open wide to accommodate the length of step of the hindquarters, else the power is lost and the step is shortened.

There should be no interference of one hock with the other, but the rear stance of the breed is comparatively narrow. The legs must never appear to spraddle. The hocks should be absolutely parallel one to the other, standing or moving. Any tendency toward barrel or bandy legs on the one hand or toward cow-hocks on the other hand is a sign of unsoundness and is not to be tolerated. (Some of the German judges who have officiated in America are more lenient toward cow-hocks than are most American judges. The fact remains that they are a serious fault.)

Cow-hocks sometimes result from excessive high jumping especially in puppyhood, in which case they tend not to reappear in the dog's progeny. However, the larger part of cow-hocks are inherited and tend to be transmitted to the progeny. It is unsafe to breed from a cow-hocked dog. Judges have no way of knowing whether cow-hocks are acquired or inherited, and therefore have no alternative but to penalize them whenever they are found.

In the craze for excessive angulation of the hindquarters there has developed a tendency for the hocks to turn forward from the vertical when the dog is standing at ease. This formation is often referred to as "saber hocks." Its effect is the weakening of the hock joint, an added tension upon the muscles. Saber hocks are deceptive in that at first consideration they appear as added angulation,

149

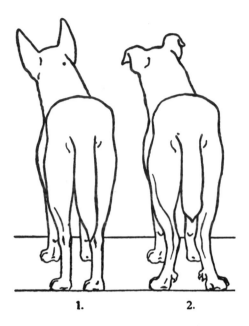

1. **2.**

HINDLEGS, EARS AND TAIL
(Dog standing still)

1. Good stand and position.

2. Faulty. Knock-kneed, legs like riding britches. Dew or
   wolf's claws (single on left foot, double on right foot).
   Double spurs. Ears badly tipping over (too heavy).
   Stumpy tail.

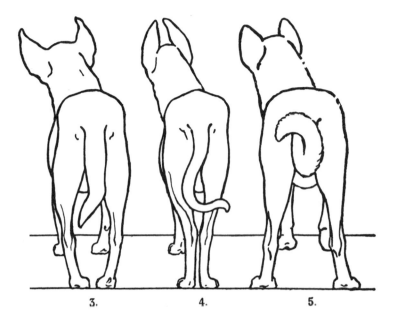

3.   4.   5.

3. Faulty. Bandy-legged. Ears too large and too deep-set. Slightly hook-like tail, bending sideways.

4. Faulty. Weak, sidewards-sloping buttocks like a pig. Turned-out knees. Fox-like loins. Bad position on the ground. Ears too near together, too thin and too long. Tail bent sideways.

5. Faulty. Broad, coarse buttocks with broad steep stand. Bear's feet. Short thick ears. Beginning of a ring tail.

but the angulation is in the wrong place. They are spectacular and may fool the uninitiated, but they exemplify weakness rather than strength.

Coat

The coat of the German Shepherd Dog may be of various lengths, textures, natures, and qualities. However, in America only the smooth coat is found and accepted. This smooth coat is found with some variation in length and density, but it is essentially alike on all dogs, and it is seldom open to much criticism.

It consists in a pily, woolly, slightly oily underjacket through which grow long, straight guard hairs. The head is comparatively smooth, the front legs smooth with a fringe of slightly longer hair at the back, a heavy coat around the neck and on the back, and a profuse growth of hair on the hips and tail. There is some variation in the profusion of coat in summer and winter weather.

The coat of a German Shepherd Dog, except for its condition, is seldom open to criticism. The guard hairs on the back will range in length from 1½ inches to 2½ inches, although without measuring the coat it may not appear to be so long. The shorter hair gives a dog a deceptive refinement of outline, which is not truly characteristic of the breed. The longer hair is, on the whole, to be preferred. While the absolutely correct coat is straight, a slightly crinkled or curled coat is not highly objectionable. Such crinkled coats are likely to be of heavier texture and less dense than one with straight guard hairs.

While little is likely to be found wrong with the nature of the coat, its condition is so important that it may defeat a dog entered in competition. That it must be healthy, alive, and lustrous goes without saying. Excessive grooming with a fine comb or rake may pull out the undercoat, leaving the guard hair lying flat to the skin, or the dog may simply fail to grow an undercoat. When it has been pulled out through excessive grooming it will grow again and no harm may accrue. A judge has no means of knowing whether a dog lacking undercoat fails to grow one or whether it has been pulled out. That undercoat is essential to a dog as protection against excessive heat, cold, sleet, rain, or snow, and even against insect bites. The German Shepherd Dog is an all-weather

152

dog, and, while in America he seldom is compelled to rough it, he must have a protective covering that enables him to endure unfavorable conditions. Along with his superior intelligence, it is accommodation to all climates and environments that makes him the best all around dog for any purpose—in addition to his specific function as a herdsman.

Dew Claws

Dew claws are fifth toes sometimes found on the inside of the hock and on forefeet. They are unsightly excrescences and are usually removed surgically from hock while the dog is a puppy in the nest. They tend to appear as recessives in certain strains and are to be avoided. Just why they should interfere with the action of the dog that carries them is not clear, but the fact is that a dog with dew claws seldom moves well. The dew claw may be on only one hock or on both. Less frequently they are found in double form with two extra toes, with two nails, on each foot.

A Picture of Your Dog

We have now gone carefully over the dog and examined him critically. We have explored him with the hands as well as with the eyes. We have found major or minor faults in his structure and have noted those departments and attributes in which he particularly excels. We have perhaps been able to stand our dog alongside another of acknowledged excellence and noted the differences between them. We have at least been able to compare the dog with the pictures of great dogs shown in this book.

It is to be remembered that no dog is perfect, and in any comparison with a living dog or with a pictured one allowance must be made for the possibility that in some details the dog under examination may excel the other. Dogs are photographed in positions to exploit their best features and to conceal their shortcomings. Photographs are even sometimes faked and doctored to make dogs appear better than they are. This must be taken into consideration before we condemn a dog for some minor fault wherein he appears to fall short or some particularly striking picture.

In many pictures the subject is stretched and drawn out in a

153

mistaken effort to make the dog appear long and to accent his angulation. Just because your dog when posed naturally is not stretched all out of shape is no reason to compare him unfavorably with the photograph, which would be a better portrait without the distortion.

While we may gain from a photograph a concept of how a dog should appear standing, his structure and proportions, yet, we must emphasize that his structure is no better than the use he makes of it. We must see the dog in action to arrive at a true evaluation of him.

For this we require a considerable space, a straightaway of 100 feet or even more. The small judging rings in too many dog shows hamper the judging of this particular breed, which is evaluated particularly upon its gait. In a small ring the judge is able, because he must, to make his decisions between exhibits in which there is considerable disparity. It is impossible in small space to make a complete evaluation of a dog in action, as it is also impossible to arrive at an accurate comparative decision between two or more evenly matched exhibits.

Gait

In our examination of the dog we shall take into account a powerful rear action, whether we shall find it or not. If it is lacking, it may still be possible to win at indoor shows or those with limited ring space. However, we have ample room for our examination and without a powerful drive our German Shepherd Dog is somewhat short of perfection.

Let us proceed to the consideration of the dog's manner of going.

Standing directly behind the dog, have the assistant walk the animal away from you, turn directly around and walk toward you. In this part of the examination, the dog is not called upon to exert himself. The trueness of his action is all that we are seeking to observe. Are his hocks parallel one to the other, as they should be? Or is there some evidence of cow-hocks or of bandy legs? Are the hindquarters trussed or spraddled out? Or are they possibly so close together as to interfere? These are seen as the dog moves away. As he returns, note the parallelism of the front legs. Are the front

154

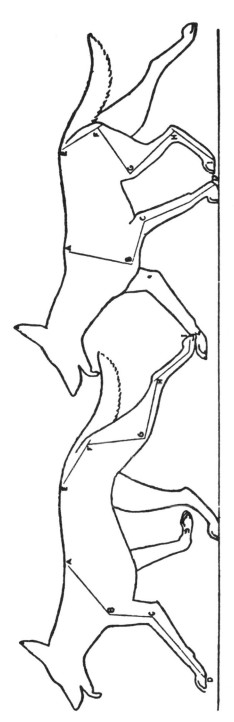

LONG SWEEPING TROT, WITH BACK-ACTION

Left, the dog supports himself with the right hind foot, which he has brought over the place of the right forefoot.

Right, the dog supports himself on the left fore-foot, which in a moment will step forward.

The Advance: After the left foreleg has begun its motion, the hindleg takes a step and pushes the weight of the body on to the right foot which, in the meantime, has been completing its step—and so on. This is the "follow through."

A–B	∴	Shoulder Blade
B–C	∴	Upper Arm
C–D	∴	Lower Arm with Metacarpus and Paw
E–F	∴	Iliac
F–G	∴	Thigh
G–H	∴	Thigh
H–I	∴	Metatarsus and Paw

Ch. Hessian's Baldur, R.O.M. Select.

Grand Victrix, Ch. Hessian's Vogue, R.O.M.

Ch. Hessian's Exaktor.

Int. Ch. Hamilton Erich v. Grafenwerth at 11 years of age.

Ch. Keno of Long-Worth.

158

legs so tightly attached to the shoulders as to cause them to cross or weave or even to tend to do so? On the other hand, are they so loosely attached as to cause the dog to paddle like a side-wheeler? One is as bad as the other. If he "frenches" while standing, it is impossible for him to move without throwing his feet sidewise, but this is not the same movement as looseness of shoulder in which the whole body lurches from side to side, supporting the weight first on one side and then on the other.

These tests are for ordinary soundness and can be made in a comparatively small space. Unless he possess ordinary or garden variety of soundness, a dog cannot be expected to perform well at more rapid gaits.

There are of course degrees of soundness. While we may desire it to be absolute, a dog may deviate slightly from being perfectly sound without condemnation. It is better that he exhibit several such minute deviations than a single gross one. A trace of cow hocks plus a trace of looseness of shoulder is to be preferred to gross cow hocks. Or a very slight spraddle plus a trace of frenchiness is to be preferred to a badly frenched front. It is hardly to be anticipated that perfection will be found in any part, although it may be. It is better to find numerous minute and hardly noticeable faults than a single bad one. The analogy of the engine again applies: a machine may function fairly well with numerous small maladjustments, whereas another machine perfect in all its parts but one and that one part grossly wrong may function very badly or not at all.

It is hardly necessary to observe the dog in profile at the walk. At this gait, the length of stride will not be demonstrated, nor will a roached or sagging back be more apparent than in the standing position.

In order to see these features, it is necessary that the dog be moved at a moderate fast trot, which is best seen from the dog's side. Stand well back from his path and have him moved with enough freedom to lower his head, if he desires to do so and if he needs to preserve his balance with his neck. The further away from him you stand, the better you can observe him.

Note whether his stride is long and flexible, as it should be, or short and choppy, wasteful of motion and of energy. A dog properly angulated, fore and aft, will extend his hind leg far under his

159

body, grasp the floor (or better the earth) firmly, and, extending his leg in a powerful follow through, throw the distance behind him. The power thus generated is transmitted through the spine to the shoulder, which, if properly angulated, opens to compensate for the long rear stride with an equally long stride in front.

There is little purpose in ample angulation, in the rear, however well used it may be, if the angle at the points of the shoulder is not sufficient to absorb the stride. It is equally futile to possess great angulation of shoulder without ample angulation in the rear and ample use of it to produce the power for transmission. A moderate and equalized angulation both aft and before is to be preferred to perfect hindquarters with an upright shoulder or to a perfect shoulder with inadequate hindquarters. Of course we want perfection of both ends of the dog, as open a shoulder as possible and as much angulation of hindquarters as the musculature can support. Excessive rear angulation without the muscles to support and articulate it results in weakness. The rear angulation is merely a series of long levers that will fall together without muscular tension. Indeed, angulation is an added burden for a standing dog, and, except in action, a dog is better for possessing mere props.

The loss of their powerful stride in our modern dogs is due to a loss of the muscular power to propel the dog, and a prevalence of straight shoulders. It is not due to a loss or *rear* angulation. There are more well-angled dogs and dogs with better angulation than in the early heyday of superb movers; they have simply lost their ability to utilize the rear angulation they possess. Some dogs with sufficient front and rear angulation also lack the driving power required. This leaves us open to the doubt that the action of the breed has actually deteriorated. We may well ask ourselves whether our current crop of dogs is receiving the exercise, especially in their puppyhood, to develop the muscles of their hindquarters to carry them over the ground with the agility and power their great-grandfathers displayed.

The stride of the forequarters should be as long as the stride behind, else at every trotting step the amount of the difference in those lengths will be lost. This is best seen from standing back a considerable way from the dog and having him led past one at a trot. The exact length of the over-step, as it is called, can be ascertained by sprinkling a thin layer of powder, flour, or even fine sand

160

Ch. Lahngold's April, owned by Ernest Loeb.

Ch. Cito v.d. Herrman Schleuse, owned by Gustave Schindler.

over the dog's·path to obtain footprints and measuring the distance by which the rear stride exceeds the front stride. There should be no difference in these measurements.

High, hackney-like action of the front feet is often mistakenly admired, being assumed to give the dog style. It is usually accompanied by a high carriage of the head. It results in waste of effort and is not at all desirable. It is not, however, so bad a fault as the excessive lifting of the hind leg in its forward thrust. This last is exceedingly wasteful of energy, serves no useful purpose whatever, and is awkward. It may occur in either leg or both legs, and gives the impression of string halt.

In action, the feet should just fairly clear the ground without any semblance of dragging. This conservation of energy may appear futile, when it is realized that the dog wastes so much energy in play and in useless activity; but in emergency of herding (or even of police service) the German Shepherd Dog is called upon to cover ground with the greatest celerity and to display tremendous endurance and stamina. In evaluating the merits of a dog, it becomes necessary to consider him in relation to the greatest exertion a member of the breed will ever be called upon to make. It is not enough that he can rather easily perform all the tasks you are likely to demand of him; but to be a typical specimen of his breed he must be structurally fit for intense and arduous service.

In fast trot, the dog should stretch out, with back entirely level and without undulation. His movement should be long, lithe, and powerful, and with no apparent effort. He should skim the ground with his feet. The best gait is not light or feathery, but the step should be firm, throwing the ground behind him. The tail may be raised to or beyond the horizontal, but it should not attain a vertical position or be turned over the back. It need not be perceptibly raised at all. This fast trot is the final test of the dog's worth. If the gait is correct, the structure of the skeleton needs must be correct.

Style

A German Shepherd Dog is theoretically merely a machine for herding sheep. What contributes to his efficiency as a herding dog makes for excellence, and whatever detracts from his herding ability is deemed a fault. This utilitarian theory is essentially true, and it is

162

1969 Grand Victor, Arno v.d. Kurpfalzhalle,
owned by Sam Lawrence.

1969 Grand Victrix, Ch. DeCloudt's Heidi,
owned by Mr. and Mrs. F. W. Cloudt.

Ch. Santana's Man O' War, R.O.M., owned by Barbara Lee Williams.

Ch. Gernda's Ludwig, R.O.M., whelped 1948. A Best in Show winner.
Owned by Mr. and Mrs. Robert M. Stoddard.

adhered to (or was prior to the war) in Germany, the homeland of the breed. Nobility, beauty, pride were merely fortuitous attributes, and the personality of the dog counted but little in German shows.

The Americans, however, demand class in their dogs, class plus conformation to a standard A. plain dog correctly constructed may get by to a high position in an award list, but such a dog is not great. A great dog must be a noble dog, beautiful and aware of his own beauty, a dominant personality. Style, flourish, elan may in an American show carry a dog further than perfect structure. A great dog of the breed must be endowed with an indefinable divine spark. The American, and in a lesser degree, the English market was before the war making some effect upon the German breeders and judges, who were beginning to find that a dog to be salable abroad had to display a pride and a personality that make him just a little more than a mechanism for the herding of sheep.

However much style and personality a dog may possess, they can never rightly take the place of correct conformation and gait; but when they are superimposed upon conformation and gait they make for greatness.

Evaluation of Faults

The novice fancier of the German Shepherd Dog must be warned on the one hand against the condemnation of his dog for some minor and minute fault. On the other hand, he must not seek to condone a major fault and deceive himself. There are no perfect dogs, and perfection must not be anticipated in any dog. Especially shall he not attach too much importance to faults that can be remedied. Fatness or thinness is not so much the fault of the dog as of the keeper. A fat dog may be reduced in weight, or a thin one may be fattened. The possession of the correct coat at a given time is less important (except in an actual show) than his known ability to grow a correct coat. Of course, for formal exhibition it is necessary that the dog be set down with a full bloom of coat, but for informal examination the certainty that he can grow a coat, irrespective of its present condition, is all that is required. This certainty is predicated upon the fact that the dog has at some previous time had a correct coat with full undercoat. If he has grown

Orpha of Edgetowne, pictured heavy in whelp. Note beautiful structure.

a coat, he can grow one again. Neither should a dog be penalized in this examination for softness or flabbiness of musculature, which can be hardened with judicious exercise. A flabby dog in a show is almost certain to go down to defeat, but it has nothing to do with his fundamental merits, which we are here seeking to ascertain.

But the pride of ownership should not prompt us to forgive obvious faults. A square body, stilty hindlegs, an upright shoulder, a crooked front, a weak back, cow-hocks, an awkward gait, any of these faults, if pronounced, seriously handicap a dog in competition. In fact, dogs that evince such faults should not be exhibited at all. It is necessary to forget that he is your dog and to look at him objectively. Charge against him all his shortcomings, but don't make mountains out of mole-hills. He may be a good pal and able to perform all that is required of him without being a first rate show specimen. Accept him for what he is, and do not expect too much from him. A woman may be good-looking and presentable without aspiring to be a moving picture star.

Above all, consider the dog as a unit. Symmetry and balance

166

of the whole organism are more important than any of the individual parts. There is a general disposition, especially among fanciers of German Shepherd Dogs, so to analyze dogs, to take them apart and judge the pieces, that the dog as a whole, the ensemble, is lost sight of. It is only as the individual parts fit together to make a complete organism that the whole dog is good or bad or mediocre.

However excellent any part may be, if it is too large or too small to mesh together with the other parts, the dog is thrown out of balance and his symmetry is lost. It is often said that if it were possible to take some parts of one dog and other parts from another and make a composite dog we should achieve perfection. Aside from the fact that it is impossible to do, the parts would not fit together. The dog is a unit.

It is the recognition of that unity that enables the experienced judge to evaluate the merits of a dog in so short a time. He sees the animal as a whole. When a class of dogs enters the ring and parades before him, he is able to arrive at a concept of which dogs are to win, which are to be discarded. He looks for balance and symmetry. Of course his opinion must be confirmed or denied by closer examination, but it is usually confirmed. No such instant evaluation of a dog is to be expected of the amateur fancier. He must examine the individual parts to know why his dog is good or bad; but, having examined the parts, he must fit them together into a whole dog. And the whole is greater than any of its parts. If the dog has symmetry and balance, it is a good dog; and if it lacks symmetry or balance it is not so good, no matter how excellent the individual pieces of dog that make up the whole may be.

There is little difference between the sexes in this particular breed. Bitches as a rule have more quality and refinement than dogs, somewhat less bone in proportion to their size, and are usually somewhat smaller. However, a large bitch may be considerably larger than a small dog. The dog is usually more arched of neck, more stallion-like. Size, within accepted limits, is a matter of little consideration.

We sometimes see a dog that in make and shape is more fitted to be a bitch; and we sometimes see a big, slashing, aggressive bitch upon which we could graft male organs. A first rate dog should conform to the character of its sex. Dogginess in a bitch, or bitchiness in a dog is a minor fault, and is subject to some penalty.

167

Diedre of Long-Worth, pictured at 15 months.

Ch. Brigitta of Dornwald, a Pfeffer daughter, owned by Mr. and Mrs.
James A. Cole, Dornwald Kennels.

8

Glossary of German
Dog Terms and Abbreviations

by Anne Fitzgerald Paramoure

INTRODUCTION

The translation of foreign pedigrees and show reports is not easy,
even for one who is well acquainted with the language in its every-
day form. Just as the novice finds many English words used in an
unfamiliar sense, so there is a special vocabulary employed by Ger-
man-speaking breeders and exhibitors. To translate them, it may be
necessary to plow through ten or twenty variations of meaning in
the unabridged dictionary, with no certainty that one will select
the right equivalent even if it is included. As for the ordinary
abridged dictionary, more than likely it will be no help whatever.
Moreover, abbreviations are frequently used, and may be fully as
puzzling as an unfamiliar use of a familiar word.

The names of German dogs, which are likely to appear daunt-
ingly long and formidable to those who do not understand the
language, are much easier to remember if they are broken down

into their separate parts. Most of them consist of an individual name, a preposition with or without an article, and a kennel name.

Most, if not all, German breeds require litter registration, with all puppies carrying the breeder's registered kennel name. It is usual for all the dogs of a single litter to have individual names beginning with the same letter.

The kennel names often refer to the town, village or local area in which the breeder lives. Sometimes they are related to the name of the breed or the breeder, and puns are not uncommon. Thus Herr Berger, breeder of German Shepherd Dogs, used the kennel name *Bergerslust,* which could be interpreted as meaning "Shepherd's Delight" or "Berger's Delight," as one chooses.

The impressive-sounding "Fiffi v. Rhein-Herne-Kanal" means simply "Fiffi of the Rhine Canal at Herne," where her breeder lived. Wilhelm Schwaneberg took the kennel name "v.d. Schwanburg," meaning "of, or from, the Swan Castle." The owners of "Neckarlust," "Neckarstadt," and "Neckartal" all live along the Neckar River. "Zwergschnauzerheim" means nothing more than "Home of Miniature Schnauzers."

While the following pages will not supply even an elementary course in the German language, they may enable the fancier confronted with the pedigree of an imported dog, a foreign show record or an advertisement of stock for sale to understand the important items without too much difficulty. A few facts which will be useful to anyone without a reading knowledge of ordinary German are also included.

All German nouns are capitalized, not merely proper names. Adjectives are not capitalized, even though they may form part of a kennel name, unless actually used in place of a noun. The formal second person "Sie" (meaning YOU) is also regularly capitalized. When an adjective is attached to the front of a noun so as to make a single word, however, it is capitalized instead of the noun to which it is attached, as in *Kleintierzuchter,* meaning small animal breeder.

German plurals are not formed by adding *S,* but in most cases by adding *er, e* or *en* to the root of the noun. Sometimes the root vowel is changed by the addition of an umlaut (··) over a, o or u, making it ä, ö, or ü. This may be the only change or it may be in addition to the plural endings already mentioned. The umlaut

Ch. Daring By Linc of Rocky Reach, U.D., owned by Jacques Levy.

Ch. Windyridge's Arry, owned by
Richard and Marjory Robbins.

stands for an *e* which is not written. In proper names or in a word beginning with a capital the *e* is often written in place of the umlaut, and where printing is done with type which does not include the umlauts the *e* itself may likewise be used. The umlaut can be important for three reasons: it changes the pronunciation; it may be the only sign that a word is plural and not singular; in a German dictionary or index all names or words which contain an umlaut will be alphabetized as though the letter *e* were printed after the vowel over which it is used. This may mean that a name or word will be found several lines or even pages away from the same name or word without the umlaut. Moreover, the presence or absence of the umlaut may completely change the meaning of a word. For instance, *Mucke* means a whim, while *Mücke* is a gnat. Finally, the feminine of many nouns is formed by adding an umlaut to the vowel and the suffix *in* to the end of the word, so Hund, dog (general or masculine) becomes Hündin, bitch.

Other peculiarities which may confuse those not familiar with the language are: nouns have four cases, nominative, genitive (usually ending in *s* or *es* but sometimes in *e, en* or *ens*), dative and accusative. Three are three genders, masculine, feminine and neuter. Adjectives and pronouns also change their endings.

Another peculiarity is that the perfect participle of verbs is formed by adding *ge* to the *front* of the verb in most cases. Thus the participle of *decken* (meaning to breed) is *gedeckt* (bred) and the word will be found in a dictionary under *d* and not *g*. Compound verbs with *inseparable* prefixes do not add the augment *ge* for the participle, however. On the other hand, compound verbs with *separable* prefixes insert the *ge* between the prefix and the verb root, the participle of *anfangen* (to begin) being *angefangen*. In certain other tenses the separable prefix of the verb in the main clause comes at the end of the phrase or sentence, as for instance, *ich fang an* (I begin) is a form of *anfangen*. As a compound verb may have quite a different meaning from the simple one from which it is formed, non-Germans unaccustomed to this usage find it extremely confusing to discover at the end of a sentence a prefix which may unexpectedly change the whole meaning. The Teutonic word order which frequently puts the verb at the end of the sentence instead of where other people would expect it is also confusing.

Ch. Tosca v. Reck, owned by Mrs. Pauline Young Foreman.

Ch. Kurt von Bid-Scono, owned by Francis L. and Mary J. Masselle.

173

Now, to the glossary. As we have said, many words used in German pedigrees and show reports are commonly abbreviated. For easiest reference, the abbreviations are presented here with the German word or words for which they stand, together with the English translation.

German training commands are shown in quotation marks (e.g. "Fuss"), and the English translations of them are followed by exclamation marks (e.g. Heel!).

	"Ablegen"	Lie down and lie still!
	Abstammung	Origin, descent, ancestry
Abz.	Abzeichen	Markings
	Abzugen	Available, offered (e.g. for sale or at stud)
	"Achtung"	Look out! Watch! On guard!
	Ahn, Ahnen	Ancestor, ancestors
	Ahnentafel	Pedigree
	Allgemeiner Eindruck	General impression
	Alter	Age
AK	Altersklasse	Open Class
A.	Amme	Foster mother
	Angekort	Inspected and certified suitable for breeding
	Ankorung	Official inspection for breeding suitability
	Anwartschaft	Prospective championship; accumulated wins toward a championship
	"Apport"	Fetch!
	Apportierbock	Dumbbell (for training to carry or retrieve)
	"Auf"	Up! (when the dog has been sitting or lying)
	Aufbeisser	Dog with undershot mouth
	Augen	Eyes
	"Aus"	Out! Let go!
	Ausbildung	Improvement or advancement of a breed
	Ausbildungskennzeichen	Standard
	Ausdruck	Character, expression
	Austellung, Austellungen	Show, Shows

An interesting study of Ch. Cita v. Da-Rie-Mar-Hill, C.D., Ch. Calipho of Villa Marina, and Cita's puppies. Owned by Mr. and Mrs. Raymond C. Becker.

Ch. Cosalta's Rodney, C.D.X.

BDH	Bahndiensthund	Railroad service dog
B.	Band, Bände	Volume, volumes (of stud book or magazine)
	Befehl	Command, order (in training)
B.	Befriedigend	Satisfactory (used in rating on show points)
	Begleithunde	Companion or house dogs
BK	Begrenzte Klasse	Limit Class
	Behaarung	Coat, hair
	Beisskorb	Muzzle (worn by dogs)
Bel.	Belassen	Left (with dam after birth); kept
	Belegt	Bred (of bitches)
Bes.	Besitzer, Besitzerin	Owner
	Besitzwechsel	Change of ownership
	Bewertung	Qualification; value; rating (e.g. "excellent," "very good," "poor")
	Bild, Bilder	Picture, pictures
Bl.	Blau	Blue; slate-grey
	"Bleibsitzen"	Stay! Keep sitting!
B.F.H.	Blindenführer Hund	Guide dog (for the blind)
BlHPr	Blindenführerhundprufung .	Guide dog trial or examination
Br.	Braun	Brown
Brgest.	Braungestichelt (Elchfarbig)	Elk color; mixed brown, not solid color
	"Bring"	Fetch!
	Bringbock	Dumbbell (for carrying)
	Bringen	To fetch
	Bruder, Bruder	Brother, brothers
	Brustfleck	Spot on chest
	Brustgeschirr	Dog harness
CAC	....	FCI award at smaller shows, or to dogs not judged good enough for CACIB
CACIB	....	International bench championship awarded by FCI for three firsts with "Excellent" under different judges

Ch. Rikter von Liebestraum, owned by Grant E. Mann.

Am. & Can. Ch. Von Nassau's Xellentie, C.D.,
owned by Ann and Thies Mesdag.

177

	"Daun"	Down! Drop! (when dog off leash is to be halted at a distance from trainer)
	Decken	To breed, to cover by a stud
	Decken, frei, zum	At public stud (for the usual fee)
	Decktag	Breeding date
D.	Der, dem, den	The (declined like an adjective or pronoun and agreeing in gender with its noun)
	Deutsche Dogge	Great Dane
	Deutsche Schäferhund	German Shepherd Dog
	Deutscher Reichsverband fur Polizei und Schutzhunde e. V.	German Reich Association for Police and Guard Dogs, inc.
D.S.V.	Deutscher Schaferhund Verband	German Shepherd Dog Association (comparatively little known in comparison to the S.V.)
D.H.S.	Deutsches Hundestammbuch	Official all-breed German stud book
	Deutsches Kartells fur Hundewesen	Pre-Hitler all-breed German club, corresponding to the American Kennel Club
	Diensthund	Service dog; trained dog in actual service
DSuchH	Dienstsuchhund	A tracker on active police duty
DSuchHPr	Dienstsuchhundprufung	A trial or contest for trained packers
D.V.	Dobermannpinscher-Verein .	Doberman Pinscher Association
	Dogge	Bulldog (see also *Deutsche Dogge*)
	Drahthaarigen	Wire-haired
	Dressierung, Dressur	Training
DrPr	Dressurprüfung	Training test, now called Zuchtprufung
	Dritter	Third
D.	Dunkel	Dark
Dr.	Dunkelrot	Dark red

178

Ch. Cobert's Ernestine, C.D., an outstanding Bernd v. Kallen-garten daughter. Owned by Mr. and Mrs. Theodore Beckhardt.

Ch. Yuccasand's Bernina, daughter of Grand Victor Ingo Wunschel-rute, owned by Waldenmark Kennels.

Ep.	Ehrenpreis	Trophy
E.	Eigentümer	Owner
E.V.	Eingetragener Verein	Registered association (i.e., incorporated)
	Eintragung	Entry (at a show or in a stud book)
	Eintragungsbestatigung	Certificate of entry; registration
	Elchfarbig	Elk colored; a brownish mixture, not solid tan or chocolate
	Ellenbogen	Elbows
	Eltern	Parents
	Enkel, Enkelin	Grandson, granddaughter
	Entwartung	Cancellation
	Ersatzpreis	A prize given in special recognition of the runner-up to the prize-winners at a show
	Erster	First
FS (FSg)	Fachschaftssieger	Club champion dog or bitch (formerly Klubsieger)
	Fachschaft	Department; division; branch
	Farbe, farbig	Color, colored
FH	Fahrtenhund	Field trial trailing dog
	Farbe, farbig	Color, colored
	"Fass"	Take it!
FCI	Federation Cynologique Internationale	International Dog Federation which awards World Championship titles
	Fehler	Faults
F.	Fehlerhaft	Faulty
F.	Führer	Handler
	"Fuss"	Heel!
	Gang	Gait
	Gebrauchshund	Working Dog
	Gedeckt	Bred, covered
	Gefleckt	Spotted
Gb.	Gelb	Yellow
Gen.	Genannt	Called, alias, known as
	Geschlecht	Sex (also species, family, kind)
	Geschutzer	Protected

Ch. Lanna v. Kuperhof, owned by B. H. Kuper.

Ch. Atlas v. Elfenhain, SchH I. owned by Rudolph Reinkers.

	Geschutzer Zuchtname	Registered kennel name
GfH	Gesellschaft fur Hundeforschung	Association for dog research
	Gestreift	Brindled
Gestr.	Gestrommt	Brindle
	Getotet	Killed, destroyed (when a litter is too large to raise advantageously)
	Gewinkelt	Angulated
Gew.	Gewolkt	Clouded
Gew.	Geworfen	Whelped
	"Gib laut"	Speak!
	Glanz	Lustrous
	Glatthaarig	Smooth-coated
	"Gradaus"	Straight ahead! Forward! (for *gerade aus*)
	Grau	Grey
	Gross	Big, large
	Grösse	Size
	Grosseltern	Grandparents
	Grossmutter	Granddam
	Grossvater	Grandsire
G.	Gut	Good
	Haar	Coat, hair
	Hals	Neck, throat
	Halsband	Collar
	Hasenfarbig	Hare-colored, mixed brownish-grey
	Hauptgeschäftstelle	Main office, headquarters
	Hauptprufung	Championship contest or trial
HPrHt	Hauptpreishuten	Herding championship trial
	Heisst	Called, known as
	Hell	Bright, light colored
H.G.H.	Herdengrebrauchshund	Trained Herding Dog
	"Hier"	Here! Come here!
	Hinterhand	Hindquarters
Hr.	Hinterläufe	Hind legs
	Hirschrot	Reddish fawn
	Hitze	Heat, season (in bitches)
	"Hoch"	Up! Over! (command for jumping)
	Hoden	Testicles
	"Hopp"	Away! Over! (command for jumping)
H.L.E.		
	Höchstlobende Erwähnung .	Very highly commended

182

1963 Canadian Grand Victor, Am. & Can. Ch. Fant Wikingerblut, SchH III, Best in Show winning son of Ulk. Owned by Mrs. Marion T. Darling.

Ch. Viking v. Hoheluft, Speciality winner of the post-war era. A Ch. Pfeffer grandson. Owned by Maur-Ray Kennels.

	Höhe	Height
H.	Holländische	Dutch
	Hund, hunde	Dog, dogs (male or in general)
	Hundefreunde	Dog lovers, fanciers
	Hündin, Hündinnen	Bitch, bitches
	Inzucht	Inbreeding
JS, JSn	Jahressieger, Jahressiegerin	Dog and bitch winner of the annual specialty championship show, thereby becoming champions of the year
	Jahrgang	Annual volumes, year's issue of stud book or magazine
JK	Jugendklasse	Youth Class (12–18 months for German Shepherd Dogs)
	Jung	Young
	Junger, Junge	Puppy, puppies, youngsters
JunghK	Junghundklasse	Junior Class (18–24 months for German Shepherd Dogs)
	Jungtier	Young animal, youngster, puppy
K.	Kampioen	Champion (Dutch)
	Katalog	Catalog
	Katzenfuss	Cat paw
	Kind, kinder	Get (of a sire or dam)
	Kippohr	Flop ear
	Klein	Small
	Kleintierzüchter	Small animal breeder
KS, KSn	Klubsieger, Klubsiegerin ...	Club champion dog or bitch. (Winner of First Open with rating of Excellent under three different judges.)
	Knochen	Bone
	"Komm"	Come!
	Konkurrenz	Competition
	Kopf	Head
	Koppel-Klasse	Brace Class
K.B.	Körbuch des Vereins für Deutsche Schäferhunde ...	Book of breeding suitability inspection of the S.V.

184

Ch. Conde del Llano Estacado, owned by Langdon Skarda.

Ch. Von Schrief's Portrait, R.O.M., a top-winning bitch of the late '50's, owned by Mr. and Mrs. Doyle A. Williams.

Servie v. Alexyrvo Hof, owned by Dr. Leo C. Clauss.

Ch. Merrilea's Rima of Dornwald, U.D.T.

	Körzeichen	Certified as suitable for breeding
	Kräftig	Strong
	"Kriech"	Crawl! Creep!
	Kriegshund	War dog
	Kruppe	Croup
	Kurz	Short
	Langhaarig	Long-haired
	"Lass"	Let go! Out!
	Läufe	Running gear, legs
	"Leg dich"	Lie down!
	"Legen"	Lie down!
	Leine	Leash
	Leistung	Field training
	Leistungsbuch	Field trial registration book
	Leistungsprüfung	Field trial
LS, LSg	Leistungssieger Leistungssiegerin	Field trial champion dog and bitch
LWP	Leistungswanderpreis des S.V.	Field trial trophy of the S.V.
	Liebhaber	Fancier
	Links	Left, left-handed
	Lobende Erwähnung	Highly recommended
M.	Mangelhaft	Passable, mediocre
M	Maske	Mask, face
MH	Melde Hund	Army messenger dog
MHPr	Meldehundprüfung	Messenger dog trial
	Meldeschein	Registration certificate
	Meldung	Entry, registration
	Mit	With
MA	Mit Amme aufgezogen	Raised with a foster mother
	Mitglied, mitglieder	Member, members
	Monatshefte	Unbound monthly issue of a magazine
	Monatsschrift	Monthly magazine
M.	Mutter	Mother, dam
	Nachgewiesen	Indicated
	Nase	Muzzle, nose
NHSB	Nederland Hundestammbuch	Netherlands stud book (all breeds)
	Neulings-Klasse	Novice Class

N. nachgew ...	Nicht nachgewiesen	Not indicated; not shown on the record
	"Nimm"	Take it!
Nr.	Nummer	Number
O	O	Zero; failed
OK	Offenklasse	Open Class
OLK	Offeneleistungsklasse	Open Class for dogs with training degrees
	Oberschlachtig	Overshot
O.A.	Ohne Amme	Without a foster mother
	Ohren	Ears
OSV	Osterreichischer Verein fur Deutsche Schäferhunde	Austrian Association for the German Shepherd Dog
	Osterreichisches Hundestammbuch	Austrian stud book (all breeds)
	Ortsgruppe	Local group; local club
	Paar	Pair, brace
	"Pass auf"	Watch out! Alert!
Pfsiz	Pfeffer und Salz	Pepper and Salt
	Pfote, Pfoten	Paw, foot
	"Pfui"	Shame! No!
	Platz	Place (in competition)
	"Platz"	Down!
	Prämierung	Award
P.D.H. ...,....	Polizei Dienst Hund	Trained dog in actual police service
P.D.H. Pr	Polizei Dienst Hund Prufung	Test or field trial for working police dogs
P.H.	Polizehund	Police-trained dog (of any breed)
	Preis, Preise	Prize, prizes
	Preishüten	Herding Trial
	Preishüten Sieger	Herding champion
	Preishüten Siegerin	Herding champion bitch
	Prüfung	Test, trial, examination
P.D.Z.	Prüfungsverband der Zuchtvereine fur Dienst-hundrassen in Kartell	Training competition organization of specialty clubs for service dog breeds affiliated with the Kartell

Am. & Can. Ch. Bernd v. Haus Twisterling, SchH II, all-breed Best in Show winner of the mid-50's, owned by Mrs. Jessie L. Ho.

1955 Canadian Grand Victrix, Am. Ch. Alfa vom Wormser Weg, owned by George Collins.

Ch. Cent v. Funf Gebeln, owned by Dr. Eleanor Waskow and Jack LaRou.

Ch. Harald vom Haus Tigges, SchH III, F.H., owned by Erich Renner.

190

	Rasse	Breed
	Rassekennzeichen	Breed standard, breed characteristics
	Rechts	Right (right hand)
	Reichsfachgruppe Deutsches Hundewesen e. V.	Post-Hitler name for D.K.H.
R.D.H.	Reichsverband fur das Deutscher Hundewesen ..	Hitler equivalent of D.K.H.
	Reichssieger, Reichssiegerin	Hitler equivalent of Jahressieger and Jahressiegerin
	Rein	Pure, entire, solid (of color)
	Reinzucht	Pure bred
	Richter	Judge
	Richterbericht	Judge's report
R.	Rot	Red
	Rucke	Back
R.	Rude	Stud dog, male
	Rute	Tail, stern
	Salz und Pfeffer	Salt and pepper color
SH	Sanitätshund	Red Cross dog
S.	Sattel	Saddle
	Schaferhund	German Shepherd Dog
	Schau	Show
	Schecken	Parti-colored
	Scheu	Shy
	Schusscheu	Gun-shy
	Schussfest	Steady to gun
	Schonheit	Beauty, bench
	Schonheitsieger	Bench champion
	Schriftleiter	Editor
	Schulhalsband	Spiked training collar
	Schulter	Shoulder
	Schulterhohe	Shoulder height
	Schusscheu	Gun-shy
	Schussfest	Steady to gun
SchH I	Schutzhundprüfung I	Obedience trial
SchH II	Schutzhundprüfung II	Trial for protection dogs
SchH III	Schutzhundprüfung III	Trial for trained police dogs
Schwz.	Schwarz	Black
	Schwarz mit braunen abzeichen	Black with brown markings; black and tan
	Schwarzgelb	Tawny; dark yellow
	Schwarzrot	Dark red

191

SHSB	Schweitzer Hundestammbuch	Swiss stud book
	Schwester	Sister
Sg.	Sehr gut	Very good (rating next below "excellent")
	"Setzen"	Sit!
S.	Sieger, Siegerin	Dog or bitch awarded VA-1 at annual Sieger show
	Siegerausstellung	Championship show
	Siegeranwärter, Siegeranwärterin	Certificate winner; prospective champion dog or bitch with wins toward the Fachschaftsieger or Klubsieger title
	Siegeranwartschaft	Prospect of a championship
	Siegerprufung	Championship contest
Sbgr	Silbergrau	Silver grey
StP	Stattspreis für Zucht oder Gebrauchsleistung	Government prize for Obedience or work training
	Sonderausstellung	Specialty Show
	Sonderverein	Specialty club
	Sprungwand	Hurdle; jump used for training to scale fences, etc.
	"Such"	Seek! Trail!
	"Such, verloren"	Seek a lost object!
SuchH	Suchhund der Polizei	Police tracker
SuchHPr	Suchhundprufung	Trailing test
S.V.	See Verein fur Deutsche Schaferhunde	
T.	Teil ...,..................	Part, section, volume
	Tiefschwarz	Solid black
	Tier	Animal
	Toten	To destroy (as unwanted puppies in a litter)
	Totgeboren	Stillborn
	Ubung	Training exercise
	Unbekannt	Unknown
U.	Und	And
	Unterschrift	Signature
	Urgrosseltern	Great-grandparents
	Urgrossenkel, urgrossenkelin	Great-great-grandson or great-great-granddaughter

Doctor of Long-Worth.

Ch. Critic of Kola-Marc, C.D., owned by Mr. and Mrs. A. R. Birrell.

193

Three Grettamarc Kennels' champions, all with obedience titles: Ch. Rhapsody, C.D.; Ch. Kalea, C.D.; and Ch. Nocturne, C.D.

Am. & Can. Ch. Frack von der Burg Arkenstede, SchH II, A.D., owned by Von Nassau Kennels.

	Urgrossmutter	Great-granddam
	Urgrossvater	Great-grandsire
	Ururgrosseltern	Great-great-grandparents
V.	Vater	Sire
	Verbindung	Mating
V.	Verein	Club, association
S.V.	Verein für Deutsche Schäferhunde e V.	German Shepherd Dog Association, Inc.
	Verbegung	Award, bestowal
	Vierter	Fourth
	Vorderbrust	Forechest
	Vorderhand	Forequarters
	Vorderpfote	Forepaw
	Vorprüfung	Preliminary trial
	Vorsitzender	President, chairman
	"Vorwärts"	Go ahead!
V.	Vorzüglich	Excellent (highest rating)
	Wanderpreis	Challenge trophy (best of breed)
	Wanderzuchtpreis	Breeder's challenge trophy
WA	Wasserhundprüfung	Water dog trial
W	Weiss	White
	Weitsprung	Broad jump
	Welp, Welpen	Young puppy, young puppies
WS	Weltsieger, Weltsiegerin	World champion dog or bitch
	Werfen·	To produce, to whelp
	Wesen	Character, temperament, disposition
	Winkelung	Angulation
	Wurf	Litter
WF	Wurfdatum	Whelping Date
	Wurfmeldung	Litter entry, litter registration
W.	Wurfstärke	Size of litter
	Zimmerrein	House-broken
Zh	Zotthaarig	Shaggy-coated
	Zucht	Breeding, breed, race
	Zuchtbuch	Stud Book
SZ	Zuchtbuch fur Deutsche Schaferhunde	German Shepherd Dog stud book

SZ–Nr	Zuchtbuch Nummer	Stud Book number
	Zuchbuchamt	Stud Book office
Z	Züchter, Züchterin	Breeder (masculine and feminine)
	Zuchtgruppe	Team
	Zuchthundin	Brood bitch
ZP	Zuchtpreis	Bred by exhibitor prize
	Zuchtprüfung	
	Schutzhundprufung	Obedience test. (Not exactly corresponding to those given in this country, but required of dogs not having a more advanced training degree in order to be eligible for championship.)
	Zuchtverein	Specialty club
	Zulassung	Allowed, permitted point or characteristic
	"Zur Spur"	Trail!
	"Zur Wache"	Watch! Guard!
	Zur Zucht nicht zugelassen	Not to be used for breeding
	Zur Zucht nur mit Genehmigung des Zuchtbuchamtes zugelassen	Can be used for breeding only with approval of the Stud Book office
	Zweiter	Second
	Zwinger	Kennel
	Zwingerklasse	Team class
	Zwingername	Kennel name

Lahngold's Admiration, R.O.M., owned by Hessian Kennels.

Ch. Kern Delta's Exakta, R.O.M., a daughter of Ch. Quell v. Fredeholz.
Owned by Art and Helen Hess.

197

Leu vom Kahlgrund, SchH III, handsome gray, strong in
Odin vom Stolzenfels breeding, imported in 1949 by
Grant Mann and Marian McDermott.

Ch. Harry vom Donauki, sire of the two-time German Sieger Volker v.
Zollgrenzeschutz-Haus.

9

The German Shepherd Dog
in Post-War Germany

by Gerda M. Umlauff
Hamburg, Germany

Note: These two reports, the first written in 1949 and the second in 1966, provide a progressive picture of the breed in Germany after World War II. We believe that the inclusion of the 1949 report just as it was written at the time will give the reader a richer appreciation of the problems that faced German breeders.

1949:

T HIS is addressed to the friends of the German Shepherd all over the world who are interested in learning what has become of the breed in its native country and of the club, which was once the greatest organization of its kind in the world—what has happened after six years of war in this country, after air raids which disturbed the houses of the breeders, who had already given to the army many of their dogs and who, when there were no more bombs, had to endure the hunger and suffering which followed, during one of the coldest winters in twenty years.

It is a cold day in January, 1949, as I am sitting opposite Dir. Kremhelmer in Augsburg. Dir. Kremhelmer is now—since Dr. Roesebeck and Dir. Schaeller died two years ago, almost at the same time—the leader of the Shepherd Club, and he willingly answers my questions.

When the Nazi regime ceased, the old name of the "Verein fur deutsche Schaferhunde (S.V.) e.V. Augsburg" was restored at once.

Due to the division of Germany, the exact number of members cannot be determined but it is between 35,000 and 42,000. In the office of the club, which has survived two wars, revolution, inflation, deflation, Nazi regime and capitulation, forty officials are working today. The registrations in the stud book have increased along with the growing membership. The records show:

1945 . . . . 11,000 registrations
1946 23,000   "
1947 25,000   "
1948 40,000   "

From 1945 through 1948, there have been from 80 to 200 shows every year and at each of them at least 100 Shepherds were exhibited. The show with the highest number of dogs of this era had 550 entries. Herding trials took place in 1947 in both North and South Germany, but only in North Germany in 1948 on account of an epidemic among the sheep in South Germany.

We find that adverse conditions could in no way stifle interest in dogs in Germany, in spite of the fact that numerous dogs were lost through the war and others at the present time are lost to the shows in the western zone through the division of Germany. Nevertheless, the dogs of the Russian zone of Germany are also registered in Augsburg. On the other hand, the total loss of animals was not so great as to make it necessary to register Shepherds without pedigrees, as some other clubs were forced to do. Also in the case of refugees, the office at Augsburg has been very careful and only if there were absolutely clear proofs and no doubt about the origin of the particular dog, was the lost pedigree certified once more.

Has the Military Government required valuable breeding stock since 1945, and has the quality become poor since that time through careless breeding or the demand of foreign customers?

The Military Government has requested dogs for the army. However, there is an arrangement with the S. V. that only those dogs named by that organization would be taken and so the breeding stock will remain in this country. The breeding results of beginners have very little influence on the whole, but the knowledge and experience of old breeders have improved the breed more and more. Prominent judges and experts state that Germany is still one of the leaders with its dogs, and reports on the new stock verify this fact. At the international show which took place at Konstanz at the Swiss frontier last year, breeders had the opportunity to see and compare the breeding products with those of Switzerland. Our young dogs exhibit great possibilities and there are a lot of requests for our stud dogs, especially from Austria, Belgium, and the Netherlands. Even the advent of the new currency did not stop the fancy in Germany, and it is reported that there have been from 60 to 70% more dogs at the shows since 1946.

American soldiers staying in Germany are much interested in Shepherds and are eager to improve their knowledge of this breed. Novices very often select dogs according to their color and want pale-colored dogs, not knowing that fading colors in Shepherds are signs of degeneracy. Therefore it is the aim of all serious German breeders to keep the Shepherds' color as dark as possible. American fanciers have reported that interest in working dogs is increasing and we are sure that the time is not far distant when dogs in the U.S.A. will be inspected and certified suitable for breeding.

If one should wonder how it has been possible to maintain the high quality of the dogs through the chaos of the past years, the answer is that it could be accomplished only through the enduring love of the breeders for their dogs. Misery and all kinds of trouble, lack of accommodations, food, and money, want of all kind could not kill the passion of the German breeder, who found a ready market for his dogs because so many people had lost their families and friends through the war, had become lonely, and were longing for the love of a living being.

The German breeder receives much support from his organization, advice in every way, and food and medicine for the dogs. Faults are pointed out and advice given on how to avoid them. There are now and then dogs who lack good teeth and the breeders are advised not to mate two such dogs. Breeders are also advised to avoid breeding with dogs whose hair has become too long. Therefore Shepherds with long hair are no longer registered. The height differs at times. Some dogs had become too large, and small stud dogs were chosen for breeding such bitches. Therefore we must now take heed that underheight and underweight do not increase.

The Schaferhund-Verein arranges meetings for the oldest and most experienced breeders and judges for the purpose of discussing and working out the best ways for breeding better dogs. It is ordered that only absolutely healthy dogs be used for breeding purposes. The male must be at least two years old and the female not less than 20 to 22 months. The male may not be bred to more than 40 bitches each year; but in the first, seventh and eighth year, only 25 to 30 times. The requirement for working dogs demands that both parents and also all grandparents must have passed the guard-dog trial. The club also makes official inspections for breeding suitability, which is demanded of both parents.

Once every year the former champion show, now called the "Chief Breed Show" (*Hauptzuchtschau*), takes place, and there are always many dogs entered in competition. If only one dog were to receive the champion title, the bloodlines would by-and-by become too narrow, and therefore there has been created the "selection class" (*Ausleseklasse*), in which all winning dogs have the same value. Prior to 1947 the title "Schutzhund I" was required for dogs shown in this class, but since that time dogs must have the title "Schutzhund II" if they are to compete in the selection class.

The Schaferhund-Verein has ruled that breeders may export only dogs who fulfill the following conditions: age, at least one year old; guard-dog trial passed; and, at shows, judged at least "very good."

The Schaferhund-Verein and its breeders do not neglect the organization for blind people, and supply them with many guide dogs.

The planned Shepherd breeding during the last fifty years has shown that there are many bloodlines, which guarantee that the whole Shepherd breeding need not fear too much inbreeding. Nevertheless, to avoid this, there are two kennels, "v.Blasienberg" and "v.Hain," which are trying to build up certain old bloodlines and obtain new bloodlines.

Cralo v. Haunstetten, SchH II, a select male of 1946, 1947, 1948, and 1949.

Ottilla Preussenblut, a select bitch of 1948.

It is no secret that it is possible, as well as important, to breed animals whose hereditary tendencies will guarantee the greatest probability of improving the most desired attributes. Therefore it is necessary to know the most important male bloodlines occurring in German Shepherd dogs. The blood is carried into the breed of today through many different bloodlines, most of which lead to the Horand-line, which has a lot of important branches. Twenty-eight different lines have been counted from him but there are still more branches; some of the most famous we shall mention in the following lines:

Here is one in which we find a very strong consolidation of the Pollux-Horand-Hektor blood: "Utz v. Haus Schutting" 331999 (Obedience test) —"Erich v. Grafenwerth" 71141 (Police trained dog) —"Alex v. Westphalenheim" 59298—"Hettel Uckermark" 3897 (trained herding dog) —"Horand v. Grafrath" 1 and from him to the oldest breeding Shepherds "Kastor" and "Pollux."

Another good line is: "Sultan v. Blasienberg" 182065 (trained herding dog and protection dog) —"Caro v. Blasienberg" 97750—"Curt v. d. Morgensonne" 66087—"Alex v. Westphalenheim" 59298 —"Heinz"—"Hektor v. Schwaben" 13—"Horand v. Grafrath" 1.

Many other branches of the breed are influenced by: "Jungtell v. d. Kriminalpolizei" 24511 (Police dog) —"Luchs v. Kalsmunt Wetzlar" 3371—"Graf Eberhard v. Hohen Esp" 1135—"Pilot" 111 —"Hektor v. Schwaben" 13—"Horand v. Grafrath" 1.

Very well known is also: "Erich v. Glockenbrink" 275752 (Protection dog) —"Erich v. Grafenwerth" 71141 (Police dog) —"Alex v. Westphalenheim" 59298—"Heinz"—"Hektor v. Schwaben" 13— "Horand v. Grafrath" 1.

As a final observation, it can be said that the Alex-lines mentioned are famous for the tendency to transmit a good-sized, powerful, and deep body, which is the ideal breeding aim for German Shepherds.

1966:

The 1965 Sieger or chief championship show (*Siegerhauptschau*) of the *Verein fur Deutsche Schaferhunde* (*SV*) took place in September at Mannheim, West Germany. The tremendous audience included many visitors from foreign lands—from Austria, the Bahamas, Belgium, Brazil, Canada, Chile, Denmark (some 30 people), Finland, France (about 50 people), Great Britain (also about 50), Ireland, Italy (about 30), Japan, Lebanon, Luxembourg, the Netherlands (about 40), Norway, Puerto Rico, Rhodesia, Sweden (about 35), Switzerland (more than a hundred), Spain, South Africa, and about 35 from the United States—in all, more than 400 enthusiastic friends of the German Shepherd Dog from 24 different countries.

The club now has a membership of about 40,000, and has set its goal at 45,000. Despite the fact that ten shows scheduled in 1965 had been cancelled because of the rabies, 662 German Shepherd Dogs were benched at Mannheim. Included were 34 entries from foreign countries: Austria 3, Belgium 1, France 6, Italy 12, Japan 1, Netherlands 4, Sweden 1, Switzerland 3, and the United States 3.

There were 15 entries for the *Zuchtgruppen* (in which dogs are entered as a group from a kennel, and judged on their uniformity), but only 8 groups were rated. The winning kennel was "v.d. Wiederau" (4 dogs, from 2 litters of different sires and dams), owned by W. Martin, Viernheim. Second was "Grubenstolz," with dogs from 3 litters, from 3 sires and dams, owned by W. Dorner, Cologne-Bocklemund. Third was "v. Elbachtal," represented by 3 litters, from 3 sires and dams, owned by H. Druck, Hadamar. Fourth was a second group from the "v. Elbachtal" kennel; fifth, "Colonia Agrippina" kennel; sixth "v. Westgermanien"; seventh, "v.d. Starenheimat;" and eighth, "v. Felsteral."

In accordance with tradition, Dr. Werner Funk, president of the club, judged the male division of the *Gebrauchshundklasse* (Working Dog class), first choice of which becomes the Sieger of the Year. In his report, Dr. Funk warned against the German Shepherd Dog being allowed to again become too big, as it had been in the years from 1920 to 1930. The ideal height is between 62 and 63 cms. (1 inch = 2.54 cms.) measured at the shoulder, but many of the dogs at Mannheim were in the 64.5 to 66 cms. range. In previous years, there had been concern about faulty forequarters, but this situation Dr. Funk found much improved. He did, however, warn breeders to take heed of loose elbows.

Almost half of the dogs entered received an "Excellent," and among those in the other half that were rated only "Very Good" were many that had gotten an "Excellent" at some previous show.

Best in this male Working class, earning the Sieger title, was Hanko v. d. Hetschmuhle, 1029585 SchH II, whelped June 4, 1962 (by Witz v. Haus Schutting, 971570 SchH II ex Eva v. d. Hetschmuhle, 949259 SchH III).

Five other dogs were rated select:

Cyru v. d. Baltikum, 1014049 SchH III, FH
Basko v. d. Khaler Heide, 1045002, SchH II
Condor v. Zollgrenzschutz-Haus, 1038960 SchH III
Alf v. Convent, 1044501 SchH II
Harras v. Rustenhugel, 1038747 SchH I

Herr W. Trox judged the bitches. In his report, he stated that of the 96 bitches entered, 83 had the right middle size, and the other 14 were a little bit higher. But none was too small.

Eight bitches were selected as best. The Siegerin award went to Landa v. d. Wienerau, 1029754, SchH III, FH, whelped May 20, 1962 (by Jalk v. Fohlenbrunnen, 973652 SchH III ex Dixie v. d. Wienerau, 980594 SchH I).

The other seven were:
Heidi v. Furstenhugel, 1038749 SchH I
Cilly v. Oranien Nassau, 1015315 SchH II
Gladys v. d. Burg Waldeck, 1015857 SchH I
Kascha v. Wiedenbrucker Land, 1010703 SchH I
Bessie v. Ihletal, 1001065 SchH III, FH
Xenia v. Elbbachtal, 1011620 SchH III, FH
Assi v. Luvenicher Land, 1023864, SchH I

In the *Sonderklasse* or Herding Dog class (dogs that are actually working with flocks of sheep), five males were judged. Best was Dolf v. Altenbachtal, 1048035, HGH, whelped April 21, 1963 (by Jalk v. Fohlenbrunnen, SchH III ex Centi v. Kirschental, SchH II, FH, HGH). Best of the ten bitches was Dolf's half-sister, Bora v. Altenbachtal, 1009711, HGH, whelped April 7, 1961 (by Valet v. Busecker-Schloss, SchH III ex Centi v. Kirschental).

The chief working trial of 1965 took place at Treysa. Winner of the *Hutensieger* title for the year with 98 points was Flink v. Sumpfbach, 1053032, HGH, whelped January 21, 1963. In second place with 95 points was Guss v. Sumpfbach, 1057025, HGH. Placing third, with 90 points, was Mutz v. Stammherde Ramholz, 1025903, HGH.

The *Bundessiegerprufung* (championship contest) took place at Ulm. Champion for 1965, with 291 points and an "Excellent," was the male Bleck v. Unteren Wallberg, 995614 SchH III.

The championship contest for dogs belonging to official agencies also took place at Ulm, and the championship title was won by Falk v. Hitdorfer Land, 1025369, DH II, FH, belonging to the police at Northrhine, Westphalia. Falk scored 288 of a possible 300 points, and received an "Excellent."

The breed continues to zoom in Germany. In 1961, 17,000 puppies were registered in the stud book. In 1965, a total of 23,000 were registered, for an increase of 35%.

German Sieger for 1959 and 1960, Volker vom Zollgrenzschutz-Haus, SchH III, bred and owned by Josef Wasserman.

10

The Siegers
and Siegerins-Germany

Note: The Sieger and Siegerin are selected each year at the *Siegerhauptschau* or championship show of the Verein fur Deutsche Schaferhunde (SV), the parent breed club. The Sieger is chosen by the judge of the *Gebrauchshund Klasse—Ruden* (Working dog class—males), and the Siegerin by the judge of the *Gebrauchshund Klasse—Hundinnen* (Working dog class—bitches).

Up to and inclusive of 1937, a Sieger and Siegerin were chosen from out of the class. However, the feeling grew that this put an undue emphasis on the bloodline of just one dog and one bitch. To give recognition to other bloodlines, beginning in 1938, a group of dogs considered outstanding for breeding were selected each year rather than just one, and were called the *Auslese* or select group.

In 1955, the Sieger title was reinstated. The dogs of the *Vorzuglich Auslese* (Excellent Select) group are rated, and the dog that is VA–1 becomes the Sieger. Similarly, the bitch that is VA–1 becomes the Siegerin.

To qualify for the *Gebrauchshund Klasse*, a dog must be two years old and must have at least a SchH I working degree. To be eligible for a V (Excellent) or VA (Excellent Select) rating, the dogs must pass a gun test at the show, and—in an adjoining ring—pass an aggressiveness test designed to show their desire to protect their owners. No dog can place in the *Auslese* group unless both parents are *angekort*—approved for breeding. Also, since 1967, only dogs with the "a" rating (free from hip dysplasia) can become *Auslese*. In fact, the "a" rating is taken into consideration in the selection of V dogs.

Other important classes at the Sieger show include a *Jugend Klasse* (divided for males and bitches) for 12–18 months old dogs, and a *Junghund Klasse* (also with separate judging for males and bitches) for dogs 18–24 months old.

Flora von der Warte, SZ–4831, German Grand Champion 1908.

1956 German Siegerin, Lore vom Tempelblick, owned by Dr. Otto Schales.

1958 Siegerin Mascha v. Stuhri-Gau.

1899 Jorg v. d. Krone
1900 Hektor v. Schwaben
1901 Hektor v. Schwaben,
1902 Peter v. Pritschen, KrH
1903 Roland v. Park
1904 Arlbert v. Grafrath
1905 Beowulf v. Nahegau
1906 Roland v. Starkenburg
1907 Roland v. Starkenburg
1908 Luchs v. Kalsmunt Wetzlar
1909 Hettel Uckermark, HGH
1910 Tell v. d. Kriminalpoizei
1911 Norbert v. Kohlwald, PH
1912 Norbert v. Kohlwald, PH
1913 Arno v. d. Eichenburg
1914–1918   Not Awarded
1919 Dolf v. Dusternbrook, PH
1920 Erich v. Grafenwerth, PH
1921 Harras v. d. Juch, PH
1922 Cito Bergerslust, SchH
1923 Cito Bergerslust, SchH
1924 Donar v. Overstolzen, SchH
1925 Klodo v. Boxberg, SchH
1926 Erich v. Glockenbrink, SchH
1927 Arko v. Sadowaberg, SchH
1928 Erich v. Glockenbrink, SchH
1929 Utz v. Haus Schutting, ZPr
1930 Herold a. d. Niederlausitz, SchH
1931 Herold a. d. Niederlausitz, SchH
1932 Hussan v. Haus Schutting, ZPr
1933 Odin v. Stolzenfels, ZPr
1934 Cuno v. Georgentor, ZPr
1935 Jalk v. Pagensgrub, ZPr
1936 Arras a. d. Stadt-Velbert, ZPr
1937 Pfeffer v. Bern, ZPr MH 1

1955 Alf v. Nordfelsen

1969 Sieger, Heiko v. Oranien Nassau.

1956   Hardt v. Stuveschacht
1957   Arno v. Haus Gersie
1958   Condor v. Hohenstamm
1959   Volker v. Zollgrenzschutz-Haus
1960   Volker v. Zollgrenzschutz-Haus
1961   Veus v. Starrenburg
1962   Mutz a. d. Kuckstrasse
1963   Ajax v. Haus Dexel
1964   Zibu v. Haus Schutting
1965   Hanko v. Hetschmuhle
1966   Basko v. d. Kahler Heide
1967   Bodo v. Lierberg
1968   Gin v. Lierberg
1969   Heiko v. Oranien Nassau

GERMAN SIEGERINS

1899 Lisie v. Schwenningen
1900 Canna
1901 Elsa v. Schwaben
1902 Hella v. Memmingen
1903 Hella v. Memmingen
1904 Regina v. Schwaben
1905 Vefi v. Niedersachsen
1906 Gretel Uckermark
1907 Hulda v. Siegestor, PH
1908 Flora v. d. Warte, PH
1909 Ella v. Erlenbrunnen
1910 Flora v. d. Kriminalpolizei
1911 Hella v. d. Kriminalpolizei
1912 Hella v. d. Kriminalpolizei
1913 Frigga v. Scharenstatten
1914–1918 Not Awarded
1919 Anni v. Humboldtpark
1920 Anni v. Humboldtpark
1921 Nanthild v. Riedekenburg
1922 Asta v. d. Kaltenweide, SchH
1923 Asta v. d. Kaltenweide, SchH
1924 Asta v. d. Kaltenweide, SchH
1925 Seffe v. Blasienberg, SchH
1926 Arna a. d. Ehrenzelle, SchH
1927 Elly v. Furstensteg, ZPr
1928 Katja v. Blasienberg, ZPr
1929 Katja v. Blasienberg, ZPr
1930 Bella v. Klosterbrunn, ZPr
1931 Illa v. Helmholtz, ZPr
1932 Birke v. Blasienberg, ZPr
1933 Jamba v. Haus Schutting, ZPr
1934 Grete a. d. Raumanskaule, SchH
1935 Stella v. Haus Schutting, SchH
1936 Stella v. Haus Schutting, SchH
1937 Traute v. Bern, ZPr

1955 Muschka v. Tempelblick

1969 Reserve Siegerin, Hexe v.d. Rheinhalle, SchH II.

1956   Lore v. Tempelblick
1957   Wilma v. Richterbach
1958   Mascha v. Stuhri-Gau
1959   Asja v. Geigerklause
1960   Mascha v. Stuhri-Gau
1961   Assie v. Hexenkalk
1962   Rike v. Colonia Agrippina
1963   Maja v. Stolperland
1964   Blanka v. Kisskamp
1965   Landa v. d. Wienerau
1966   Cita v. Gruchental
1967   Betty v. Glockenland
1968   Rommy v. Driland
1969   Connie v. Klosterbogen, SchH II.

German Shepherd Dog puppy.

11

The Most Utilitarian
Dog of All

by Jane G. Bennett

The German Shepherd Dog, as its name implies, was developed to herd sheep. As its use as a herding dog diminished, other areas were sought in which this highly intelligent animal could serve mankind as more than a companion and enjoyable family member.

The first major endeavor was to intensify the already highly developed protective sense. Dogs with a more aggressive attitude were selected to be used as police dogs. We are all aware of the tremendous work the German Shepherd Dog has done for nearly fifty years in aiding the major police departments throughout the world. In ever-increasing realization of the great asset that a well-trained dog can be in riot control, search of buildings, and as a second pair of ears for the lone patrolman walking his beat, police departments are turning to canine corps. One of the best known, and most copied, is the canine corps of London, England.

A closely related service is the privately owned, or leased, guard

The German Shepherd's sense of smell can solve problems in heavy cover.
—*Photo, with permission, from "The Koehler Method of Guard Dog Training."*

218

Up, up and over. German Shepherd Dog with Delaware State Police trainer.

Champion Arno of San Miguel, C.D.X. and companion.
(Photo, courtesy German Shepherd Dog Review.)

dog. Great is the demand for these dogs by industry, construction companies, banks, estates, and private individuals who feel the need of extra protection. In New York City alone there are over 4,000 of these dogs trained to do the job that understaffed police precincts cannot handle. In the hands of private individuals a highly trained guard dog with "attack" training can be dangerous, but only if the dog has been badly schooled, or if the handler has not been fully instructed in dealing with his four-legged anti-burglar, anti-mugger companion.

Much has been written of the enormous service the German Shepherd Dog has been to the military. Their great work for Germany and France in World War I was responsible for the tremendous, and unfortunate, popularity of the breed in the 1920's. In the military they have been of invaluable service as messengers, wire carriers, aid to medical corps men, scout dogs, munition sniffers, airplane spotters, and as guards. (After war-time use of various breeds, the War Department in 1946 named the German Shepherd Dog as the official U.S. Army dog.)

Their service in Vietnam has been reported almost weekly, and returning servicemen tell repeatedly of how the alerting actions of scout dogs have saved platoon after platoon.

In recent years, a new service has been found for the keenness of scent this breed possesses. With the drug problem increasing, dogs are now being used at several major airports and steamship terminals to sniff out shipments hitherto undetectable. Famed television star Jack Webb, always an ardent German Shepherd Dog fan, documented the use of a trained "dope dog" in a recent Dragnet program, using one of the dogs actually trained for the Los Angeles Police Department.

One of the most spectacular uses of the working dog is as an "Avalanche Dog." In Switzerland, hundreds of people each year owe their lives to the keen senses of the dog who can find humans under many feet of snow and/or rocks. Wherever the breed is available, and avalanches are a danger, teams of man and dog are trained and ready for duty.

"Search and Rescue" work is also becoming widely acclaimed throughout the United States, as sheriff offices more and more recognize the assistance readily available from teams being developed on a voluntary basis. Outstanding search and rescue work has been attributed recently to a group in the area of Seattle, Washington. This group, with an assist from the German Shepherd Dog Club of America, Inc., is now attempting to promote this service in far-flung areas.

Of all the services for mankind performed by the German Shepherd Dog none has been of greater benefit than his work in guide-dog harness. The contribution to this work made by Mrs. Harrison Eustis' Fortunate Fields strain of German Shepherd Dogs is legendary. The experiments in breeding conducted at Fortunate Fields brought out the capabilities of this amazing breed. This work was continued by Elliott Humphrey in this country at the Seeing Eye, Inc. at Morristown, N. J. All other guide dog institutions in the United States employ much the same methods that have been proven over the years at Seeing Eye, Inc.

In his work leading the sightless, the German Shepherd Dog shows to the world his great intelligence, devotion, sense of discrimination, and reasoning power. He must sublimate all of his own canine desires, and live for his master alone. His great heart has brought many people out of despair, enabling them once more to walk among the sighted.

The German Shepherd Dog has been developed by devoted breeders everywhere to maintain a gait *unique* to the breed, conformation of great beauty, and intelligence unequalled by any other breed. In service to mankind, no breed can match the variety of its endeavors. If you own just one, do not miss the great enjoyment you can have—*train your dog*.

A graduate from the world-famous Seeing Eye School at Morristown, N.J., leaving with his guide dog. Thousands of German Shepherd Dogs have been thus trained since the inception of the school forty years ago.

223

Ch. Giralda's Lola, C.D. (whelped 1928) and family.

Part II

GENERAL CARE AND TRAINING OF YOUR DOG

by

Elsworth S. Howell

Milo G. Denlinger

A. C. Merrick, D.V.M.

Introduction

THE normal care and training of dogs involve no great mysteries. The application of common sense and good judgment is required, however. The pages that follow distill the combined experience and knowledge of three authorities who have devoted most of their lives to dogs.

Milo Denlinger wrote many books out of his rich and varied experience as a breeder, exhibitor and owner of a commercial kennel. Elsworth Howell has been a fancier since young boyhood and claims intimate knowledge of 25 different breeds; he is an American Kennel Club delegate and judge of the sporting breeds. Dr. A. C. Merrick is a leading veterinarian with a wide practice.

The chapter on "Training and Simple Obedience" covers the basic behavior and performance every dog should have to be accepted by your friends, relatives, neighbors and strangers. The good manners and exercises described will avoid costly bills for damage to the owner's or neighbor's property and will prevent heartbreaking accidents to the dog and to the people he meets. The instructions are given in simple, clear language so that a child may easily follow them.

"The Exhibition of Dogs" describes the kinds of dog shows, their classes and how an owner may enter his dog and show it. If one practices good sportsmanship, shows can be enjoyable.

The chapter on feeding offers sound advice on feeding puppies,

3

adult dogs, the stud dog and the brood bitch. The values of proteins, carbohydrates, fats, minerals and vitamins in the dog's diet are thoroughly covered. Specific diets and quantities are not given because of the many variations among dogs, even of the same breed or size, in their individual needs, likes, dislikes, allergies, etc.

"The Breeding of Dogs" contains the fundamental precepts everyone who wishes to raise puppies should know. Suggestions for choosing a stud dog are given. The differences among outcrossing, inbreeding and line breeding are clearly explained. Care tips for the pregnant and whelping bitch will be found most helpful.

The material on "External Vermin and Parasites" gives specific treatments for removing and preventing fleas, lice, ticks and flies. With today's wonder insecticides and with proper management there is no excuse for a dog to be infested with any of these pests which often cause secondary problems.

"Intestinal Parasites and Their Control" supplies the knowledge dog owners must have of the kinds of worms that invade dogs and the symptoms they cause. While drugs used for the removal of these debilitating dog enemies are discussed, dosages are not given because it is the authors' and publisher's belief that such treatment is best left in the hands of the veterinarian. These drugs are powerful and dangerous in inexperienced hands.

The chapter on "Skin Troubles" supplies the information and treatments needed to recognize and cure these diseases. The hints appearing on coat care will do much to prevent skin problems.

One of the most valuable sections in this book is the "instant" advice on "FIRST AID" appearing on pages 95-98. The publisher strongly urges the reader to commit this section to memory. It may save a pet's life.

The information on diseases will help the dog owner to diagnose symptoms. Some dog owners rush their dogs to the veterinarian for the slightest, transitory upsets.

Finally, the chapters on "Housing for Dogs" and "Care of the Old Dog" round out this highly useful guide for all dog lovers.

Training and
Simple Obedience

E VERY DOG that is mentally and physically sound can be taught good manners and simple obedience by any normal man, woman, or child over eight years old.

Certain requirements must be met by the dog, trainer and the environment if the training is to be enjoyable and effective. The dog must be rested and calm. The trainer must be rested, calm, gentle, firm, patient and persistent. The training site should be dry, comfortable and, except for certain exercises, devoid of distractions.

Proper techniques can achieve quick and sure results. Always use short, strong words for commands and always use the *same* word or words for the same command. Speak with authority; never scream or yell. Teach one command or exercise at a time and make sure the dog understands it and performs it perfectly before you proceed to the next step. Demand the dog's undivided attention; if he wavers or wanders, speak his name or pat him smartly or jerk his leash. Use pats and praise plentifully; avoid tidbit training if at all possible because tidbits may not always be available in an emergency and the dog will learn better without them. Keep lessons short; when the dog begins to show boredom, stop and do not resume in less than two hours. One or two ten-minute lessons a day should be ample, especially for a young puppy. Dogs have their good and bad days; if your well dog seems unduly lazy, tired, bored or off-color, put off the lesson until tomorrow. Try to make lessons a joy, a happy time both for you and the dog, but do demand and get the desired action. Whenever correction or punishment is needed, use ways and devices that the dog does not connect with you; some of these means are given in the following instructions. Use painful punishment only as a last resort.

"NO!"

The most useful and easily understood command is "NO!" spoken in a sharp, disapproving tone and accompanied with a shaking finger. At first, speak the dog's name following with "NO!" until the meaning of the word—your displeasure—is clear.

"COME!"

Indoors or out, let the dog go ten or more feet away from you. Speak his name following at once with "COME!" Crouch, clap your hands, pick up a stick, throw a ball up and catch it, or create any other diversion which will lure the dog to you. When he comes, praise and pat effusively. As with all commands and exercises repeat the lesson, until the dog *always* comes to you.

THE FIRST NIGHTS

Puppies left alone will bark, moan and whine. If your dog is not to have the run of the house, put him in a room where he can do the least damage. Give him a Nylabone and a strip of beef hide (both available in supermarkets or pet shops and excellent as teething pacifiers). A very young puppy may appreciate a loud-ticking clock which, some dog trainers say, simulates the heart-beat of his former litter mates. Beyond providing these diversions, grit your teeth and steel your heart. If in pity you go to the howling puppy, he will howl every time you leave him. Suffer one night, two nights or possibly three, and you'll have it made.

The greatest boon to dog training and management is the wooden or wire crate. Any two-handed man can make a ⅜″ plywood crate. It needs only four sides, a top, a bottom, a door on hinges and with a strong hasp, and a fitting burlap bag stuffed with shredded newspaper, cedar shavings or 2″ foam rubber. Feed dealers or seed stores should give you burlap bags; be sure to wash them thoroughly to remove any chemical or allergy-causing material. The crate should be as long, as high and three times as wide as the dog will be full grown. The crate will become as much a sanctuary to your dog as a cave was to his prehistoric ancestor; it will also help immeasurably in housebreaking.

HOUSEBREAKING

The secret to housebreaking a healthy normal dog is simple: take him out every hour if he is from two to six months old when you get him; or the first thing in the morning, immediately after every meal, and the last thing at night if he is over six months.

For very young puppies, the paper break is indicated. Lay eight or ten layers of newspapers in a room corner most remote from the puppy's bed. By four months of age or after two weeks in a new home if older, a healthy puppy should not need the paper *IF* it is exercised outdoors often and *IF* no liquid (including milk) is given after 5 P.M. and *IF* it is taken out not earlier than 10 P.M. at night and not later than 7 A.M. the next morning.

When the dog does what it should when and where it should, praise, praise and praise some more. Be patient outdoors: keep the dog out until action occurs. Take the dog to the same general area always; its own traces and those of other dogs thus drawn to the spot will help to inspire the desired action.

In extreme cases where frequent exercising outdoors fails, try to catch the dog in the act and throw a chain or a closed tin can with pebbles in it near the dog but not on him; say "NO!" loudly as the chain or can lands. In the most extreme case, a full 30-second spanking with a light strap may be indicated but be sure you catch the miscreant *in the act*. Dog memories are short.

Remember the crate discussed under "THE FIRST NIGHTS." If you give the dog a fair chance, he will NOT soil his crate.

Do not rub his nose in "it." Dogs have dignity and pride. It is permissible to lead him to his error as soon as he commits it and to remonstrate forcefully with "NO!"

7

COLLAR AND LEASH TRAINING

Put on a collar tight enough not to slip over the head. Leave it on for lengthening periods from a few minutes to a few hours over several days. A flat collar for shorthaired breeds; a round or rolled collar for longhairs. For collar breaking, do NOT use a choke collar; it may catch on a branch or other jutting object and strangle the dog.

After a few days' lessons with the collar, attach a heavy cord or rope to it without a loop or knot at the end (to avoid snagging or catching on a stump or other object). Allow the dog to run free with collar and cord attached a few moments at a time for several days. Do not allow dog to chew cord!

When the dog appears to be accustomed to the free-riding cord, pick up end of the cord, loop it around your hand and take your dog for a walk (not the other way around!). DON'T STOP WALK-ING if the dog pulls, balks or screams bloody murder. Keep going and make encouraging noises. If dog leaps ahead of you, turn sharply left or right whichever is *away* from dog's direction— AND KEEP MOVING! The biggest mistake in leash training is stopping when the dog stops, or going the way the dog goes when the dog goes wrong. You're the leader; make the dog aware of it. This is one lesson you should continue until the dog realizes who is boss. If the dog gets the upper leg now, you will find it difficult to resume your rightful position as master. Brutality, no; firmness, yes!

If the dog pulls ahead, jerk the cord—or by now, the leash— backward. Do not pull. Jerk or snap the leash only!

JUMPING ON PEOPLE

Nip this annoying habit at once by bumping the dog with your knee on his chest or stepping with authority on his rear feet. A sharp "NO!" at the same time helps. Don't permit this action when you're in your work clothes and ban it only when dressed in glad rags. The dog is not Beau Brummel, and it is cruel to expect him to distinguish between denim and silk.

THE "PROBLEM" DOG

The following corrections are indicated when softer methods fail. Remember that it's better to rehabilitate than to destroy.

Biting. For the puppy habit of mouthing or teething on the owner's hand, a sharp rap with a folded newspaper on the nose, or snapping the middle finger off the thumb against the dog's nose, will usually discourage nibbling tactics. For the biter that means it, truly drastic corrections may be preferable to destroying the dog. If your dog is approaching one year of age and is biting in earnest, take him to a professional dog trainer and don't quibble with his methods unless you would rather see the dog dead.

Chewing. For teething puppies, provide a Nylabone (trade mark) and beef hide strips (see "THE FIRST NIGHTS" above). Every time the puppy attacks a chair, a rug, your hand, or any other chewable object, snap your finger or rap a newspaper on his nose, or throw the chain or a covered pebble-laden tin can near him, say "NO!" and hand him the bone or beef hide. If he persists, put him in his crate with the bone and hide. For incorrigible chewers, check diet for deficiencies first. William Koehler, trainer of many movie dogs including *The Thin Man's* Asta, recommends in his book, *The Koehler Method of Dog Training,* that the chewed object or part of it be taped crosswise in the dog's mouth until he develops a hearty distaste for it.

Digging. While he is in the act, throw the chain or noisy tin can and call out "NO!" For the real delinquent Koehler recommends filling the dug hole with water, forcing the dog's nose into it until the dog thinks he's drowning and he'll never dig again. Drastic perhaps, but better than the bullet from an angry neighbor's gun, or a surreptitious poisoning.

The Runaway. If your dog wanders while walking with you, throw the chain or tin can and call "COME!" to him. If he persists, have a friend or neighbor cooperate in chasing him home. A very long line, perhaps 25 feet or more, can be effective if you permit the dog to run its length and then snap it sharply to remind him not to get too far from you.

Car Chasing. Your dog will certainly live longer if you make him car-wise; in fact, deathly afraid of anything on wheels. Ask a friend or neighbor to drive you in *his* car. Lie below the windows and as your dog chases the car throw the chain or tin can while your neighbor or friend says "GO HOME!" sharply. Another method is to shoot a water pistol filled with highly diluted ammonia at the dog. If your dog runs after children on bicycles, the latter device is especially effective but may turn the dog against children.

The Possessive Dog. If a dog displays overly protective habits, berate him in no uncertain terms. The chain, the noisy can, the rolled newspaper, or light strap sharply applied, may convince him that, while he loves you, there's no percentage in overdoing it.

The Cat Chaser. Again, the chain, the can, the newspaper, the strap—or the cat's claws if all else fails, but only as the last resort.

The Defiant, or Revengeful, Wetter. Some dogs seem to resent being left alone. Some are jealous when their owners play with another dog or animal. Get a friend or neighbor in this case to heave the chain or noisy tin can when the dog relieves himself in sheer spite.

For other canine delinquencies, you will find *The Koehler Method of Dog Training* effective. William Koehler's techniques have been certified as extremely successful by directors of motion pictures featuring dogs and by officers of dog obedience clubs.

OBEDIENCE EXERCISES

A well-mannered dog saves its owner money, embarrassment and possible heartbreak. The destruction of property by canine delinquents, avoidable accidents to dogs and children, and other unnecessary disadvantages to dog ownership can be eliminated by simple obedience training. The elementary exercises of heeling, sitting, staying and lying down can keep the dog out of trouble in most situations.

The only tools needed for basic obedience training are a slip collar made of chain link, leather or nylon and a strong six-foot leather leash with a good spring snap. Reviewing the requirements and basic techniques given earlier, let's proceed with the dog's schooling.

Heeling. Keep your dog on your left side, with the leash in your left hand. Start straight ahead in a brisk walk. If your dog pulls ahead, jerk (do not pull) the leash and say "Heel" firmly. If the dog persists in pulling ahead, stop, turn right or left and go on for several yards, saying "Heel" each time you change direction.

If your dog balks, fix leash *under* his throat and coax him forward by repeating his name and tapping your hip.

Whatever you do, don't stop walking! If the dog jumps up or "fights" the leash, just keep moving briskly. Sooner than later he will catch on and with the repetition of "Heel" on every correction, you will have him trotting by your side with style and respect.

Sit. Keeping your dog on leash, hold his neck up and push his rump down while repeating "Sit." If he resists, "spank" him lightly several times on his rump. Be firm, but not cruel. Repeat this lesson often until it is learned perfectly. When the dog knows the command, test him at a distance without the leash. Return to him every time he fails to sit and repeat the exercise.

Stay. If you have properly trained your dog to "Sit," the "Stay" is simple. Take his leash off and repeat "Stay" holding your hand up, palm toward dog, and move away. If dog moves toward you, you must repeat the "sit" lesson until properly learned. After your

11

dog "stays" while you are in sight, move out of his sight and keep repeating "Stay." Once he has learned to "stay" even while you are out of his sight, you can test him under various conditions, such as when another dog is near, a child is playing close to him, or a car appears on the road. (Warning: do not tax your dog's patience on the "stay" until he has learned the performance perfectly.)

Down. For this lesson, keep your dog on leash. First tell him to "sit." When he has sat for a minute, place your shoe over his leash between the heel and sole. Slowly pull on the leash and repeat "Down" while you push his head down with your other hand. Do this exercise very quietly so that dog does not become excited and uncontrollable. In fact, this performance is best trained when the dog is rather quiet. Later, after the dog has learned the voice signal perfectly, you can command the "Down" with a hand signal, sweeping your hand from an upright position to a downward motion with your palm toward the dog. Be sure to say "Down" with the hand signal.

For more advanced obedience the following guides by Blanche Saunders are recommended:

The Complete Novice Obedience Course
The Complete Open Obedience Course
The Complete Utility Obedience Course (with Tracking)
Dog Training for Boys and Girls (includes simple tricks.)

All are published by Howell Book House at $3.00 each.

OBEDIENCE TRIALS

Booklets covering the rules and regulations of Obedience Trials may be obtained from The American Kennel Club, 51 Madison Avenue, New York, N.Y. 10010. In Canada, write The Canadian Kennel Club, 667 Yonge Street, Toronto, Ontario.

Both these national clubs can give you the names and locations of local and regional dog clubs that conduct training classes in obedience and run Obedience Trials in which trained dogs compete for degrees as follow: CD (Companion Dog), CDX (Companion Dog Excellent), UD (Utility Dog), TD (Tracking Dog) and UDT (Utility Dog, Tracking.)

12

The Exhibition
of Dogs

NOBODY should exhibit a dog in the shows unless he can win without gloating and can lose without rancor. The showing of dogs is first of all a sport, and it is to be approached in a sportsmanlike spirit. It is not always so approached. That there are so many wretched losers and so many supercilious winners among the exhibitors in dog shows is the reason for this warning.

The confidence that one's dog is of exhibition excellence is all that prompts one to enter him in the show, but, if he fails in comparison with his competitors, nobody is harmed. It is no personal disgrace to have a dog beaten. It may be due to the dog's fundamental faults, to its condition, or to inexpert handling. One way to avoid such hazards is to turn the dog over to a good professional handler. Such a man with a flourishing established business will not accept an inferior dog, one that is not worth exhibiting. He will put the dog in the best possible condition before he goes into the ring with him, and he knows all the tricks of getting out of a dog all he has to give. Good handlers come high, however. Fees for taking a dog into the ring will range from ten to twenty-five dollars, plus any cash prizes the dog may win, and plus a bonus for wins made in the group.

Handlers do not win all the prizes, despite the gossip that they do, but good handlers choose only good dogs and they usually

13

finish at or near the top of their classes. It is a mistake to assume that this is due to any favoritism or any connivance with the judges; the handlers have simply chosen the best dogs, conditioned them well, and so maneuvered them in the ring as to bring out their best points.

The services of a professional handler are not essential, however. Many an amateur shows his dogs as well, but the exhibitor without previous experience is ordinarily at something of a disadvantage. If the dog is good enough, he may be expected to win.

The premium list of the show, setting forth the prizes to be offered, giving the names of the judges, containing the entry form, and describing the conditions under which the show is to be held, are usually mailed out to prospective exhibitors about a month before the show is scheduled to be held. Any show superintendent is glad to add names of interested persons to the mailing list.

Entries for a Licensed show close at a stated date, usually about two weeks before the show opens, and under the rules no entry may be accepted after the advertised date of closing. It behooves the exhibitor to make his entries promptly. The exhibitor is responsible for all errors he may make on the entry form of his dog; such errors cannot be rectified and may result in the disqualification of the exhibit. It therefore is wise for the owner to double check all data submitted with an entry. The cost of making an entry, which is stated in the premium list, is usually from six to eight dollars. An unregistered dog may be shown at three shows, after which he must be registered or a statement must be made to the American Kennel Club that he is ineligible for registry and why, with a request for permission to continue to exhibit the dog. Such permission is seldom denied. The listing fee for an unregistered dog is twenty-five cents, which must be added to the entry fee.

Match or Sanctioned shows are excellent training and experience for regular bench shows. Entry fees are low, usually ranging from fifty cents to a dollar, and are made at the show instead of in advance. Sanctioned shows are unbenched, informal affairs where the puppy may follow his owner about on the leash and become accustomed to strange dogs, to behaving himself in the ring, and to being handled by a judge. For the novice exhibitor, too, Sanctioned shows will provide valuable experience, for ring procedure is similar to that at regular bench shows.

14

The classes open at most shows and usually divided by sex are as follows: Puppy Class (often Junior Puppy for dogs 6 to 9 months old, and Senior Puppy for dogs 9 to 12 months); Novice Class, for dogs that have never won first in any except the Puppy Class; Bred-by-Exhibitor Class, for dogs of which the breeder and owner are the same person or persons; the American-bred Class, for dogs whose parents were mated in America; and the Open Class, which is open to all comers. The respective first prize winners of these various classes compete in what is known as the Winners Class for points toward championship. No entry can be made in the Winners Class, which is open without additional charge to the winners of the earlier classes, all of which are obligated to compete.

A dog eligible to more than one class can be entered in each of them, but it is usually wiser to enter him in only one. A puppy should, unless unusually precocious and mature, be placed in the Puppy Class, and it is unfair to so young a dog to expect him to defeat older dogs, although an exceptional puppy may receive an award in the Winners Class. The exhibitor who is satisfied merely that his dog may win the class in which he is entered is advised to place him in the lowest class to which he is eligible, but the exhibitor with confidence in his dog and shooting for high honors should enter the dog in the Open Class, where the competition is usually the toughest. The winner of the Open Class usually (but by no means always) is also the top of the Winners Class; the runner-up to this dog is named Reserve Winners.

The winner of the Winners Class for dogs competes with the Winners Bitch for Best of Winners, after competing for Best of Breed or Best of Variety with any Champions of Record which may be entered for Specials Only. In the closing hours of the show, the Best of Breed or Best of Variety is eligible to compete in the respective Variety Group to which his breed belongs. And if, perchance, he should win his Variety Group, he is obligated to compete for Best Dog in Show. This is a major honor which few inexperienced exhibitors attain and to which they seldom aspire.

Duly entered, the dog should be brought into the best possible condition for his exhibition in the show and taught to move and to pose at his best. He should be equipped with a neat, strong collar without ornaments or spikes, a show lead of the proper length, width and material for his size and coat, and a nickel bench chain

15

of strong links with which to fasten him to his bench. Food such as the dog is used to, a bottle of the water he is accustomed to drink, and all grooming equipment should be assembled in a bag the night before departure for the show. The exhibitor's pass, on which the dog is assigned a stall number, is sent by mail by the show superintendent and should not be left behind, since it is difficult to have the pass duplicated and it enables the dog's caretaker to leave and return to the show at will.

The time of the opening of the show is stated in the premium list, and it is wise to have one's dog at the show promptly. Late arrivals are subject to disqualification if they are protested.

Sometimes examination is made by the veterinarian at the entrance of the show, and healthy dogs are quickly passed along. Once admitted to the show, if it is a "benched" show, it is wise to find one's bench, the number of which is on the exhibitor's ticket, to affix one's dog to the bench, and not to remove him from it except for exercising or until he is to be taken into the ring to be judged. A familiar blanket or cushion for the bench makes a dog feel at home there. It is contrary to the rules to remove dogs from their benches and to keep them in crates during show hours, and these rules are strictly enforced. Many outdoor shows are not "benched," and you provide your own crate or place for your dog.

At bench shows some exhibitors choose to sit by their dog's bench, but if he is securely chained he is likely to be safe in his owner's absence. Dogs have been stolen from their benches and others allegedly poisoned in the shows, but such incidents are rare indeed. The greater danger is that the dog may grow nervous and insecure, and it is best that the owner return now and again to the bench to reassure the dog of his security.

The advertised program of the show permits exhibitors to know the approximate hour of the judging of their respective breeds. Although that time may be somewhat delayed, it may be depended upon that judging will not begin before the stated hour. The dog should have been groomed and made ready for his appearance in the show ring. When his class is called the dog should be taken unhurriedly to the entrance of the ring, where the handler will receive an arm band with the dog's number.

When the class is assembled and the judge asks that the dogs be paraded before him, the handler should fall into the counter-clock-wise line and walk his dog until the signal to stop is given. In moving in a circle, the dog should be kept on the inside so that he may be readily seen by the judge, who stands in the center of the ring. In stopping the line, there is no advantage to be gained in maneuvering one's dog to the premier position, since the judge will change the position of the dogs as he sees fit.

Keep the dog alert and facing toward the judge at all times. When summoned to the center of the ring for examination, go briskly but not brashly. It is unwise to enter into conversation with the judge, except briefly to reply to any questions he may ask. Do not call his attention to any excellences the dog may possess or excuse any shortcomings; the judge is presumed to evaluate the exhibit's merits as he sees them.

If asked to move the dog, he should be led directly away from the judge and again toward the judge. A brisk but not too rapid trot is the gait the judge wishes to see, unless he declares otherwise. He may ask that the movement be repeated, with which request the handler should respond with alacrity. It is best not to choke a dog in moving him, but rather to move him on a loose lead. The judge will assign or signal a dog to his position, which should be assumed without quibble.

Fig. 1

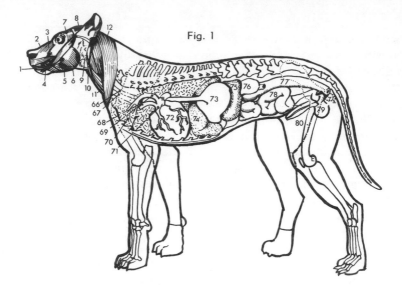

Fig. 2

Fig. 1

1 Orbicularis oris.
2 Levator nasolabialis.
3 Levator labii superioris proprius (levator of upper lip).
4 Dilator naris lateralis.
5 Zygomaticus.
6 Masseter (large and well developed in the dog).
7 Scutularis.
8 Parotid Gland.
9 Submaxillary Gland.
10 Parotido-auricularis.
11 Sterno-hyoideus.
12 Brachio-cephalicus.

(Between figures 8 and 12 on top the Elevator and Depressor muscles of the ear are to be seen.)

66 Œsophagus (gullet).
67 Trachea (wind pipe).
68 Left Carotid Artery.
69 Anterior Aorta.
70 Lungs.
71 Posterior Aorta.
72 Heart.
73 Stomach.

74 Liver. (The line in front of Liver shows the Diaphragm separating Thoracic from Abdominal cavity.)
75 Spleen.
76 Kidney (left).
77 Rectum.
77A Anal Glands (position) just inside rectum.
78 Intestine.
79 Testicle.
80 Penis.
   (Midway between 76 and 79 is the seat of the Bladder and behind this the seat of the Prostate gland in males, uterus in females.)

Fig. 2

Section of Head and Neck.
1 Nasal septum.
2 Tongue.
3 Cerebrum.
4 Cerebellum.
5 Medulla oblongata.
6 Spinal Cord.
7 Œsophagus (gullet).
8 Trachea (wind pipe).
9 Hard palate.
10 Soft palate.
11 Larynx, containing vocal cords.

18

The Feeding of Dogs,
Constitutional Vigor

IN selecting a new dog, it is quite as essential that he shall be of sound constitution as that he shall be of the correct type of his own particular breed. The animal that is thoroughly typical of his breed is likely to be vigorous, with a will and a body to surmount diseases and ill treatment, but the converse of this statement is not always true. A dog may have constitutional vigor without breed type. We want both.

Half of the care and effort of rearing a dog is saved by choosing at the outset a puppy of sound constitution, one with a will and an ability to survive and flourish in spite of such adversity and neglect as he may encounter in life. This does not mean that the reader has any intention of obtaining a healthy dog and ill treating it, trusting its good constitution to bring it through whatever crises may beset it. It only means that he will save himself work, expense, and disappointment if only he will exercise care in the first place to obtain a healthy dog, one bred from sound and vigorous parents and one which has received adequate care and good food.

The first warning is not to economize too much in buying a dog. Never accept a cull of the litter at any price. The difference in first cost between a fragile, ill nourished, weedy, and unhealthy puppy and a sound, vigorous one, with adequate substance and the will to survive, may be ten dollars or it may be fifty dollars. But whatever it may be, it is worthwhile. A dog is an investment and it is not the cost but the upkeep that makes the difference. We may save fifty dollars on the first price of a dog, only to lay out twice or five times that sum for veterinary fees over and above what it would cost to rear a dog of sound fundamental constitution and structure.

The vital, desirable dog, the one that is easy to rear and worth the care bestowed upon him, is active, inquisitive, and happy. He is sleek, his eyes free from pus or tears, his coat shining and alive, his flesh adequate and firm. He is not necessarily fat, but a small amount of surplus flesh, especially in puppyhood, is not undesirable. He is free from rachitic knobs on his joints or from crooked bones resultant from rickets. His teeth are firm and white and even. His breath is sweet to the smell. Above all, he is playful and responsive. Puppies, like babies, are much given to sleep, but when they are awake the sturdy ones do not mope lethargically around.

An adult dog that is too thin may often be fattened; if he is too fat he may be reduced. But it is essential that he shall be sound and healthy with a good normal appetite and that he be active and full of the joy of being alive. He must have had the benefit of a good heredity and a good start in life.

A dog without a fundamental inheritance of good vitality, or one that has been neglected throughout his growing period is seldom worth his feed. We must face these facts at the very beginning. Buy only from an owner who is willing to guarantee the soundness of his stock, and before consummating the purchase, have the dog, whether puppy or adult, examined by a veterinarian in order to determine the state of the dog's health.

If the dog to be cared for has already acquired, there is nothing to do but to make the best of whatever weaknesses or frailties he may possess. But, when it is decided to replace him with another, let us make sure that he has constitutional vigor.

THE FEEDING AND NUTRITION OF
THE ADULT DOG

The dog is a carnivore, an eater of meat. This is a truism that cannot be repeated too often. Dog keepers know it but are prone to disregard it, although they do so at their peril and the peril of their dogs. Despite all the old-wives' tales to the contrary, meat does not cause a dog to be vicious, it does not give him worms nor cause him to have fits. It is his food. This is by no means all that is needed to know about food for the dog, but it is the essential knowledge. Give a dog enough sound meat and he will not be ill fed.

The dog is believed to have been the first of the animals that was brought under domestication. In his feral state he was almost exclusively an eater of meat. In his long association with man, however, his metabolism has adjusted itself somewhat to the consumption of human diet until he now can eat, even if he cannot flourish upon, whatever his master chooses to share with him, be it caviar or corn pone. It is not to be denied that a mature dog can survive without ill effects upon an exclusive diet of rice for a considerable period, but it is not to be recommended that he should be forced to do so.

Even if we had no empirical evidence that dogs thrive best upon foods of animal origin, and we possess conclusive proof of that fact, the anatomy and physiology of the dog would convince us of it. An observation of the structure of the dog's alimentary canal, superimposed upon many trial and error methods of feeding, leads us to the conclusion that a diet with meat predominating is the best food we can give a dog.

To begin with, the dental formation of the dog is typical of the carnivores. His teeth are designed for tearing rather than for mastication. He bolts his food and swallows it with a minimum of chewing. It is harmless that he should do this. No digestion takes place in the dog's mouth.

The capacity of the dog's stomach is great in comparison with the size of his body and with the capacity of his intestines. The amounts of carbohydrates and of fats digested in the stomach are minimal. The chief function of the dog's stomach is the digestion of proteins. In the dog as in the other carnivores, carbohydrates

21

and fats are digested for the most part in the small intestine, and absorption of food materials is largely from the small intestine. The enzymes necessary for the completion of the digestion of proteins which have not been fully digested in the stomach and for the digestion of sugars, starches, and fats are present in the pancreatic and intestinal juices. The capacity of the small intestine in the dog is not great and for that reason digestion that takes place there must be rapid.

The so-called large intestine (although in the dog it is really not "large" at all) is short and of small capacity in comparison with that of animals adapted by nature to subsist wholly or largely upon plant foods. In the dog, the large gut is designed to serve chiefly for storage of a limited and compact bulk of waste materials, which are later to be discharged as feces. Some absorption of water occurs there, but there is little if any absorption there of the products of digestion.

It will be readily seen that the short digestive tract of the dog is best adapted to a concentrated diet, which can be quickly digested and which leaves a small residue. Foods of animal origin (flesh, fish, milk, and eggs) are therefore suited to the digestive physiology of the dog because of the ease and completeness with which they are digested as compared with plant foods, which contain considerable amounts of indigestible structural material. The dog is best fed with a concentrated diet with a minimum of roughage.

This means meat. Flesh, milk, and eggs are, in effect, vegetation partly predigested. The steer or horse eats grain and herbage, from which its long digestive tract enables it to extract the food value and eliminate the indigestible material. The carnivore eats the flesh of the herbivore, thus obtaining his grain and grass in a concentrated form suitable for digestion in his short alimentary tract. Thus it is seen that meat is the ideal as a chief ingredient of the dog's ration.

Like that of all other animals, the dog's diet must be made up of proteins, carbohydrates, fats, minerals, vitamins, and water. None of these substances may be excluded if the dog is to survive. If he fails to obtain any of them from one source, it must come from another. It may be argued that before minerals were artificially supplied in the dog's diet and before we were aware of the existence of the various vitamins, we had dogs and they (some of them) appeared to thrive. However, they obtained such substances in their foods, although we were not aware of it. It is very likely that few dogs obtained much more than their very minimum of requirements of the minerals and vitamins. It is known that rickets were more prevalent before we learned to supply our dogs with ample calcium, and black tongue, now almost unknown, was a common canine disease before we supplied in the dog's diet that fraction of the vitamin B complex known as nicotinic acid. There is no way for us to know how large a portion of our dogs died for want of some particular food element before we learned to supply all the necessary ones. The dogs that survived received somewhere in their diet some of all of these compounds.

PROTEIN

The various proteins are the nitrogenous part of the food. They are composed of the amino acids, singly or in combination. There are at least twenty-two of these amino acids known to the nutritional scientists, ten of which are regarded as dietary essentials, the others of which, if not supplied in the diet, can be compounded in the body, which requires an adequate supply of all twenty-two. When any one of the essential ten amino acids is withdrawn from the diet of any animal, growth ceases or is greatly retarded. Thus, a high protein content in any food is not an assurance of its food value if taken alone; it may be lacking in one or more of the essential ten amino acids. When the absent essential amino acids are added to it in sufficient quantities or included separately in the diet, the protein may be complete and fully assimilated.

Proteins, as such, are ingested and in the digestive tract are broken down into the separate amino acids of which they are composed. These amino acids have been likened to building stones, since they are taken up by the blood stream and conveyed to the various parts of the animal as they may be required, where they are deposited and re-united with other complementary amino acids again to form bone and muscles in the resumed form of protein.

To correct amino acid deficiencies in the diet, it is not necessary to add the required units in pure form. The same object may be accomplished more efficiently by employing proteins which contain the required amino acids.

Foods of animal origin—meat, fish, eggs, and milk—supply proteins of high nutritive value, both from the standpoint of digestibility and amino acid content. Gelatin is an exception to that statement, since gelatin is very incomplete.

Even foods of animal origin vary among themselves in their protein content and amino acid balance. The protein of muscle meat does not rank quite as high as that of eggs or milk. The glandular tissues—such as liver, kidneys, sweetbreads or pancreas—contain proteins of exceptionally high nutritive value, and these organs should be added to the dog's diet whenever it is possible to do so. Each pint of milk contains two-thirds of an ounce (dry weight) of particularly high class protein, in addition to minerals, vitamins, carbohydrates, and fats. (The only dietary necessity absent

24

from milk is iron.) Animal proteins have a high content of dietary-essential amino acids, which makes them very effective in supplementing many proteins of vegetable origin. The whites of eggs, while somewhat inferior to the yolks, contain excellent proteins. The lysine of milk can be destroyed by excessive heat and the growth promoting value of its protein so destroyed. Evaporated tinned milk has not been subjected to enough heat to injure its proteins.

Thus we can readily see why meat with its concentrated, balanced, and easily assimilated proteins should form the major part of dry weight of a dog's ration.

It has never been determined how much protein the dog requires in his diet. It may be assumed to vary as to the size, age, and breed of the dog under consideration; as to the individual dog, some assimilating protein better, or utilizing more of it than others; as to the activity or inactivity of the subject; and as to the amino acid content of the protein employed. When wheat protein gliadin is fed as the sole protein, three times as much of it is required as of the milk protein, lactalbumin. It has been estimated that approximately twenty to twenty-five percent of animal protein (dry weight) in a dog's diet is adequate for maintenance in good health, although no final conclusion has been reached and probably never can be.

Our purpose, however, is not to feed the dog the minimum ration with which he can survive or even the minimum ration with which he can flourish. It is rather to give him the maximum food in quantity and balance which he can digest and enjoy without developing a paunch. Who wants to live on the minimum diet necessary for adequate sustenance? We all enjoy a full belly of good food, and so do our dogs.

Roy G. Daggs found from experimentation that milk production in the dog was influenced by the different kinds of proteins fed to it. He has pointed out that relatively high protein diets stimulate lactation and that, in the bitch, animal proteins are better suited to the synthesis of milk than plant proteins. He concluded that liver was a better source of protein for lactation than eggs or round steak.

25

THE CARBOHYDRATES

The carbohydrates include all the starches, the sugars, and the cellulose and hemicellulose, which last two, known as fiber, are the chief constituents of wood, of the stalks and leaves of plants, and of the coverings of seeds. There remains considerable controversy as to the amount of carbohydrates required or desirable in canine nutrition. It has been shown experimentally that the dog is able to digest large quantities of cornstarch, either raw or cooked. Rice fed to mature dogs in amounts sufficient to satisfy total energy requirements has been found to be 95 percent digested. We know that the various commercial biscuits and meals which are marketed as food for dogs are well tolerated, especially if they are supplemented by the addition of fresh meat. There seems to be no reason why they should not be included in the dog's ration.

Carbohydrates are a cheap source of energy for the dog, both in their initial cost and in the work required of the organism for their metabolism. Since there exists ample evidence that the dog has no difficulty in digesting and utilizing considerable amounts of starches and sugars for the production of energy, there is no reason why they should be excluded from his diet. Some carbohydrate is necessary for the metabolism of fats. The only danger from the employment of carbohydrates is that, being cheap, they may be employed to the exclusion of proteins and other essential elements of the dog's diet. It should be noted that meat and milk contain a measure of carbohydrates as well as of proteins.

Thoroughly cooked rice or oatmeal in moderate quantities may well be used to supplement and cheapen a meat diet for a dog without harm to him, as may crushed dog biscuit or shredded wheat waste or the waste from manufacture of other cereal foods. They are not required but may be used without harm.

Sugar and candy, of which dogs are inordinately fond, used also to be *verboten*. They are an excellent source of energy—and harmless. They should be fed in only moderate quantities.

FATS

In the dog as in man, body fat is found in largest amounts under the skin, between the muscles and around the internal organs. The fat so stored serves as a reserve source of heat and energy when the caloric value of the food is insufficient, or for temporary periods when no food is eaten. The accumulation of a certain amount of fat around vital organs provides considerable protection against cold and injury.

Before fats can be carried to the body cells by means of the circulating blood, it is necessary for them to be digested in the intestines with the aid of enzymes. Fats require a longer time for digestion than carbohydrates or proteins. For this reason, they are of special importance in delaying the sensations of hunger. This property of fats is frequently referred to as "staying power."

It is easily possible for some dogs to accumulate too much fat, making them unattractive, ungainly, and vaguely uncomfortable. This should be avoided by withholding an excess of fats and carbohydrates from the diets of such dogs whenever obesity threatens them. There is greater danger, however, that dogs may through inadequacy of their diets be permitted to become too thin.

Carbohydrates can in part be transformed to fats within the animal body. The ratio between fats and carbohydrates can therefore be varied within wide limits in the dog's ration so long as the requirements for proteins, vitamins, and minerals are adequately met. Some dogs have been known to tolerate as much as forty percent of fat in their diets over prolonged periods, but so much is not to be recommended as a general practice. Perhaps fifteen to twenty percent of fat is adequate without being too much.

Fat is a heat producing food, and the amount given a dog should be stepped up in the colder parts of the year and reduced in the summer months. In a ration low in fat it is particularly important that a good source of the fat-soluble vitamins be included or that such vitamins be artificially supplied. Weight for weight, fat has more than twice the food value of the other organic food groups—carbohydrates and proteins. The use of fat tends to decrease the amount of food required to supply caloric needs. The fats offer a means of increasing or decreasing the total sum of energy in the diet with the least change in the volume of food intake.

27

It is far less important that the dog receive more than a minimum amount of fats, however, than that his ration contain an adequate amount and quality balance of proteins. Lean meat in adequate quantities will provide him with such proteins, and fats may be added to it in the form of fat meat, suet, or lard. Small quantities of dog biscuits, cooked rice, or other cereals in the diet will supply the needed carbohydrates. However, cellulose or other roughage is not required in the diet of the carnivore. It serves only to engorge the dog's colon, which is not capacious, and to increase the volume of feces, which is supererogatory.

MINERALS

At least eleven minerals are present in the normal dog, and there are probably others occurring in quantities so minute that they have not as yet been discovered. The eleven are as follows: Calcium (lime), sodium chloride (table salt), copper, iron, magnesium, manganese, phosphorus, zinc, potassium, and iodine.

Of many of these only a trace in the daily ration is required and that trace is adequately found in meat or in almost any other normal diet. There are a few that we should be at pains to add to the diet. The others we shall ignore.

Sodium chloride (salt) is present in sufficient quantities in most meats, although, more to improve the flavor of the food than to contribute to the animal's nutrition, a small amount of salt may be added to the ration. The exact amount makes no material difference, since the unutilized portions are eliminated, largely in the urine. If the brand of salt used is iodized, it will meet the iodine requirements, which are very small. Iodine deficiency in dogs is rare, but food crops and meats grown in certain areas contain little or no iodine, and it is well to be safe by using iodized salt.

Sufficient iron is usually found in meat and milk, but if the dog appears anemic or listless the trace of iron needed can be supplied with one of the iron salts—ferric sulphate, or oxide, or ferrous gluconate. Iron is utilized in the bone marrow in the synthesis of hemoglobin in the blood corpuscles. It is used over and over; when a corpuscle is worn out and is to be replaced, it surrenders its iron before being eliminated.

When more iron is ingested than can be utilized, some is stored in the liver, after which further surplus is excreted. The liver of the newborn puppy contains enough iron to supply the organism up until weaning time. No iron is present in milk, which otherwise provides a completely balanced ration.

A diet with a reasonable content of red meat, especially of liver or kidney, is likely to be adequate in respect to its iron. However, bitches in whelp require more iron than a dog on mere maintenance. It is recommended that the liver content of bitches' diets be increased for the duration of pregnancy.

Iron requires the presence of a minute trace of copper for its utilization, but there is enough copper in well nigh any diet to supply the requirements.

Calcium and phosphorous are the only minerals of which an insufficiency is a warranted source of anxiety. This statement may not be true of adult dogs not employed for breeding purposes, but it does apply to brood bitches and to growing puppies. The entire skeleton and teeth are made largely from calcium and phosphorus, and it is essential that the organism have enough of those minerals.

If additional calcium is not supplied to a bitch in her diet, her own bone structure is depleted to provide her puppies with their share of calcium. Moreover, in giving birth to her puppies or shortly afterward she is likely to go into eclampsia as a result of calcium depletion.

The situation, however, is easily avoided. The addition of a small amount of calcium phosphate diabasic to the ration precludes any possible calcium deficiency. Calcium phosphate diabasic is an inexpensive substance and quite tasteless. It may be sprinkled in or over the food, especially that given to brood bitches and puppies. It is the source of strong bones and vigorous teeth of ivory whiteness.

But it must be mentioned that calcium cannot be assimilated into the bone structure, no matter how much of it is fed or otherwise administered, except in the presence of vitamin D. That is D's function, to facilitate the absorption of calcium and phosphorus. This will be elaborated upon in the following discussion of the vitamins and their functions.

VITAMINS

Vitamins have in the past been largely described by diseases resulting from their absence. It is recognized more and more that many of the subacute symptoms of general unfitness of dogs may be attributable to an inadequate supply in the diet of one or more of these essential food factors. It is to be emphasized that vitamins are to be considered a part of the dog's food, essential to his health and well being. They are not to be considered as medication. Often the morbid conditions resultant from their absence in the diet may be remedied by the addition of the particular needed vitamin.

The requirements of vitamins, as food, not as medication, in the diet cannot be too strongly emphasized. These vitamins may be in the food itself, or they may better be added to it as a supplement to insure an adequate supply. Except for vitamin D, of which it is remotely possible (though unlikely) to supply too much, a surplus of the vitamin substances in the ration is harmless. They are somewhat expensive and we have no disposition to waste them, but if too much of them are fed they are simply eliminated with no subsequent ill effect.

It must be realized that vitamins are various substances, each of which has a separate function. It is definitely not safe to add to a dog's (or a child's) diet something out of a bottle or box indefinitely labeled "Vitamins," as is the practice of so many persons. We must know which vitamins we are giving, what purpose each is designed to serve, and the potency of the preparation of the brand of each one we are using.

Any one of the "shotgun" vitamin preparations is probably adequate if administered in large enough dosages. Such a method may be wasteful, however; to be sure of enough of one substance, the surplus of the others is wasted. It is much better to buy a product that contains an adequate amount of each of the needed vitamins and a wasteful surplus of none. Such a procedure is cheaper in the long run.

There follows a brief description of each of the various vitamins so far discovered and a statement of what purpose in the diet they are respectively intended to serve:

Vitamin A—This vitamin in some form is an absolute requisite for good health, even for enduring life itself. Symptoms of ad-

31

vanced deficiency of vitamin A in dogs are an eye disease with resulting impaired vision, inflammation of the conjunctiva or mucous membranes which line the eyelid, and injury to the mucous membranes of the body. Less easily recognized symptoms are an apparent lowered resistance to bacterial infection, especially of the upper respiratory tract, retarded growth, and loss of weight. Diseases due to vitamin A deficiency may be well established while the dog is still gaining in weight. Lack of muscular coordination and paralysis have been observed in dogs and degeneration of the nervous system. Some young dogs deprived of vitamin A become wholly or partially deaf.

The potency of vitamin A is usually calculated in International Units, of which it has been estimated that the dog requires about 35 per day for each pound of his body weight. Such parts as are not utilized are not lost, but are stored in the liver for future use in time of shortage. A dog well fortified with this particular vitamin can well go a month or more without harm with none of it in his diet. At such times he draws upon his liver for its surplus.

It is for its content of vitamins A and D that cod-liver oil (and the oils from the livers of other fish) is fed to puppies and growing children. Fish liver oils are an excellent source of vitamin A, and if a small amount of them is included in the diet no anxiety about deficiency of vitamin A need be entertained. In buying cod-liver oil, it pays to obtain the best grade. The number of International Units it contains per teaspoonful is stated on most labels. The vitamin content of cod-liver oil is impaired by exposure to heat, light, and air. It should be kept in a dark, cool place and the bottle should be firmly stopped.

Another source of vitamin A is found in carrots but it is almost impossible to get enough carrots in a dog to do him any good. It is better and easier to use a preparation known as carotene, three drops of which contains almost the vitamin A in a bushel of carrots.

Other natural sources of vitamin A are liver, kidney, heart, cheese, egg yolks, butter and milk. If these foods, or any one of them, are generously included in the adult dog's maintenance ration, all other sources of vitamin A may be dispensed with. The ration for all puppies, however, and for pregnant and lactating bitches should be copiously fortified either with fish liver oil or with tablets containing vitamin A.

32

Vitamin B. What was formerly known as a single vitamin B has now been found to be a complex of many different factors. Some of them are, in minute quantities, very important parts of the diets of any kind of animals. The various factors of this complex, each a separate vitamin, are designated by the letter B followed by an inferior number, as B_1, B_2, or B_6.

The absence or insufficiency in the diet of Vitamin B_1, otherwise known as thiamin, has been blamed for retarded growth, loss of weight, decreased fertility, loss of appetite, and impaired digestion. A prolonged shortage of B_1 may result in paralysis, the accumulation of fluid in the tissues, and finally in death, apparently from heart failure.

It is not easy to estimate just how much B_1 a dog requires per pound of body weight, since dogs as individuals vary in their needs, and the activity of an animal rapidly depletes the thiamin in his body. The feeding of 50 International Units per day per pound of body weight is probably wasteful but harmless. That is at least enough.

Thiamin is not stored in the system for any length of time and requires a daily dosage. It is destroyed in part by heat above the boiling point. It is found in yeast (especially in brewer's yeast), liver, wheat germ, milk, eggs, and in the coloring matter of vegetables. However, few dogs or persons obtain an optimum supply of B_1 from their daily diet, and it is recommended that it be supplied to the dog daily.

Brewer's yeast, either in powdered or tablet form affords a cheap and rather efficient way to supply the average daily requirements. An overdose of yeast is likely to cause gas in the dog's stomach.

Another factor of the vitamin B complex, riboflavin, affects particularly the skin and hair. Animals fed a diet in which it is deficient are prone to develop a scruffy dryness of the skin, especially about the eyes and mouth, and the hair becomes dull and dry, finally falling out, leaving the skin rough and dry. In experiments with rats deprived of riboflavin the toes have fallen off.

Riboflavin is present in minute quantities in so many foods that a serious shortage in any well balanced diet is unlikely. It is especially to be found in whey, which is the explanation of the smooth skin and lively hair of so many dogs whose ration contains cottage cheese.

33

While few dogs manifest any positive shortage of riboflavin, experiments on various animals have shown that successively more liberal amounts of it in their diets, up to about four times as much as is needed to prevent the first signs of deficiency, result in increased positive health.

Riboflavin deteriorates with exposure to heat and light. Most vitamin products contain it in ample measure.

Dogs were immediately responsible for the discovery of the existence of vitamin B_2, or nicotinic acid, formerly known as vitamin G. The canine disease of black tongue is analogous with the human disease called pellagra, both of which are prevented and cured by sufficient amounts of nicotinic acid in the diet. Black tongue is not a threat for any dog that eats a diet which contains even a reasonable quantity of lean meat, but it used to be prevalent among dogs fed exclusively upon corn bread or corn-meal mush, as many were.

No definite optimum dosage has been established. However, many cases of vaguely irritated skin, deadness of coat, and soft, spongy, or bleeding gums have been reported to be remedied by administration of nicotinic acid.

It has been demonstrated that niacin is essential if a good sound healthy appetite is to be maintained. Pantothenic acid is essential to good nerve health. Pyridoxin influences proper gastro-intestinal functions. Vitamin B_{12}, the "animal protein factor," is essential for proper growth and health in early life. And the water soluble B factor affects the production of milk.

Vitamin C, the so-called anti-scorbutic vitamin, is presumed to be synthesized by the dog in his own body. The dog is believed not to be subject to true scurvy. Vitamin C, then, can well be ignored as pertains to the dog. It is the most expensive of the vitamins, and, its presence in the vitamin mixture for the dog will probably do no good.

Vitamin D, the anti-rachitic vitamin, is necessary to promote the assimilation of calcium and phosphorus into the skeletal structure. One may feed all of those minerals one will, but without vitamin D they will pass out of the system unused. It is impossible to develop sound bones and teeth without its presence. Exposure to sunshine unimpeded by glass enables the animal to manufacture vitamin D in his system, but sunshine is not to be depended upon for an entire supply.

Vitamin D is abundant in cod-liver oil and in the liver oils of some other fish, or it may be obtained in a dry form in combination with other vitamins. One International Unit per pound of body weight per day is sufficient to protect a dog from rickets. From a teaspoonful to a tablespoonful of cod-liver oil a day will serve well instead for any dog.

This is the only one of the vitamins with which overdosage is possible and harmful. While a dog will not suffer from several times the amount stated and an excess dosage is unlikely, it is only fair to warn the reader that it is at least theoretically possible.

Vitamin E is the so-called fertility vitamin. Whether it is required for dogs has not as yet been determined. Rats fed upon a ration from which vitamin E was wholly excluded became permanently sterile, but the finding is not believed to pertain to all animals. Some dog keepers, however, declare that the feeding of wheat germ oil, the most abundant source of vitamin E, has prevented early abortions of their bitches, has resulted in larger and more vigorous litters of puppies, has increased the fertility of stud dogs, has improved the coats of their dogs and furthered the betterment of their general health. Whether vitamin E or some other factor or factors in the wheat germ oil is responsible for these alleged benefits is impossible to say.

Vitamin E is so widely found in small quantities in well nigh all foods that the hazard of its omission from any normal diet is small.

Numerous other vitamins have been discovered and isolated in recent years, and there are suspected to be still others as yet unknown. The ones here discussed are the only ones that warrant the use of care to include them in the dog's daily ration. It is well to reiterate that vitamins are not medicine, but are food, a required part of the diet. Any person interested in the complete nutrition of his dog will not neglect them.

It should go without saying that a dog should have access to clean, fresh, pure drinking water at all times, of which he should be permitted to drink as much or as little as he chooses. The demands of his system for drinking water will depend in part upon the moisture content of his food. Fed upon dry dog biscuits, he will probably drink considerable water to moisten it; with a diet which contains much milk or soup, he will need little additional water.

35

That he chooses to drink water immediately after a meal is harmless. The only times his water should be limited (but not entirely withheld from him) is after violent exercise or excitement, at which times his thirst should be satisfied only gradually.

The quantities of food required daily by dogs are influenced and determined by a number of factors: the age, size, individuality, and physical condition of the animal; the kind, quality, character, and proportions of the various foods in the ration; the climate, environment and methods of management; and the type and amount of work done, or the degree of exercise. Of these considerations, the age and size of the dog and the kind and amount of work are particularly important in determining food requirements. During early puppyhood a dog may require two or three (or even more) times as much food per pound of body weight as the same dog will require at maturity.

Any statement we should make here about the food requirements of a dog as to weight or volume would be subject to modification. Dogs vary in their metabolism. One dog might stay fat and sleek on a given amount of a given ration, whereas his litter brother in an adjoining kennel might require twice or only half as much of the same ration to maintain him in the same state of flesh.

The only sound determiners of how much to feed a dog are his appetite and his condition. As a general rule, a dog should have as much food for maintenance as he will readily clean up in five or ten minutes, unless he tends to lay on unwanted fat, in which case his intake of food should be reduced, especially its content of fats and carbohydrates. A thin dog should have his ration increased and be urged to eat it. The fats in his ration should be increased, and he may be fattened with a dessert of candy, sugar, or sweet cake following his main meal. These should never be used before a meal, lest they impair the appetite, and they should not be given to a fat dog at all. Rightly employed, they are useful and harmless, contrary to the prevalent belief.

Growing puppies require frequent meals, as will be discussed later. Pregnant and lactating bitches and frequently used stud dogs should have at least two meals, and better three, each day. For the mere maintenance of healthy adult dogs, one large meal a day appears to suffice as well as more smaller ones. Many tender-hearted dog keepers choose to divide the ration into two parts

36

and to feed their dogs twice each day. There can be no objection offered to such a program except that it involves additional work for the keeper. Whether one meal or two, they should be given at regular hours, to which dogs soon adjust and expect their dinner at a given time.

It is better to determine upon an adequate ration, with plenty of meat in it, and feed it day after day, than to vary the diet in the assumption that a dog tires of eating the same thing. There is no evidence that he does, and it is a burden upon his carnivorous digestion to be making constant adjustments and readjustments to a new diet.

Today there are available for dogs many brands of canned foods, some good and others not so good. But it is safe to feed your dog exclusively—if you do not object to the cost—a canned dog food which has been produced by a reliable concern. Many of the producers of canned dog foods are subject to Federal inspection because they also process meat and meat products for human consumption. The Federal regulations prohibit the use of diseased or unsuitable by-products in the preparation of dog food. Some of the canned dog foods on the market are mostly cereal. A glance at the analysis chart on the label will tell you whether a particular product is a good food for your dog.

If fish is fed, it should be boned—thoroughly. The same is true of fowl and rabbit meats. Small bones may be caught in the dog's throat or may puncture the stomach or intestines. Large, raw shank bones of beef may be given to the dog with impunity, but they should be renewed at frequent intervals before they spoil. A dog obtains much amusement from gnawing a raw bone, and some nutrition. Harm does not accrue from his swallowing of bone fragments, which are dissolved by the hydrochloric acid in his stomach. If the dog is fed an excessive amount of bones, constipation may result. When this occurs, the best way to relieve the condition is by the use of the enema bag. Medicinal purges of laxatives given at this time may cause irreparable damage.

Meat for dogs may be fed raw, or may be roasted, broiled, or boiled. It is not advisable to feed fried foods to dogs. All soups, gravies and juices from cooked meat must be conserved and included in the food, since they contain some of the minerals and vitamins extracted from the meat.

37

A well-known German physician selected a medium sized, strong, healthy bitch, and after she had been mated, he fed her on chopped horse meat from which the salts were to a large extent extracted by boiling for two hours in distilled water. In addition to this she was given each day a certain quantity of fried fat. As drink she had only distilled water. She gave birth to six healthy puppies, one of which was killed immediately, and its bones found to be strong and well built and free from abnormalities. The other puppies did not thrive, but remained weak, and could scarcely walk at the end of a month, when four died from excessive feebleness. And the sixth was killed two weeks' later. The mother in the meantime had become very lean but was tolerably lively and had a fair appetite. She was killed one hundred and twenty-six days after the beginning of the experiment, and it was then found that the bones of her spine and pelvis were softened—a condition known to physicians as osteomalacia.

The results of this experiment are highly interesting and instructive, showing clearly as they do that the nursing mother sends out to her young, in her milk, a part of her store of lime, which is absolutely essential to their welfare. They show also that if proper food is denied her, when in whelp and when nursing, not only her puppies but she as well must suffer greatly in consequence. And in the light of these facts is uncovered one of the most potential causes of rickets, so common among large breeds.

It may therefore be accepted that bitches in whelp must have goodly quantities of meat; moreover, that while cooking may be the rule if the broth is utilized, it is a wise plan to give the food occasionally in the raw state.

There is little choice among the varieties of meat, except that pork is seldom relished by dogs, usually contains too much fat, and should be cooked to improve its digestibility when it is used at all. Beef, mutton, lamb, goat, and horse flesh are equally valuable. The choice should be made upon the basis of their comparative cost and their availability in the particular community. A dog suddenly changed from another diet to horse flesh may develop a harmless and temporary diarrhea, which can be ignored. Horse flesh is likely to be deficient in fats, which may be added in the form of suet, lard or pure corn oil.

The particular cuts of whatever meat is used is of little consequence. Liver and kidney are especially valuable and when it is possible they should be included as part of the meat used. As the only meat in the ration, liver and kidney tend to loosen the bowels. It is better to include them as a part of each day's ration than to permit them to serve as the sole meat content one or two days a week.

It makes no difference whether meat is ground or is fed to the dog in large or medium sized pieces. He is able to digest pieces of meat as large as he can swallow. The advantage of grinding meat is that it can be better mixed with whatever else it is wished to include in the ration, the dog being unable to pick out the meat and reject the rest. There is little harm in his doing so, except for the waste, since it is the meat upon which we must depend for the most part for his nutrition.

Fresh ground meat can be kept four or five days under ordinary refrigeration without spoiling. It may be kept indefinitely if solidly frozen. Frozen ground horse meat for dogs is available in many markets, is low in price, and is entirely satisfactory for the purpose intended.

A suggested ration is made as follows: Two-thirds to three-quarters by weight of ground meat including ten to twenty percent of fat and a portion of liver or kidney, with the remainder thoroughly cooked rice or oatmeal, or shredded wheat, or dog biscuit, or wheat germ, with a sprinkling of calcium phosphate diabasic. Vitamins may be added, or given separately.

If it is desired to offer the dog a second meal, it may be of shredded wheat or other breakfast cereal with plenty of milk, with or without one or more soft boiled eggs. Evaporated canned milk or powdered milk is just as good food for the dog as fresh milk. Cottage cheese is excellent for this second meal.

These are not the only possible rations for the dog, but they will prove adequate. Leavings from the owner's table can be added to either ration, but can hardly be depended upon for the entire nourishment of the dog.

The dog's food should be at approximately body heat, tepid but never hot.

Little consideration is here given to the costs of the various foods. Economies in rations and feeding practices are admittedly desirable, but not if they are made at the expense of the dog's health.

SOME BRIEF PRECEPTS ABOUT FEEDING

Many dogs are overfed. Others do not receive adequate rations. Both extremes should be avoided, but particularly overfeeding of grown dogs. Coupled with lack of exercise, overfeeding usually produces excessive body weight and laziness, and it may result in illness and sterility. Prolonged undernourishment causes loss of weight, listlessness, dull coats, sickness, and death.

An adequate ration will keep most mature dogs at a uniform body weight and in a thrifty, moderately lean condition. Observation of condition is the best guide in determining the correct amount of food.

The axiom, "One man's meat is another man's poison," is applicable to dogs also. Foods that are not tolerated by the dog or those that cause digestive and other disturbances should be discontinued. The use of moldy, spoiled, or rotten food is never good practice. Food should be protected from fouling by rats or mice, especially because rats are vectors of leptospirosis. The excessive use of food of low energy content and low biological values will often result in poor condition and may cause loss of weight and paunchiness.

All feeding and drinking utensils must be kept scrupulously clean. They should be washed after each using.

It is usually desirable to reduce the food allotment somewhat during hot weather. Dogs should be fed at regular intervals, and the best results may be expected when regular feeding is accompanied by regular, but not exhausting, exercise.

Most dogs do not thrive on a ration containing large amounts of sloppy foods, and excessive bulk is to be avoided especially for hardworking dogs, puppies, and pregnant or lactating bitches. If the ration is known to be adequate and the dog is losing weight or is not in good condition, the presence of intestinal parasites is to be suspected. However, dogs sometimes go "off feed" for a day or two. This is cause for no immediate anxiety, but if it lasts more than two or three days, a veterinarian should be consulted.

FOOD FOR THE STUD DOG

The stud dog that is used for breeding only at infrequent intervals requires only the food needed for his maintenance in good health, as set forth in the foregoing pages. He should be well fed with ample meat in his diet, moderately exercised to keep his flesh firm and hard, and not permitted to become too thin or too fat.

More care is required for the adequate nutrition of the dog offered at public stud and frequently employed for breeding. A vigorous stud dog may very handily serve two bitches a week over a long period without a serious tax upon his health and strength if he is fully nourished and adequately but not excessively exercised. Such a dog should have at least two meals a day, and they should consist of even more meat, milk (canned is as good as fresh), eggs, cottage cheese, and other foods of animal origin than is used in most maintenance rations. Liver and some fat should be included, and the vitamins especially are not to be forgotten. In volume this will be only a little more than the basic maintenance diet, the difference being in its richness and concentration.

An interval of an hour or two should intervene between a dog's meal and his employment for breeding. He may be fed, but only lightly, immediately after he has been used for breeding.

The immediate reason that a stud dog should be adequately fed and exercised is the maintenance of his strength and virility. The secondary reason is that a popular stud dog is on exhibition at all times, between the shows as well as at the shows. Clients with bitches to be bred appear without notice to examine a dog at public stud, and the dog should be presented to them in the best possible condition—clean, hard, in exactly the most becoming state of flesh, and with a gleaming, lively coat. These all depend largely upon the highly nutritious diet the dog receives.

FOOD FOR THE BROOD BITCH

Often a well fed bitch comes through the ordeal of rearing a large litter of puppies without any impairment of her vitality and flesh. In such case she may be returned to a good maintenance ration until she is ready to be bred again. About the time she weans her puppies her coat will be dead and ready to drop out, but if she is healthy and well fed a new and vigorous coat will grow in, and she will be no worse off for her maternal ordeal. Some bitches, either from a deficient nutrition or a constitutional disposition to contribute too much of their own strength and substance to the nutrition of the puppies, are thin and exhausted at the time of weaning. Such a bitch needs the continuance of at least two good and especially nutritious meals a day for a month or more until her flesh and strength are restored before she is returned to her routine maintenance ration, upon which she may be kept until time comes to breed her again.

At breeding time a bitch's flesh should be hard, and she should be on the lean side rather than too fat. No change in her regular maintenance diet need be made until about the fourth or fifth week of her pregnancy. The growth of the fetus is small up until the middle of the pregnancy, after which it becomes rapid.

The bitch usually begins to "show in whelp" in four to six weeks after breeding, and her food consumption should be then gradually stepped up. If she has been having only one meal a day, she should be given two; if she has had two, both should be larger. Henceforth until her puppies are weaned, she must eat not merely for two, as is said of the pregnant woman, but for four or five, possibly for ten or twelve. She is not to be encouraged to grow fat. Especial emphasis should be laid upon her ration's content of meat, including liver, milk, calcium phosphate, and vitamins A and D, both of which are found in cod-liver oil.

Some breeders destroy all but a limited number of puppies in a litter in the belief that a bitch will be unable adequately to nourish all the puppies she has whelped. In some extreme cases it may be necessary to do this or to obtain a foster mother or wet nurse to share the burden of rearing the puppies. However, the healthy bitch with normal metabolism can usually generate enough milk to feed adequately all the puppies she has produced, provided she is well enough fed and provided the puppies are fed additionally as soon as they are able to eat.

After whelping until the puppies are weaned, throughout the lactating period, the bitch should have all the nourishing food she can be induced to eat—up to four or five meals a day. These should consist largely of meat and liver, some fat, a small amount of cereals, milk, eggs, cottage cheese, calcium phosphate, and vitamins, with especial reference to vitamins A and D. At that time it is hardly possible to feed a bitch too much or to keep her too fat. The growth of the puppies is much more rapid after they are born than was their growth in the dam's uterus, and the large amount of food needed to maintain that rapid growth must pass through the bitch and be transformed to milk, while at the same time she must maintain her own body.

THE FEEDING OF PUPPIES

If the number of puppies in a litter is small, if the mother is vigorous, healthy, and a good milker, the youngsters up until their weaning time may require no additional food over and above the milk they suck from their dam's breasts. If the puppies are numerous or if the dam's milk is deficient in quality or quantity, it is wise to begin feeding the puppies artificially as soon as they are able and willing to accept food. This is earlier than used to be realized.

It is for the sake of the puppies' vigor rather than for the sake of their ultimate size that their growth is to be promoted as rapidly as possible. Vigorous and healthy puppies attain early maturity if they are given the right amounts of the right quality of food. The ultimate size of the dog at maturity is laid down in his germ plasm, and he can be stunted or dwarfed, if at all, only at the expense of his type. If one tries to prevent the full growth of a dog by withholding from him the food he needs, one will wind up with a rachitic, cowhocked dog, one with a delicate digestive apparatus, a sterile one, one with all of these shortcomings combined, or even a dead dog.

Growth may be slowed with improper food, sometimes without serious harm, but the dog is in all ways better off if he is forced along with the best food and encouraged to attain his full size at an early age. Dogs of the smaller breeds usually reach their full maturity several months earlier than those of the larger breeds. A well grown dog reaches his sexual maturity and can be safely used for limited breeding at one year of age.

As soon as teeth can be felt with the finger in a puppy's mouth, which is usually at about seventeen or eighteen days of age, it is safe to begin to feed him. His first food (except for his mother's milk) should be of scraped raw beef at body temperature. The first day he may have ¼ to 2 teaspoonfuls, according to size. He will not need to learn to eat this meat; he will seize upon it avidly and lick his chops for more. The second day he may have ⅓ to 3 teaspoonfuls, according to size, with two feedings 12 hours apart. Thereafter, the amount and frequency of this feeding may be rapidly increased. By the twenty-fifth day the meat need not be scraped, but only finely ground. This process of the early feeding of raw meat to puppies not only gives them a good start in life, but

44

it also relieves their mother of a part of her burden of providing milk for them.

At about the fourth week, some cereal (thoroughly cooked oatmeal, shredded wheat, or dried bread) may be either moistened and mixed with the meat or be served to the puppies with milk, fresh or canned. It may be necessary to immerse their noses into such a mixture to teach them to eat it. Calcium phosphate and a small amount of cod-liver oil should be added to such a mixture, both of which substances the puppies should have every day until their maturity. At the fourth week, while they are still at the dam's breast, they may be fed three or four times a day upon this extra ration, or something similar, such as cottage cheese or soft boiled egg. By the sixth week their dam will be trying to wean them, and they may have four or five meals daily. One of these may be finely broken dog biscuit thoroughly soaked in milk. One or two of the meals should consist largely or entirely of meat with liver.

The old advice about feeding puppies "little and often" should be altered to "much and often." Each puppy at each meal should have all the food he will readily clean up. Food should not be left in front of the puppies. They should be fed and after two or three minutes the receptacle should be taken away. Young puppies should be roly-poly fat, and kept so up to at least five or six months of age. Thereafter they should be slightly on the fat side, but not pudgy, until maturity.

The varied diet of six-week-old puppies may be continued, but at eight or nine weeks the number of meals may be reduced to four, and at three months, to three large rations per day. After six months the meals may be safely reduced again to two a day, but they must be generous meals with meat, liver, milk, cod-liver oil, and calcium phosphate. At full maturity, one meal a day suffices, or two may be continued.

The secret of turning good puppies into fine, vigorous dogs is to keep them growing through the entire period of their maturation. The most important item in the rearing of puppies is adequate and frequent meals of highly nourishing foods. Growth requires two or three times as much food as maintenance. Time between meals should be allowed for digestion, but puppies should never be permitted to become really hungry. Water in a shallow dish should be available to puppies at all times after they are able to walk.

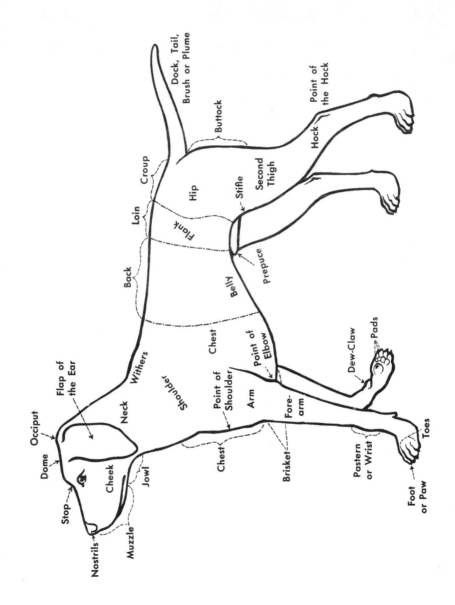

46

The Breeding
of Dogs

HERE, if anywhere in the entire process of the care
and management of dogs, the exercise of good judgment is involved.
Upon the choice of the two dogs, male and female, to be mated
together depends the future success or failure of one's dogs. If the
two to be mated are ill chosen, either individually or as pertains
to their fitness as mates, one to the other, all the painstaking care
to feed and rear the resultant puppies correctly is wasted. The
mating together of two dogs is the drafting of the blueprints and
the writing of the specifications of what the puppies are to be
like. The plans, it is true, require to be executed; the puppies,
when they arrive, must be adequately fed and cared for in order
to develop them into the kinds of dogs they are in their germ plasm
designed to become. However, if the plans as determined in the
mating are defective, just so will the puppies that result from them
be defective, in spite of all the good raising one can give them.

The element of luck in the breeding of dogs cannot be discounted,
for it exists. The mating which on paper appears to be the best
possible may result in puppies that are poor and untypical of
their breed. Even less frequently, a good puppy may result from
a chance mating together of two ill chosen parents. These results
are fortuitous and unusual, however. The best dogs as a lot come
from parents carefully chosen as to their individual excellences and
as to their suitability as mates for each other. It is as unwise as

47

it is unnecessary to trust to luck in the breeding of dogs. Careful planning pays off in the long run, and few truly excellent dogs are produced without it.

Some breeders without any knowledge of genetics have been successful, without knowing exactly why they succeeded. Some of them have adhered to beliefs in old wives' tales and to traditional concepts that science has long since exploded and abandoned. Such as have succeeded have done so in spite of their lack of knowledge and not because of it.

There is insufficient space at our disposal in this book to discuss in detail the science of genetics and the application of that science to the breeding of dogs. Whole books have been written about the subject. One of the best, clearest, and easiest for the layman to understand is *The New Art of Breeding Better Dogs,* by Philip Onstott, which may be obtained from Howell Book House, the publisher. In it and in other books upon the subject of genetics will be found more data about the practical application of science to the breeding of livestock than can be included here.

The most that can be done here is to offer some advice soundly based upon the genetic laws. Every feature a dog may or can possess is determined by the genes carried in the two reproductive cells, one from each parent, from the union of which he was developed. There are thousands of pairs of these determiners in the life plan of every puppy, and often a complex of many genes is required to produce a single recognizable attribute of the dog.

These genes function in pairs, one member of each pair being contributed by the father and the other member of the pair coming from the mother. The parents obtained these genes they hand on from their parents, and it is merely fortuitous which half of any pair of genes present in a dog's or a bitch's germ plasm may be passed on to any one of the progeny. Of any pair of its own genes, a dog or a bitch may contribute one member to one puppy and the other member to another puppy in the same litter or in different litters. The unknown number of pairs of genes is so great that there is an infinite number of combinations of them, which accounts for the differences we find between two full brothers or two full sisters. In fact, it depends upon the genes received whether a dog be a male or a female.

We know that the male dog contributes one and the bitch the

48

other of every pair of genes that unite to determine what the puppy will be like and what he will grow into. Thus, the parents make exactly equal contributions to the germ plasm or zygote from which every puppy is developed. It was long believed that the male dog was so much more important than the bitch in any mating that the excellence or shortcomings of the bitch might be disregarded. This theory was subsequently reversed and breeders considered the bitch to be more important than the dog. We now know that their contribution in every mating and in every individual puppy is exactly equal, and neither is to be considered more than the other.

There are two kinds of genes—the recessive genes and the dominant. And there are three kinds of pairs of genes: a recessive from the sire plus a recessive from the dam; a dominant from the sire plus a dominant from the dam; and a dominant from one parent plus a recessive from the other. It is the last combination that is the source of our trouble in breeding. When both members of a pair of genes are recessive, the result is a recessive attribute in the animal that carries them; when both members of the pair are dominant, the result is a pure dominant attribute; but when one member of the pair is recessive and the other member dominant, the result will be a wholly or only partially dominant attribute, which will breed true only half of the time. This explains why a dog or a bitch may fail to produce progeny that looks at all like itself.

If all the pairs of a dog's genes were purely dominant, we could expect him to produce puppies that resembled himself in all particulars, no matter what kind of mate he was bred to. Or if all his genes were recessive and he were mated to a bitch with all recessive genes, the puppies might be expected to look quite like the parents. However, a dog with mixed pairs of genes bred to a bitch with mixed pairs of genes may produce anything at all, puppies that bear no resemblance to either parent.

Long before the Mendelian laws were discovered, some dogs were known to be "prepotent" to produce certain characters, that is the characters would show up in their puppies irrespective of what their mates might be like. For instance, some dogs, themselves with dark eyes, might be depended upon never to produce a puppy with light eyes, no matter how light eyed the mate to which he was bred. This was true despite the fact that the dog's litter brother which had equally dark eyes, when bred to a light eyed bitch might produce a large percentage of puppies with light eyes.

Before it is decided to breed a bitch, it is well to consider whether she is worth breeding, whether she is good enough as an individual and whether she came from a good enough family to warrant the expectations that she will produce puppies worth the expense and trouble of raising. It is to be remembered that the bitch contributes exactly half the genes to each of her puppies; if she has not good genes to contribute, the time and money involved in breeding her and rearing her puppies will be wasted.

It is conceded that a bad or mediocre bitch when bred to an excellent dog will probably produce puppies better than herself. But while one is "grading up" from mediocre stock, other breeders are also grading upward from better stock and they will keep just so far ahead of one's efforts that one can never catch up with them. A merely pretty good bitch is no good at all for breeding. It is better to dispose of a mediocre bitch or to relegate her to the position of a family pet than to breed from her. It is difficult enough, with all the care and judgment one is able to muster, to obtain superlative puppies even from a fine bitch, without cluttering the earth with inferior puppies from just any old bitch.

If one will go into the market and buy the best possible bitch from the best possible family one's purse can afford and breed her sensibly to the best and most suitable stud dog one can find, success is reasonably sure. Even if for economy's sake, the bitch is but a promising puppy backed up by the best possible pedigree, it will require only a few months until she is old enough to be bred. From such a bitch, one may expect first-rate puppies at the first try, whereas in starting with an inferior bitch one is merely lucky if in two or three generations he obtains a semblance of the kind of dog he is trying to produce.

Assuming it is decided that the bitch is adequate to serve as a brood bitch, it becomes necessary to choose for her a mate in collaboration with which she may realize the ultimate of her possibilities. It is never wise to utilize for stud the family pet or the neighbor's pet just because he happens to be registered in the studbook or because his service costs nothing. Any dog short of the best and most suitable (wherever he may be and whoever may own him) is an extravagance. If the bitch is worth breeding at all, she is worth shipping clear across the continent, if need be, to obtain for her a mate to enable her to realize her possibilities. Stud fees may range from fifty to one hundred dollars or even more. The average value of each puppy, if well reared, should at the time of weaning approximate the legitimate stud fee of its sire. With a good bitch it is therefore profitable to lay out as much as may be required to obtain the services of the best and most suitable stud dog—always assuming that he is worth the price asked. However, it is never wise to choose an inferior or unsuitable dog just because he is well ballyhooed and commands an exorbitant stud fee.

There are three considerations by which to evaluate the merits of a stud dog—his outstanding excellence as an individual, his pedigree and the family from which he derived, and the excellence or inferiority of the progeny he is known to have produced.

As an individual a good stud dog may be expected to be bold and aggressive (not vicious) and structurally typical of his breed, but without any freakish exaggerations of type. He must be sound, a free and true mover, possess fineness and quality, and be a gentleman of his own breed. Accidentally acquired scars or injuries such as broken legs should not be held against him, because he can transmit only his genes to his puppies and no such accidents impair his genes.

A dog's pedigree may mean much or little. One of two litter brothers, with pedigrees exactly alike, may prove to be a superlative show and stud dog, and the other worth exactly nothing for either purpose. The pedigree especially is not to be judged on its length, since three generations is at most all that is required, although further extension of the pedigree may prove interesting to a curious owner. No matter how well-bred his pedigree may show a dog to be, if he is not a good dog the ink required to write the pedigree was wasted.

The chief value of a pedigree is to enable us to know from which of a dog's parents, grandparents, or great-grandparents, he derived his merits, and from which his faults. In choosing a mate for him (or for her, as the case may be) one seeks to reinforce the one and to avoid the other. Let us assume that one of the grandmothers was upright in shoulder, whereas the shoulder should be well laid back; we can avoid as a mate for such a dog one with any

51

tendency to straight shoulders or one from straight shouldered ancestry. The same principle would apply to an uneven mouth, a light eye, a soft back, splayed feet, cowhocks, or to any other inherited fault. Suppose, on the other hand, that the dog himself, the parents, and all the grandparents are particularly nice in regard to their fronts; in a mate for such a dog, one desires as good a front as is obtainable, but if she, or some of her ancestors are not too good in respect to their fronts, one may take a chance anyway and trust to the good fronted dog with his good fronted ancestry to correct the fault. That then is the purpose of the pedigree as a guide to breeding.

A stud dog can best be judged, however, by the excellence of the progeny he is known to have produced, if it is possible to obtain all the data to enable the breeder to evaluate that record. A complete comparative evaluation is perhaps impossible to make, but one close enough to justify conclusions is available. Not only the number but the quality of the bitches to which the dog has been bred must enter into the consideration. A young dog may not have had the opportunity to prove his prowess in the stud. He may have been bred to few bitches and those few of indifferent merits, or his get may not be old enough as yet to hit the shows and establish a record for themselves or for their sire. Allowance may be made for such a dog.

On the other hand, a dog may have proved himself to be phenomenal in the show ring, or may have been made to seem phenomenal by means of the owner's ballyhoo and exploitation. Half of the top bitches in the entire country may have been bred to him upon the strength of his winning record. Merely from the laws of probability such a dog, if he is not too bad, will produce some creditable progeny. It is necessary to take into consideration the opportunities a dog has had in relation to the fine progeny he has produced.

That, however, is the chief criterion by which a good stud dog may be recognized. A dog which can sire two or three excellent puppies in every litter from a reasonably good bitch may be considered as an acceptable stud. If he has in his lifetime sired one or two champions each year, and especially if one or two of the lot are superlative champions, top members of their breed, he is a great stud dog. Ordinarily and without other considerations, such a dog is to be preferred to one of his unproved sons, even though the son be as good or better an individual. In this way one employs genes one knows to produce what one wants. The son may be only hybrid dominant for his excellent qualities.

In the choice of a stud dog no attention whatever need be paid to claims that he sires numerically big litters. Unless the sire is deficient in sperm, the number of puppies in the litter, provided there are any puppies at all, depends entirely upon the bitch. At one service, a dog deposits enough spermatozoa to produce a million puppies, if there were so many ova to be fertilized. In any event, the major purpose should be to obtain good puppies, not large numbers of them.

There are three methods of breeding employed by experienced breeders—outcrossing, inbreeding, and line breeding. By outcrossing is meant the breeding together of mates of which no blood relationship can be traced. It is much favored by novice breeders, who feel that the breeding together of blood relatives is likely to result in imbecility, constitutional weakness, or some other kind of degeneration. Inbreeding is the mating together of closely related animals—father to daughter, mother to son, brother to sister, half brother to half sister. Some of the best animals ever produced have been bred from some such incestuous mating, and the danger from such practices, if they are carried out by persons who know what they are about, is minimal. Line breeding is the mating together of animals related one to another, but less closely—such as first cousins, grandsire to granddaughter, granddam to grandson, uncle to niece, or aunt to nephew.

Absolute outcrossing is usually impossible, since all the good dogs in any breed are more or less related—descended from some common ancestor in the fifth or sixth or seventh generation of their pedigrees. In any event, it is seldom to be recommended, since the results from it in the first generation of progeny are usually not satisfactory. It may be undertaken by some far-sighted and experienced breeder for the purpose of bringing into his strain some particular merit lacking in it and present in the strain of the unrelated dog. While dogs so bred may obtain an added vigor from what is known in genetics as *heterosis,* they are likely to manifest a coarseness and a lack of uniformity in the litter which is not to be found in more closely bred puppies. Good breeders never outcross if it is possible to obtain the virtues they want by sticking to their own strain. And when they do outcross, it is for the purpose of utilizing the outcrossed product for further breeding. It is not an end in itself.

Inbreeding (or incest breeding, as it is sometimes called) involves no such hazards as are and in the past have been attributed to it. It produces some very excellent dogs when correctly employed, some very bad ones even when correctly employed, and all bad ones when carelessly used. All the standard breeds of dogs were established as uniform breeds through intense inbreeding and culling over many generations. Inbreeding brings into manifestation undesirable recessive genes, the bearers of which can be discarded and the strain can thus be purged of its bad recessives.

Dogs of great soundness and excellence, from excellent parents and grandparents, all of them much alike, may be safely mated together, no matter how closely they may be related, with reasonable hope that most of the progeny will be sound and typical with a close resemblance to all the members of their ancestry. However, two such superlative and well-bred dogs are seldom to be found. It is the way to make progress rapidly and to establish a strain of dogs much alike and which breeds true. The amateur with the boldness and courage to try such a mating in the belief that his dogs are good enough for it is not to be discouraged. But if his judgment is not justified by the results, let him not complain that he has not been warned.

Line breeding is the safest course between the Scylla of outcrossing and the Charybdis of inbreeding for the inexperienced navigator in the sea of breeding. It, too, is to be used with care, because when it succeeds it partakes much of the nature of inbreeding. At any rate, its purpose is the pairing of like genes.

Here the pedigrees come into use. We examine the pedigree of the bitch to be bred. We hope that all the dogs named in it are magnificent dogs, but we look them over and choose the best of the four grandparents. We check this grandparent's breeding and find it good, as it probably is if it is itself a dog or bitch of great excellence. We shall assume that this best dog in the bitch's pedigree is the maternal grandsire. Then our bitch may be bred back to this particular grandsire, to his full brother if he has one of equal excellence, to his best son or best grandson. In such a fashion we compound the genes of this grandsire, and hope to obtain some puppies with his excellences intensified.

The best name in the pedigree may be some other dog or bitch, in which case it is his or her germ plasm that is to be doubled to serve for the foundation of the pedigrees of the puppies of the projected litter.

In making a mating, it is never wise to employ two dogs with the same positive fault. It is wise to use two dogs with as many of the same positive virtues as it is possible to obtain. Neither should faults balance each other, as one with a front too wide, the other with a front too narrow; one with a sway back, the other roach backed. Rather, one member of the mating should be right where the other is wrong. We cannot trust to obtain the intermediate, if we overcompensate the fault of one mate with a fault of the other.

NEGOTIATIONS TO USE THE STUD DOG

Plans to use a stud dog should be laid far enough in advance to enable one to make sure that the services of the dog will be available when they are required. Most men with a dog at public stud publish "stud cards," on which are printed the dog's pedigree and pertinent data pertaining to its record. These should be requested for all the dogs one contemplates using. Most such owners reserve the right to refuse to breed their dogs to bitches they deem unsuitable for them; they wish to safeguard their dog's reputation as a producer of superior puppies, by choosing the bitches to which he shall be bred. Therefore, it is advisable to submit a description of the bitch, with or without a picture of her, and her pedigree to the stud dog's owner at the time the application to use him is made.

Notification should be sent to the owner of the dog as soon as the bitch begins to show in heat, and she should be taken or sent by air or by railway express to the dog's owner about the time she is first recognized to be in full heat and ready to breed. The stud dog's owner should be advised by telegram or telephone just how she has been sent and just when she may be expected, and instruction should be given about how she is to be returned.

Extreme care should be used in securely crating a bitch for shipment when she is in heat. Such bitches are prone to chew their way out of insecure boxes and escape to be bred by some vagrant mongrel. A card containing a statement of the bitch's condition should be attached to the crate as a warning to the carrier to assure her greater security.

MATING

The only time the bitch may become pregnant is during her period of oestruation, a time also variously referred to as the "oestrus," "the season," and as being in "heat." A bitch's first season usually occurs when she is between six and nine months of age, with the average age being eight months. In rare instances it may occur as early as five months or as late as thirteen months of age. After the first season, oestrus usually recurs at intervals of approximately six months, though this too is subject to variation. Also, the bitch's cycle may be influenced by factors such as a change of environment or a change of climate, and her cycle will, of course, be changed if it is interrupted by pregnancy. Most bitches again come in season four to six months after whelping.

There is a decided controversy among breeders as to the wisdom of breeding a bitch during her first season. Some believe a really fine bitch should be bred during her first season in order that she may produce as many puppies as possible during the fertile years of her life span. Others feel that definite physical harm results from breeding a bitch at her first season. Since a normal healthy bitch can safely produce puppies until she is about nine years old, she can comfortably yield eight to ten litters with rests between them in her life. Any breeder should be satisfied with this production from one animal. It seems wiser, therefore, to avoid the risk of any harm and pass her first season. Bitches vary in temperament and in the ages at which they reach sufficient maturity for motherhood and its responsibilities. As with the human animal, stability comes with age and a dam is much more likely to be a good mother if she is out of the puppy phase herself. If the bitch is of show quality, she might become a champion between her first and second heats if not bred.

Usually, oestruation continues for a period of approximately three weeks, but this too is subject to variation. Prior to the beginning of the oestrus, there may be changes in the bitch's actions and demeanor; she may appear restless, or she may become increasingly affectionate. Often there is increased frequency of urination and the bitch may be inclined to lick her external parts. The breeder should be alert for any signs of the approach of oestrus since the bitch must be confined and protected at this time in order to preclude the possibility of the occurrence of a mating with any but the selected stud.

The first physical sign of oestrus is a bloody discharge of watery consistency. The mucous membrane lining the vulva becomes congested, enlarged, and reddened, and the external parts become puffy and swollen. The color of the discharge gradually deepens during the first day or two until it is a rich red color; then it gradually becomes lighter until by the tenth to twelfth day it has only a slightly reddish, or straw-colored, tinge. During the next day or so it becomes almost clear. During this same period, the swelling and hardness of the external parts gradually subside, and by the time the discharge has lost most of its color, the parts are softened and spongy. It is at this time that ovulation, the production of ripened ova (or eggs), takes place, although physical manifestations of oestrus may continue for another week.

A normal bitch has two ovaries which contain her ova. All the eggs she will produce during her lifetime are present in the ovaries at birth. Ordinarily, some of the ova ripen each time the bitch comes in season. Should a bitch fail to ovulate (produce ripened ova), she cannot, of course, become pregnant. Actually, only one ovary is necessary for ovulation, and loss of or damage to one ovary without impairment of the other will not prevent the bitch from producing puppies.

If fertilization does not occur, the ova (and this is also true of the sperm of the male) live only a short time—probably a couple of days at the most. Therefore, if mating takes place too long before or after ovulation, a bitch will not conceive, and the unfertilized ova will pass through the uterus into the vagina. Eventually they will either be absorbed or will pass out through the vulva by the same opening through which urination takes place. If fertilization does occur, the fertilized eggs become implanted on the inner surface of the uterus and grow to maturity.

Obviously, the breeder must exercise great care in determining when the dog and the bitch should be put together. Because the length of time between the beginning of the oestrus and the time of ovulation varies in different bitches, no hard and fast rule can be established, although the twelfth to fourteenth day is in most cases the correct time. The wise breeder will keep a daily record of the changes in the bitch's condition and will arrange to put the bitch

58

and dog together when the discharge has become almost clear and the external parts are softened and spongy. If the bitch refuses the advances of the dog, it is preferable to separate the two, wait a day, then again permit the dog to approach the bitch.

Ordinarily, if the bitch is willing to accept the dog, fertilization of the ovum will take place. Usually one good service is sufficient, although two at intervals of twenty-four to forty-eight hours are often allowed.

Male dogs have glands on the penis which swell after passing the sphincter muscle of the vagina and "tie" the two animals together. The time may last for a period of a few minutes, a half hour, or occasionally up to an hour or more, but will end naturally when the locking glands have deflated the needful amount. While tying may increase the probability of success, in many cases no tie occurs, yet the bitches become pregnant.

Sperm are produced in the dog's testicles and are stored in the epididymis, a twisting tube at the side of the testicle. The occasional male dog whose testicles are not descended (a cryptorchid) is generally conceded to be sterile, although in a few instances it has been asserted that cryptorchids were capable of begetting progeny. The sterility in cryptorchids is believed to be due to the fact that the sperm are destroyed if the testicle remains within the abdominal cavity because the temperature is much higher there than in the normally descended testicle. Thus all sperm produced by the dog may be destroyed if both testicles are undescended. A monorchid (a dog with one testicle descended, the other undescended) may be fertile. Nevertheless, it is unwise to use a monorchid for stud purposes, because monorchidism is believed to be a heritable trait, and the monorchid, as well as the cryptorchid, is ineligible for the show ring.

After breeding, a bitch should be confined for a week to ten days to avoid mismating with another dog.

WHELPING CALENDAR

Find the month and date on which your bitch was bred in one of the left-hand columns. Directly opposite that date, in the right-hand column, is her expected date of whelping, bearing in mind that 61 days is as common as 63.

Each pair of columns shows **Date bred** (left) and **Date due to whelp** (right).

January	March	February	April	March	May	April	June	May	July	June	August	July	September	August	October	September	November	October	December	November	January	December	February
1	5	1	5	1	3	1	3	1	3	1	3	1	2	1	3	1	3	1	3	1	3	1	2
2	6	2	6	2	4	2	4	2	4	2	4	2	3	2	4	2	4	2	4	2	4	2	3
3	7	3	7	3	5	3	5	3	5	3	5	3	4	3	5	3	5	3	5	3	5	3	4
4	8	4	8	4	6	4	6	4	6	4	6	4	5	4	6	4	6	4	6	4	6	4	5
5	9	5	9	5	7	5	7	5	7	5	7	5	6	5	7	5	7	5	7	5	7	5	6
6	10	6	10	6	8	6	8	6	8	6	8	6	7	6	8	6	8	6	8	6	8	6	7
7	11	7	11	7	9	7	9	7	9	7	9	7	8	7	9	7	9	7	9	7	9	7	8
8	12	8	12	8	10	8	10	8	10	8	10	8	9	8	10	8	10	8	10	8	10	8	9
9	13	9	13	9	11	9	11	9	11	9	11	9	10	9	11	9	11	9	11	9	11	9	10
10	14	10	14	10	12	10	12	10	12	10	12	10	11	10	12	10	12	10	12	10	12	10	11
11	15	11	15	11	13	11	13	11	13	11	13	11	12	11	13	11	13	11	13	11	13	11	12
12	16	12	16	12	14	12	14	12	14	12	14	12	13	12	14	12	14	12	14	12	14	12	13
13	17	13	17	13	15	13	15	13	15	13	15	13	14	13	15	13	15	13	15	13	15	13	14
14	18	14	18	14	16	14	16	14	16	14	16	14	15	14	16	14	16	14	16	14	16	14	15
15	19	15	19	15	17	15	17	15	17	15	17	15	16	15	17	15	17	15	17	15	17	15	16
16	20	16	20	16	18	16	18	16	18	16	18	16	17	16	18	16	18	16	18	16	18	16	17
17	21	17	21	17	19	17	19	17	19	17	19	17	18	17	19	17	19	17	19	17	19	17	18
18	22	18	22	18	20	18	20	18	20	18	20	18	19	18	20	18	20	18	20	18	20	18	19
19	23	19	23	19	21	19	21	19	21	19	21	19	20	19	21	19	21	19	21	19	21	19	20
20	24	20	24	20	22	20	22	20	22	20	22	20	21	20	22	20	22	20	22	20	22	20	21
21	25	21	25	21	23	21	23	21	23	21	23	21	22	21	23	21	23	21	23	21	23	21	22
22	26	22	26	22	24	22	24	22	24	22	24	22	23	22	24	22	24	22	24	22	24	22	23
23	27	23	27	23	25	23	25	23	25	23	25	23	24	23	25	23	25	23	25	23	25	23	24
24	28	24	28	24	26	24	26	24	26	24	26	24	25	24	26	24	26	24	26	24	26	24	25
25	29	25	29	25	27	25	27	25	27	25	27	25	26	25	27	25	27	25	27	25	27	25	26
26	30	26	30	26	28	26	28	26	28	26	28	26	27	26	28	26	28	26	28	26	28	26	27
27	31	27	May 1	27	29	27	29	27	29	27	29	27	28	27	29	27	29	27	29	27	29	27	28
28	Apr. 1	28	2	28	30	28	30	28	30	28	30	28	29	28	30	28	30	28	30	28	30	28	Mar. 1
29	2			29	31	29	July 1	29	31	29	31	29	30	29	31	29	Dec. 1	29	31	29	31	29	2
30	3			30	June 1	30	2	30	Aug. 1	30	Sep. 1	30	Oct. 1	30	Nov. 1	30	2	30	Jan. 1	30	Feb. 1	30	3
31	4			31	2			31	2			31	2	31	2			31	2			31	4

THE PREGNANCY AND WHELPING
OF THE BITCH

The "period of gestation" of the bitch, by which is meant the duration of her pregnancy, is usually estimated at sixty-three days. Many bitches, especially young ones, have their puppies as early as sixty days after they are bred. Cases have occurred in which strong puppies were born after only fifty-seven days, and there have been cases that required as many as sixty-six days. However, if puppies do not arrive by the sixty-fourth day, it is time to consult a veterinarian.

For the first five to six weeks of her pregnancy, the bitch requires no more than normal good care and unrestricted exercise. For that period, she needs no additional quantity of food, although her diet must contain sufficient amounts of all the food factors, as is stated in the division of this book that pertains to food. After the fifth to sixth week, the ration must be increased and the violence of exercise restricted. Normal running and walking are likely to be better for the pregnant bitch than a sedentary existence but she should not be permitted to jump, hunt, or fight during the latter half of her gestation. Violent activity may cause her to abort her puppies.

About a week before she is due to whelp, a bed should be prepared for her and she be persuaded to use it for sleeping. This bed may be a box of generous size, big enough to accommodate her with room for activity. It should be high enough to permit her to stand upright, and is better for having a hinged cover. An opening in one side will afford her ingress and egress. This box should be placed in a secluded location, away from any possible molestation by other dogs, animals, or children. The bitch must be made confident of her security in her box.

A few hours, or perhaps a day or two, before her whelping, the bitch will probably begin arranging the bedding of the box to suit herself, tearing blankets or cushions and nosing the parts into the corners. Before the whelping actually starts, however, it is best to substitute burlap sacking, securely tacked to the floor of the box. This is to provide traction for the puppies to reach the dam's breast.

The whelping may take place at night without any assistance from the owner. The box may be opened in the morning to reveal

61

the happy bitch nursing a litter of complacent puppies. But she may need some assistance in her parturition. If whelping is recognized to be in process, it is best to help the bitch.

As the puppies arrive, one by one, the enveloping membranes should be removed as quickly as possible, lest the puppies suffocate. Having removed the membrane, the umbilical cord should be severed with clean scissors some three or four inches from the puppy's belly. (The part of the cord attached to the belly will dry up and drop off in a few days.) There is no need for any medicament or dressing of the cord after it is cut.

The bitch should be permitted to eat the afterbirth if she so desires, and she normally does. If she has no assistance, she will probably remove the membrane and sever the cord with her teeth. The only dangers are that she may delay too long or may bite the cord too short. Some bitches, few of them, eat their newborn puppies (especially bitches not adequately fed during pregnancy). This unlikelihood should be guarded against.

As they arrive, it is wise to remove all the puppies except one, placing them in a box or basket lined and covered by a woolen cloth, somewhere aside or away from the whelping bed, until all have come and the bitch's activity has ceased. The purpose of this is to prevent her from walking or lying on the whelps, and to keep her from being disturbed by the puppies' whining. A single puppy should be left with the bitch to ease her anxiety.

It is best that the "midwife" be somebody with whom the bitch is on intimate terms and in whom she has confidence. Some bitches exhibit a jealous fear and even viciousness while they are whelping. Such animals are few, and most appear grateful for gentle assistance through their ordeal.

The puppies arrive at intervals of a few minutes to an hour until all are delivered. It is wise to call a veterinarian if the interval is greater than one hour. Though such service is seldom needed, an experienced veterinarian can usually be depended upon to withdraw with obstetrical forceps an abnormally presented puppy. It is possible, but unlikely, that the veterinarian will recommend a Caesarian section. This surgery in the dog is not very grave, but it should be performed only by an expert veterinarian. It is unnecessary to describe the process here, or the subsequent management of the patient, since, if a Caesarian section should be necessary, the veterinarian will provide all the needed instructions.

Some bitches, at or immediately after their whelping period, go into a convulsive paralysis, which is called *eclampsia*. This is unlikely if the bitch throughout her pregnancy has had an adequate measure of calcium in her rations. The remedy for eclampsia is the intravenous or intramuscular administration of parenteral calcium. The bitch suspected of having eclampsia should be attended by a veterinarian.

Assuming that the whelping has been normal and without untoward incident, all of the puppies are returned to the bitch, and put, one by one, to the breast, which strong puppies will accept with alacrity. The less handling of puppies for the first four or five hours of their lives, the better. However, the litter should be looked over carefully for possible defectives and discards, which should be destroyed as soon as possible. There is no virtue in rearing hare-lipped, crippled, or mismarked puppies.

It is usually unwise to destroy sound, healthy puppies just to reduce the number in the litter, since it is impossible to sort young puppies for excellence and one may be destroying the best member of the litter, a future champion. Unless a litter is extraordinarily numerous, the dam, if well fed, can probably suckle them all. If it is found that her milk is insufficient, the litter may be artificially fed or may be divided, and the surplus placed on a foster mother if it is possible to obtain one. The foster mother need not be of the same breed as the puppies, a mongrel being as good as any. She should be approximately the same size as the actual mother of the puppies, clean, healthy, and her other puppies should be of as nearly the same age as the ones she is to take over as possible. She should be removed from her own puppies (which may well be destroyed) and her breasts be permitted to fill with milk until she is somewhat uncomfortable, at which time her foster puppies can be put to her breasts and will usually be accepted without difficulty. Unless the services of the foster mother are really required, it is better not to use her.

The whelping bitch may be grateful for a warm meal even between the arrivals of her puppies. As soon as her chore is over, she should be offered food in her box. This should be of cereal and milk or of meat and broth, something sloppy. She will probably not leave her puppies to eat and her meals must be brought to her.

It is wise to give a mild laxative for her bowels, also milk of magnesia. She will be reluctant to get out of her box even to relieve herself for about two days, but she should be urged, even forced, to do so regularly. A sensible bitch will soon settle down to care for her brood and will seldom give further trouble. She should be fed often and well, all that she can be induced to eat during her entire lactation.

As a preventive for infections sometimes occurring after whelping, some experienced breeders and veterinarians recommend injecting the bitch with penicillin or another antibiotic immediately following the birth of the last puppy. Oral doses of the same drug may be given daily thereafter for the first week. It is best to consult your veterinarian about this treatment.

ACID MILK

Occasionally a bitch produces early milk (colostrum) so acid that it disagrees with, sometimes kills, her puppies. The symptoms of the puppies are whining, disquiet, frequently refusal to nurse, frailty, and death. It is true that all milk is slightly acid, and it should be, turning blue litmus paper immersed in it a very light pink. However, milk harmfully on the acid side will readily turn litmus paper a vivid red. It seems that only the first two or three days milk is so affected. Milk problems come also from mastitis and other infections in the bitch.

This is not likely to occur with a bitch that throughout her pregnancy has received an adequate supply of calcium phosphate regularly in her daily ration. That is the best way to deal with the situation—to see to the bitch's correct nutrition in advance of her whelping. The owner has only himself to blame for the bitch's too acid milk, since adequate calcium in advance would have neutralized the acid.

If it is found too late that her milk is too acid, the puppies must be taken from her breast and either given to a foster mother or artificially fed from bottle or by medicine dropper. Artificial feeding of very young puppies seldom is successful. Sometimes the acidity of the dam's milk can be neutralized by giving her large doses of bicarbonate of soda (baking soda), but the puppies should not be restored to her breasts until her milk ceases to turn litmus paper red.

If it is necessary to feed the puppies artificially, "Esbilac," a commercial product, or the following orphan puppy formula, may be used.

7 oz. whole milk

1 oz. cream (top milk)

1 egg yolk

2 tbsp. corn syrup

2 tbsp. lime water

REARING THE PUPPIES

Puppies are born blind and open their eyes at approximately the ninth day thereafter. If they were whelped earlier than the full sixty-three days after the breeding from which they resulted, the difference should be added to the nine days of anticipated blindness. The early eye color of young puppies is no criterion of the color to which the eyes are likely to change, and the breeder's anxiety about his puppies' having light eyes is premature.

In breeds that require the docking of the tail, this should be done on the third day and is a surgical job for the veterinarian. Many a dog has had his tail cut off by an inexperienced person, ruining his good looks and his possibility for a win in the show ring. Dew claws should be removed at the same time. There is little else to do with normal puppies except to let them alone and permit them to grow. The most important thing about their management is their nutrition, which is discussed in another chapter. The first two or three weeks, they will thrive and grow rapidly on their mother's milk, after which they should have additional food as described.

Puppies sleep much of the time, as do other babies, and they should not be frequently awakened to be played with. They grow more and more playful as they mature.

After the second week their nails begin to grow long and sharp. The mother will be grateful if the puppies' nails are blunted with scissors from time to time so that in their pawing of the breast they do not lacerate it. Sharp nails tend to prompt the mother to wean the whelps early, and she should be encouraged to keep them with her as long as she will tolerate them. Even the small amount of milk they can drain from her after the weaning process is begun is the best food they can obtain. It supplements and makes digestible the remainder of their ration.

Many bitches, after their puppies are about four weeks of age, eat and regurgitate food, which is eaten by the puppies. This food is warmed and partly digested in the bitch's stomach. This practice, while it may appear digusting to the novice keeper of dogs, is perfectly normal and should not be discouraged. However, it renders it all the more necessary that the food of the bitch be sound, clean, and nutritious.

It is all but impossible to rear a litter of puppies without their becoming infested with roundworms. Of course, the bitch should be wormed, if she harbors such parasites, before she is bred, and her teats should be thoroughly washed with mild soap just before she whelps to free them from the eggs of roundworms. Every precaution must be taken to reduce the infestation of the puppies to a minimum. But, in spite of all it is possible to do, puppies will have roundworms. These pests hamper growth, reduce the puppies' normal resistance to disease, and may kill them outright unless the worms are eliminated. The worming of puppies is discussed in the chapter entitled "Intestinal Parasites and Their Control."

External Vermin
and Parasites

U NDER this heading the most common external parasites will be given consideration. Fleas, lice, ticks, and flies are those most commonly encountered and causing the most concern. The external parasite does not pose the problem that it used to before we had the new "miracle" insecticides. Today, with DDT, lindane, and chlordane, the course of extermination and prevention is much easier to follow. Many of the insecticide sprays have a four to six weeks residual effect. Thus the premises can be sprayed and the insect pests can be quite readily controlled.

FLEAS

Neglected dogs are too often beset by hundreds of blood-thirsty fleas, which do not always confine their attacks to the dogs but also sometimes feast upon their masters. Unchecked, they overrun kennels, homes, and playgrounds. Moreover, they are the intermediate hosts for the development of the kind of tapeworm most frequently found in dogs, as will be more fully discussed under the subject of *Intestinal Parasites*. Fleas are all-round bad actors and nuisances. Although it need hardly concern us in America, where the disease is not known to exist, fleas are the recognized and only vectors of bubonic plague.

There are numerous kinds and varieties of fleas, of which we shall discuss here only the three species often found on dogs. These are the human flea (*Pulex irritans*), the dog flea (*Ctenocephalides canis*), and the so-called chicken flea or sticktight flea (*Echidnophaga gallinacea*).

Of these the human flea prefers the blood of man to that of the dog, and unless humans are also bothered, are not likely to be found on the dog. They are small, nearly black insects, and occur mostly in the Mississippi Valley and in California. Their control is the same as for the dog flea.

The dog flea is much larger than his human counterpart, is dark brown in color and seldom bites mankind. On an infested dog these dog fleas may be found buried in the coat of any part of the anatomy, but their choicest habitat is the area of the back just forward from the tail and over the loins. On that part of a badly neglected dog, especially in summer, fleas by the hundreds will be found intermixed with their dung and with dried blood. They may cause the dog some discomfort or none. It must not be credited that because a dog is not kept in a constant or frequent agitation of scratching that he harbors no fleas. The coats of pet animals are soiled and roughened by the fleas and torn by the scratching that they sometimes induce. Fleas also appear to be connected with summer eczema of dogs; at least the diseased condition of the skin often clears up after fleas are eradicated.

Although the adults seldom remain long away from the dog's body, fleas do not reproduce themselves on the dog. Rather, their breeding haunts are the debris, dust, and sand of the kennel floor, and especially the accumulations of dropped hair, sand, and loose soil of unclean sleeping boxes. Nooks and cracks and crannies of the kennel may harbor the eggs or maggot-like larvae of immature fleas.

This debris and accumulation must be eliminated—preferably by incineration—after which all possible breeding areas should be thoroughly sprayed with a residual effect spray.

The adult dog may be combed well, then bathed in a detergent solution, rinsed thoroughly in warm water, and allowed to drip fairly dry. A solution of Pine Oil (1 oz. to a quart of water) is then used as a final rinse. This method of ridding the dog of its fleas is ideal in warm weather. The Pine Oil imparts a pleasant odor

68

to the dog's coat and the animal will enjoy being bathed and groomed.

The same procedure may be followed for young puppies except that the Pine Oil solution should be rinsed off. When bathing is not feasible, then a good flea powder—one containing lindane—should be used.

Sticktight fleas are minute, but are to be found, if at all, in patches on the dog's head and especially on the ears. They remain quiescent and do not jump, as the dog fleas and human fleas do. Their tiny heads are buried in the dog's flesh. To force them loose from the area decapitates them and the heads remain in the skin which is prone to fester from the irritation. They may be dislodged by placing a cotton pad or thick cloth well soaked in ether or alcohol over the flea patch, which causes them immediately to relinquish their hold, after which they can be easily combed loose and destroyed.

These sticktights abound in neglected, dirty, and abandoned chicken houses, which, if the dogs have access to them, should be cleaned out thoroughly and sprayed with DDT.

Fleas, while a nuisance, are only a minor problem. They should be eliminated not only from the dog but from all the premises he inhabits. Dogs frequently are reinfested with fleas from other dogs with which they play or come in contact. Every dog should be occasionally inspected for the presence of fleas, and, if any are found, immediate means should be taken to eradicate them.

LICE

There are even more kinds of lice than of fleas, although as they pertain to dogs there is no reason to differentiate them. They do not infest dogs, except in the events of gross neglect or of unforeseen accident. Lice reproduce themselves on the body of the dog. To rid him of the adult lice is easy. The standard Pine Oil solution used to kill fleas will also kill lice. However, the eggs or "nits" are harder to remove. Weather permitting, it is sometimes best to have the dog clipped of all its hair. In heavily infested dogs this is the only sure way to cope with the situation. When the hair is clipped, most of the "nits" are removed automatically. A good commercial flea and louse powder applied to the skin will then keep the situation under control.

69

Rare as the occurrence of lice upon dogs may be, they must be promptly treated and eradicated. Having a dog with lice can prove to be embarrassing, for people just do not like to be around anything lousy. Furthermore, the louse may serve as the intermediate host of the tapeworm in dogs.

The dog's quarters should be thoroughly sprayed with a residual spray of the same type recommended for use in the control of fleas. The problem of disinfecting kennel and quarters is not as great as it is in the case of fleas, for the louse tends to stay on its host, not leaving the dog as the flea does.

TICKS

The terms "wood ticks" and "dog ticks," as usually employed, refer to at least eight different species, whose appearances and habits are so similar that none but entomologists are likely to know them apart. It is useless to attempt to differentiate between these various species here, except to warn the reader that the Rocky Mountain spotted fever tick (*Dermacentor andersoni*) is a vector of the human disease for which it is named, as well as of rabbit fever (tularemia), and care must be employed in removing it from dogs lest the hands be infected. Some one or more of these numerous species are to be found in well nigh every state in the Union, although there exist wide areas where wood ticks are seldom seen and are not a menace to dogs.

All the ticks must feed on blood in order to reproduce themselves. The eggs are always deposited on the ground or elsewhere after the female, engorged with blood, has dropped from the dog or other animal upon which she has fed. The eggs are laid in masses in protected places on the ground, particularly in thick clumps of grass. Each female lays only one such mass, which contains 2500 to 5000 eggs. The development of the American dog tick embraces four stages: the egg, the larva or seed tick, the nymph, and the adult. The two intermediate stages in the growth of the tick are spent on rodents, and only in the adult stage does it attach itself to the dog. Both sexes affix themselves to dogs and to other animals and feed on their blood; the males do not increase in size, although the female is tremendously enlarged as she gorges. Mating occurs while the female is feeding. After some five to thirteen days, she drops from her host, lays her eggs and dies. At no time do ticks feed on anything except the blood of animals.

The longevity and hardihood of the tick are amazing. The larvae and nymphs may live for a full year without feeding, and the adults survive for more than two years if they fail to encounter a host to which they may attach. In the Northern United States the adults are most active in the spring and summer, few being found after July. But in the warmer Southern states they may be active the year around.

Although most of the tick species require a vegetative cover and wild animal hosts to complete their development, at least one species, the brown tick (*Rhipicephalus sanguinius*), is adapted to life in the dryer environment of kennels, sheds, and houses, with the dog as its only necessary host. This tick is the vector of canine piroplasmosis, although this disease is at this time almost negligible in the United States.

This brown dog tick often infests houses in large numbers, both immature and adult ticks lurking around baseboards, window casings, furniture, the folds of curtains, and elsewhere. Thus, even dogs kept in houses are sometimes infested with hundreds of larvae, nymphs, and adults of this tick. Because of its ability to live in heated buildings, the species has become established in many Northern areas. Unlike the other tick species, the adult of the brown dog tick does not bite human beings. However, also unlike the other ticks, it is necessary not only to rid the dogs of this particular tick but also to eliminate the pests from their habitat, especially the dogs' beds and sleeping boxes. A spray with a 10% solution of DDT suffices for this purpose. Fumigation of premises seldom suffices, since not only are brown dog ticks very resistant to mere fumigation, but the ticks are prone to lurk around entry ways, porches and outbuildings, where they cannot be reached with a fumigant. The spraying with DDT may not penetrate to spots where some ticks are in hiding, and it must be repeated at intervals until all the pests are believed to be completely eradicated.

Dogs should not be permitted to run in brushy areas known to be infested with ticks, and upon their return from exercise in a place believed to harbor ticks, dogs should be carefully inspected for their presence.

If a dog's infestation is light, the ticks may be picked individually

71

from his skin. To make tick release its grip, dab with alcohol or a drop of ammonia. If the infestation is heavy, it is easier and quicker to saturate his coat with a derris solution (one ounce of soap and two ounces of derris powder dissolved in one gallon of water). The derris should be of an excellent grade containing at least 3% of rotenone. The mixture may be used and reused, since it retains its strength for about three weeks if it is kept in a dark place.

If possible, the dip should be permitted to dry on the dog's coat. It should not get into a dog's eyes. The dip will not only kill the ticks that are attached to the dog, but the powder drying in the hair will repel further infestation for two or three days and kill most if not all the boarders. These materials act slowly, requiring sometimes as much as twenty-four hours to complete the kill.

If the weather is cold or the use of the dip should be otherwise inconvenient, derris powder may be applied as a dust, care being taken that it penetrates the hair and reaches the skin. Breathing or swallowing derris may cause a dog to vomit, but he will not be harmed by it. The dust and liquid should be kept from his eyes.

Since the dog is the principal host on which the adult tick feeds and since each female lays several thousand eggs after feeding, treating the dog regularly will not only bring him immediate relief but will limit the reproduction of the ticks. Keeping underbrush, weeds, and grass closely cut tends to remove protection favorable to the ticks. Burning vegetation accomplishes the same results.

Many of the ticks in an infested area may be killed by the thorough application of a spray made as follows: Four tablespoonfuls of nicotine sulphate (40% nicotine) in three gallons of water. More permanent results may be obtained by adding to this solution four ounces of sodium fluorides, but this will injure the vegetation.

Besides the ticks that attach themselves to all parts of the dog, there is another species that infests the ear specifically. This pest, the spinose ear tick, penetrates deep into the convolutions of the ear and often causes irritation and pain, as evidenced by the dog's scratching its ears, shaking its head or holding it on one side. One part derris powder (5% rotenone) mixed with ten parts medicinal mineral oil and dropped into the ear will kill spinose ear ticks. Only a few drops of the material is required, but it is best to massage the base of the ear to make sure the remedy penetrates to the deepest part of the ear to reach all the ticks.

FLIES

Flies can play havoc with dogs in outdoor kennels, stinging them and biting the ears until they are raw. Until recently the only protection against them was the screening of the entire kennel. The breeding places of flies, which are damp filth and stagnant garbage, are in most areas now happily abated, but the chief agent for control of the pest is DDT.

A spray of a 10% solution of DDT over all surfaces of the kennel property may be trusted to destroy all the flies that light on those surfaces for from two weeks to one month. It must, of course, be repeated from time to time when it is seen that the efficacy of the former treatment begins to diminish.

Intestinal Parasites and
Their Control

THE varieties of worms that may inhabit the alimentary tract of the dog are numerous. Much misapprehension exists, even among experienced dog keepers, about the harm these parasites may cause and about the methods of getting rid of them. Some dog keepers live in terror of these worms and continually treat their dogs for them whether they are known to be present or not; others ignore the presence of worms and do nothing about them. Neither policy is justified.

Promiscuous dosing, without the certainty that the dog harbors worms or what kind he may have, is a practice fraught with danger for the well-being of the animal. All drugs for the expulsion or destruction of parasites are poisonous or irritant to a certain degree and should be administered only when it is known that the dog is infested by parasites and what kind. It is hardly necessary to say that when a dog is known to harbor worms he should be cleared of them, but in most instances there is no such urgency as is sometimes manifested.

It may be assumed that puppies at weaning time are more or less infested with intestinal roundworms or ascarids (*Toxocara canis*) and that such puppies need to be treated for worms. It is all but impossible to rear a litter of puppies to weaning age free from those parasites. Once the puppies are purged of them, it is amazing to see the spurt of their growth and the renewal of their thriftiness.

Many neglected puppies surmount the handicap of their worms and at least some of them survive. This, however, is no reason that good puppies—puppies that are worth saving—should go unwormed and neglected.

The ways to find out that a dog actually has worms are to see some of the worms themselves in the dog's droppings or to submit a sample of his feces to a veterinarian or to a biological laboratory for microscopic examination. From a report of such an examination, it is possible to know whether or not a dog is a host to intestinal parasites at all and intelligently to undertake the treatment and control of the specific kind he may harbor.

All of the vermifuges, vermicides, and anthelmintic remedies tend to expel other worms besides the kind for which they are specifically intended, but it is better to employ the remedy particularly effective against the individual kind of parasite the dog is known to have, and to refrain from worm treatment unless or until it is known to be needed.

ROUNDWORMS

The ascarids, or large intestinal roundworms, are the largest of the worm parasites occurring in the digestive tract of the dog, varying in length from 1 to 8 inches, the females being larger than the males. The name "spool worms," which is sometimes applied to them, is derived from their tendency to coil in a springlike spiral when they are expelled, either from the bowel or vomited, by their hosts. There are at least two species of them which frequently parasitize dogs: *Toxocara canis* and *Toxascaris leonina,* but they are so much alike except for some minor details in the life histories of their development that it is not practically necessary for the dog keeper to seek to distinguish between them.

Neither specie requires an intermediate host for its development. Numerous eggs are deposited in the intestinal tract of the host animal; these eggs are passed out by the dog in his feces and are swallowed by the same or another animal, and hatching takes place in its small intestine. Their development requires from twelve to sixteen days under favorable circumstances.

It has been shown that puppies before their birth may be infested by roundworms from their mother. This accounts for the occasional finding of mature or nearly mature worms in very young puppies. It cannot occur if the mother is entirely free from worms, as she should be.

These roundworms are particularly injurious to young puppies. The commonest symptoms of roundworm infestation are general unthriftiness, digestive disturbances, and bloat after feeding. The hair grows dead and lusterless, and the breath may have a peculiar sweetish odor. Large numbers of roundworms may obstruct the intestine, and many have been known to penetrate the intestinal wall. In heavy infestations the worms may wander into the bile ducts, stomach, and even into the lungs and upper respiratory passages where they may cause pneumonia, especially in very young animals.

The control of intestinal roundworms depends primarily upon prompt disposal of feces, keeping the animals in clean quarters and on clean ground, and using only clean utensils for feed and water. Dampness of the ground favors the survival of worm eggs and larvae. There is no known chemical treatment feasible for the destruction of eggs in contaminated soil, but prolonged exposure to sunlight and drying has proved effective.

Numerous remedies have been in successful use for roundworms, including turpentine, which has a recognized deleterious effect upon the kidneys; santonin, an old standby; freshly powdered betel nut and its derivative, arecoline, both of which tend to purge and sicken the patient; oil of chenopodium, made from American wormseed; carbon tetrachloride, widely used as a cleaning agent; tetrachlorethylene, closely related chemically to the former, but less toxic; and numerous other medicaments. While all of them are effective as vermifuges or vermicides, if rightly employed, to each of them some valid objection can be interposed.

In addition to the foregoing, there are other vermifuges available for treatment of roundworms. Some may be purchased without a prescription, whereas others may be procured only when prescribed by a veterinarian.

HOOKWORMS

Hookworms are the most destructive of all the parasites of dogs. There are three species of them—*Ancylostoma caninum, A. braziliense,* and *Uncinaria stenocephalia*—all to be found in dogs in some parts of the United States. The first named is the most widespread; the second found only in the warmer parts of the South and Southwest; the last named, in the North and in Canada. All are similar one to another and to the hookworm that infests mankind (*Ancylostoma uncinariasis*). For purposes of their eradication, no distinction need be made between them.

It is possible to keep dogs for many years in a dry and well drained area without an infestation with hookworms, which are contracted only on infested soils. However, unthrifty dogs shipped from infested areas are suspect until it is proved that hookworm is not the cause of their unthriftiness.

Hookworm males seldom are longer than half an inch, the females somewhat larger. The head end is curved upward, and is equipped with cutting implements, which may be called teeth, by which they attach themselves to the lining of the dog's intestine and suck his blood.

The females produce numerous eggs which pass out in the dog's feces. In two weeks or a little more these eggs hatch, the worms pass through various larval stages, and reach their infective stage. Infection of the dog may take place through his swallowing the organism, or by its penetration of his skin through some lesion. In the latter case the worms enter the circulation, reach the lungs, are coughed up, swallowed, and reach the intestine where their final development occurs. Eggs appear in the dog's feces from three to six weeks after infestation.

Puppies are sometimes born with hookworms already well developed in their intestines, the infection taking place before their birth. Eggs of the hookworm are sometimes found in the feces of puppies only thirteen days old. Assumption is not to be made that all puppies are born with hookworms or even that they are likely to become infested, but in hookworm areas the possibility of either justifies precautions that neither shall happen.

Hookworm infestation in puppies and young dogs brings about a condition often called kennel anemia. There may be digestive disturbances and blood streaked diarrhea. In severe cases the feces may be almost pure blood. Infested puppies fail to grow, often lose weight, and the eyes are sunken and dull. The loss of blood results in an anemia with pale mucous membranes of the mouth and eyes. This anemia is caused by the consumption of the dog's blood by the worms and the bleeding that follows the bites. The worms are not believed to secrete a poison or to cause damage to the dog except loss of blood.

There is an admitted risk in worming young puppies before weaning time, but it is risk that must be run if the puppies are known to harbor hookworms. The worms, if permitted to persist, will ruin the puppies and likely kill them. No such immediacy is needful for the treatment of older puppies and adult dogs, although hookworm infestation will grow steadily worse until it is curbed. It should not be delayed and neglected in the belief or hope that the dog can cure himself.

If treatment is attempted at home, there are available three fairly efficacious and safe drugs that may be used: normal butyl chloride, hexaresorcinal, and methyl benzine.

If a dog is visibly sick and a diagnosis of hookworm infestation has been made, treatment had best be under professional guidance.

Brine made by stirring common salt (sodium chloride) into boiling water, a pound and a half of salt to the gallon of water, will destroy hookworm infestation in the soil. A gallon of brine should be sufficient to treat eight square feet of soil surface. One treatment of the soil is sufficient unless it is reinfested.

TAPEWORMS

The numerous species of tapeworm which infest the dog may, for practical purposes, be divided into two general groups, the armed forms and the unarmed forms. Species of both groups resemble each other in their possession of a head and neck and a chain of segments. They are, however, different in their life histories, and the best manner to deal with each type varies. This is unfortunately not well understood, since to most persons a tapeworm is a tapeworm.

The armed varieties are again divided into the single pored forms of the genera *Taenia, Multiceps,* and *Echinococcus,* and the double pored tapeworm, of which the most widespread and prevalent among dogs in the United States is the so-called dog tapeworm, *Dipylidium caninum.* This is the variety with segments shaped like cucumber-seeds. The adult rarely exceeds a foot in length, and the head is armed with four or five tiny hooks. For the person with well cared for and protected dogs, this is the only tapeworm of which it is necessary to take particular cognizance.

The dog tapeworm requires but a single intermediate host for its development, which in most cases is the dog flea or the biting louse. Thus, by keeping dogs free from fleas and lice the major danger of tapeworm infestation is obviated.

The tapeworm is bi-sexual and requires the intermediate host in order to complete its life cycle. Segments containing the eggs of the tapeworm pass out with the stool, or the detached proglottid may emerge by its own motile power and attach itself to the contiguous hair. The flea then lays its eggs on this segment, thus affording sustenance for the larva. The head of the tapeworm develops in the lung chamber of the baby flea. Thus, such a flea, when it develops and finds its way back to a dog, is the potential carrier of tapeworm. Of course, the cycle is complete when the flea bites the dog and the dog, in biting the area to relieve the itching sensation, swallows the flea.

Since the egg of the tapeworm is secreted in the segment that breaks off and passes with the stool, microscopic examination of the feces is of no avail in attempting to determine whether tapeworms infest a dog. It is well to be suspicious of a finicky eater— a dog that refuses all but the choicest meat and shows very little appetite. The injury produced by this armed tapeworm to the dog that harbors it is not well understood. Frequently it produces no symptoms at all, and it is likely that it is not the actual cause of many of the symptoms attributed to it. At least, it is known that a dog may have one or many of these worms over a long period of time and apparently be no worse for their presence. Nervous symptoms or skin eruptions, or both, are often charged to the presence of tapeworm, which may or may not be the cause of the morbid condition.

Tapeworm-infested dogs sometimes involuntarily pass segments of worms and so soil floors, rugs, furniture, or bedding. The passage by dogs of a segment or a chain of segments via the anus is a frequent cause of the dog's itching, which he seeks to allay by sitting and dragging himself on the floor by his haunches. The segments or chains are sometimes mistakenly called pinworms, but pinworms are a kind of roundworm to which dogs are not subject.

Despite that they may do no harm, few dogs owners care to tolerate tapeworms in their dogs. These worms, it has been definitely established, are not transmissible from dog to dog or to man. Without the flea or the louse, it is impossible for the adult dog tapeworm to reproduce itself, and by keeping dogs free from fleas and lice it is possible to keep them also free from dog tapeworm.

The various unarmed species of tapeworm find their intermediate hosts in the flesh and other parts of various animals, fish, crustacians and crayfish. Dogs not permitted to eat raw meats which have not been officially inspected, never have these worms, and it is needless here to discuss them at length. Hares and rabbits are the intermediate hosts to some of these worms and dogs should not be encouraged to feed upon those animals.

Little is known of the effects upon dogs of infestations of the unarmed tapeworms, but they are believed to be similar to the effects (if any) of the armed species.

The prevention of tapeworm infestation may be epitomized by saying: Do not permit dogs to swallow fleas or lice nor to feed upon uninspected raw meats. It is difficult to protect dogs from such contacts if they are permitted to run at large, but it is to be presumed that persons interested enough in caring for dogs to read this book will keep their dogs at home and protect them.

The several species of tapeworm occurring in dogs are not all

81

removable by the same treatment. The most effective treatment for the removal of the armed species, which is the one most frequently found in the dogs, is arecoline hydrobromide. This drug is a drastic purgative and acts from fifteen to forty-five minutes after its administration. The treatment should be given in the morning after the dog has fasted overnight, and food should be withheld for some three hours after dosing.

Arecoline is not so effective against the double-pored tapeworm as against the other armed species, and it may be necessary to repeat the dose after a few days waiting, since some of the tapeworm heads may not be removed by the first treatment and regeneration of the tapeworm may occur in a few weeks. The estimatedly correct dosage is not stated here, since the drug is so toxic that the dosage should be estimated for the individual dog by a competent veterinarian, and it is better that he should be permitted to administer the remedy and control the treatment.

WHIPWORMS

The dog whipworm (*Trichuris vulpis*) is so called from its fancied resemblance to a tiny blacksnake whip, the front part being slender and hairlike and the hinder part relatively thick. It rarely exceeds three inches in its total length. Whipworms in dogs exist more or less generally throughout the world, but few dogs in the United States are known to harbor them. They are for the most part confined to the caecum, from which they are hard to dislodge, but sometimes spill over into the colon, whence they are easy to dislodge.

The complete life history of the whipworm is not well established, but it is known that no intermediate host is required for its development. The eggs appear to develop in much the same way as the eggs of the large roundworm, but slower, requiring from two weeks to several months for the organisms to reach maturity.

It has not as yet been definitely established that whipworms are the true causes of all the ills of which they are accused. In many instances they appear to cause little damage, even in heavy infestations. A great variety of symptoms of an indefinite sort have been ascribed to whipworms, including digestive disturbances, diarrhea, loss of weight, nervousness, convulsions, and general unthriftiness, but it remains to be proved that whipworms were responsible.

To be effective in its removal of whipworms, a drug must enter the caecum and come into direct contact with them; but the entry of the drug into this organ is somewhat fortuitous, and to increase the chances of its happening, large doses of a drug essentially harmless to the dog must be used. Normal butyl chloride meets this requirement, but it must be given in large doses. Even then, complete clearance of whipworms from the caecum may not be expected; the best to be hoped is that their numbers will be reduced and the morbid symptoms will subside.

Before treatment the dog should be fasted for some eighteen hours, although he may be fed two hours after being treated. It is wise to follow the normal butyl chloride in one hour with a purgative dose of castor oil. This treatment, since it is not expected to be wholly effective, may be repeated at monthly intervals.

The only known means of the complete clearance of whipworms from the dog is the surgical removal of the caecum, which of course should be undertaken only by a veterinary surgeon.

HEART WORMS

Heart worms (*Dirofilaria immitis*) in dogs are rare. They occur largely in the South and Southeast, but their incidence appears to be increasing and cases have been reported along the Atlantic Seaboard as far north as New York. The various species of mosquitoes are known to be vectors of heart worms, although the flea is also accused of spreading them.

The symptoms of heart worm infestation are somewhat vague, and include coughing, shortness of breath and collapse. In advanced cases, dropsy may develop. Nervous symptoms, fixity of vision, fear of light, and convulsions may develop. However, all such symptoms may occur from other causes and it must not be assumed because a dog manifests some of these conditions that he has heart worms. The only way to be sure is a microscopic examination of the blood and the presence or absence of the larvae. Even in some cases where larvae have been found in the blood, post mortem examinations have failed to reveal heart worms in the heart.

Both the diagnosis and treatment of heart worm are functions of the veterinarian. They are beyond the province of the amateur. The drug used is a derivative from antimony known as fuadin, and many dogs are peculiarly susceptible to antimony poisoning. If proper treatment is used by a trained veterinarian, a large preponderance of cases make a complete recovery. But even the most expert of veterinarians may be expected to fail in the successful treatment of a percentage of heart worm infestations. The death of some of the victims is to be anticipated.

LESS FREQUENTLY FOUND WORMS

Besides the intestinal worms that have been enumerated, there exist in some dogs numerous other varieties and species of worms which are of so infrequent occurrence that they require no discussion in a book for the general dog keeper. These include, esophageal worms, lungworms, kidney worms, and eye worms. They are in North America, indeed, so rare as to be negligible.

COCCIDIA

Coccidia are protozoic, microscopic organisms. The forms to which the dog is a host are *Isospora rivolta, I. bigeminia* and *I. felis.* Coccidia eggs, called *oocysts,* can be carried by flies and are picked up by dogs as they lick themselves or eat their stools.

These parasides attack the intestinal wall and cause diarrhea. They are particularly harmful to younger puppies that have been weaned, bringing on fever, running eyes, poor appetite and debilitation as well as the loose stools.

The best prevention is scrupulous cleanliness of the puppy or dog, its surroundings and its playmates whether canine or human. Flies should be eliminated as described in the preceding chapter and stools removed promptly where the dog cannot touch it.

Infection can be confirmed by microscopic examination of the stool. Treatment consists of providing nourishing food, which should be force-fed if necessary, and whatever drug the veterinarian recommends. Puppies usually recover, though occasionally their teeth may be pitted as in distemper.

A dog infected once by one form develops immunity to that form but may be infected by another form.

Skin Troubles

THERE is a tendency on the part of the amateur dog keeper to consider any lesion of the dog's skin to be mange. Mange is an unusual condition in clean, well fed, and well cared for dogs. Eczema occurs much more frequently and is often more difficult to control.

MANGE OR SCABIES

There are at least two kinds of mange that effect dogs—sarcoptic mange and demodectic or red mange, the latter rare indeed and difficult to cure.

Sarcoptic mange is caused by a tiny spider-like mite (*Sarcoptes scabiei canis*) which is similar to the mite that causes human scabies or "itch." Indeed, the mange is almost identical with scabies and is transmissible from dog to man. The mite is approximately 1/100th of an inch in length and without magnification is just visible to acute human sight.

Only the female mites are the cause of the skin irritation. They burrow into the upper layers of the skin, where each lays twenty to forty eggs, which in three to seven days hatch into larvae. These larvae in turn develop into nymphs which later grow into adults. The entire life cycle requires from fourteen to twenty-one days for completion. The larvae, nymphs, and males do not burrow into the skin, but live under crusts and scabs on the surface.

The disease may make its first appearance on any part of the dog's body, although it is usually first seen on the head and muzzle, around the eyes, or at the base of the ears. Sometimes it is first noticed in the armpits, the inner parts of the thighs, the lower abdomen or on the front of the chest. If not promptly treated it may cover the whole body and an extremely bad infestation may cause the death of the dog after a few months.

Red points which soon develop into small blisters are the first signs of the disease. These are most easily seen on the unpigmented parts of the skin, such as the abdomen. As the female mites burrow into the skin, there is an exudation of serum which dries and scabs. The affected parts soon are covered with bran-like scales followed with grayish crusts. The itching is intense, especially in hot weather or after exercise. The rubbing and scratching favor secondary bacterial infections and the formation of sores. The hair may grow matted and fall out, leaving bare spots. The exuded serum decomposes and gives rise to a peculiar mousy odor which increases as the disease develops and which is especially characteristic.

Sarcoptic mange is often confused with demodectic (red) mange, ringworm, or with simple eczema. If there is any doubt about the diagnosis, a microscopic examination of the scrapings of the lesions will reveal the true facts.

It is easy to control sarcoptic mange if it is recognized in its earlier stages and treatment is begun immediately. Neglected, it may be very difficult to eradicate. If it is considered how rapidly the causative mites reproduce themselves, the necessity for early treatment becomes apparent. That treatment consists not only of medication of the dog but also of sterilization of his bedding, all tools and implements used on him, and the whole premises upon which he has been confined. Sarcoptic mange is easily and quickly transmissible from dog to dog, from area to area on the same dog, and even from dog to human.

In some manner which is not entirely understood, an inadequate or unbalanced diet appears to predispose a dog to sarcoptic mange, and few dogs adequately fed and cared for ever contract it. Once a dog has contracted mange, however, improvement in the amount of quality of his food seems not to hasten his recovery.

There are various medications recommended for sarcoptic mange, sulphur ointment being the old standby. However, it is messy, difficult to use, and not always effective. For the treatment of sarcoptic mange, there are available today such insecticides as lindane, chlordane, and DDT. The use of these chemicals greatly facilitates treatment and cure of the dogs affected with mange and those exposed to it.

A bath made by dissolving four ounces of derris powder (containing at least 5% rotenone) and one ounce of soap in one gallon of water has proved effective, especially if large areas of the surface of the dog's skin are involved. All crusts and scabs should be removed before its application. The solution must be well scrubbed into the skin with a moderately stiff brush and the whole animal thoroughly soaked. Only the surplus liquid should be taken off with a towel and the remainder must be permitted to dry on the dog. This bath should be repeated at intervals of five days until all signs of mange have disappeared. Three such baths will usually suffice.

The advantage of such all over treatment is that it protects uninfected areas from infection. It is also a precautionary measure to bathe in this solution uninfected dogs which have been in contact with the infected one.

Isolated mange spots may be treated with oil of lavender. Roll a woolen cloth into a swab with which the oil of lavender can be applied and rubbed in thoroughly for about five minutes. This destroys all mites with which the oil of lavender comes into contact.

Even after a cure is believed to be accomplished, vigilance must be maintained to prevent fresh infestations and to treat new spots immediately if they appear.

DEMODECTIC OR RED MANGE

Demodectic mange, caused by the wormlike mite *Demodex canis*, which lives in the hair follicles and the sebaceous glands of the skin, is difficult to cure. It is a baffling malady of which the prognosis is not favorable. The life cycle of the causative organism is not well understood, the time required from the egg to maturity being so far unknown. The female lays eggs which hatch into young of appearance similar to that of the adult, except that they are smaller and have but three pairs of legs instead of four.

One peculiar feature about demodectic mange is that some dogs appear to be genetically predisposed to it while others do not contract it whatever their contact with infected animals may be. Young animals seem to be especially prone to it, particularly those with short hair. The first evidence of its presence is the falling out of the hair on certain areas of the dog. The spots may be somewhat reddened, and they commonly occur near the eyes, on the hocks, elbows, or toes, although they may be on any part of the dog's body. No itching occurs at the malady's inception, and it never grows so intense as in sarcoptic mange.

In the course of time, the hairless areas enlarge, and the skin attains a copper hue; in severe cases it may appear blue or leadish gray. During this period the mites multiply and small pustules develop. Secondary invasions may occur to complicate the situation. Poisons are formed by the bacteria in the pustules, and the absorption of toxic materials deranges the body functions and eventually affects the whole general health of the dog, leading to emaciation, weakness, and the development of an acrid, unpleasant odor.

This disease is slow and subtle in its development, runs a casual course, and frequently extends over a period of two or even three years. Unless it is treated, it usually terminates in death, although spontaneous recovery occasionally occurs, especially if the dog has been kept on a nourishing diet. As in other skin diseases, correct nutrition plays a major part in recovery from demodectic mange, as it plays an even larger part in its prevention.

It is possible to confuse demodectic mange with sarcoptic mange, fungus infection, acne, or eczema. A definite diagnosis is possible only from microscopic examination of skin scrapings and of material from the pustules. The possibility of demodectic mange, particularly in its earlier stages, is not negated by the failure to find the mites under the microscope, and several examinations may be necessary to arrive at a definite diagnosis.

The prognosis is not entirely favorable. It may appear that the mange is cured and a new and healthy coat may be re-established only to have the disease manifest itself in a new area, and the whole process of treatment must be undertaken afresh.

In the treatment of demodectic mange, the best results have been obtained by the persistent use of benzine hexachloride, chlordane, rotenone, and 2-mercapto benzothiazole. Perseverance is necessary, but even then failure is possible.

EAR MITES OR EAR MANGE

The mites responsible for ear mange (*Ododectes cynotis*) are considerably larger than the ones which cause sarcoptic mange. They inhabit the external auditory canal and are visible to the unaided eye as minute, slowly moving, white objects. Their life history is not known, but is probably similar to that of the mite that causes sarcoptic mange.

These mites do not burrow into the skin, but are found deep in the ear canal, near the eardrum. Considerable irritation results from their presence, and the normal secretions of the ear are interfered with. The ear canal is filled with inflammatory products, modified ear wax, and mites, causing the dog to scratch and rub its ears and to shake its head. While ear mange is not caused by incomplete washing or inefficient drying of the ears, it is encouraged by such negligence.

The ear mange infestation is purely local and is no cause for anxiety. An ointment containing benzine hexachloride is very effective in correcting this condition. The ear should be treated every third or fourth day.

ECZEMA

Eczema is probably the most common of all ailments seen in the dog. Oftentimes it is mistaken for mange or ringworm, although there is no actual relationship between the conditions. Eczema is variously referred to by such names as "hot spots," "fungitch," and "kennel itch."

Some years ago there was near-unanimity of opinion among dog people that the food of the animal was the major contributing factor of eczema. Needless to say, the manufacturers of commercial dog foods were besieged with complaints. Some research on the cause of eczema placed most of the blame on outside environmental factors, and with some help from other sources it was found that a vegetative organism was the causative agent in a great majority of the cases.

Some dogs do show an allergic skin reaction to certain types of protein given to them as food, but this is generally referred to as the "foreign protein" type of dermatitis. It manifests itself by raising numerous welts on the skin, and occasionally the head, face, and ears will become alarmingly swollen. This condition can be controlled by the injection of antihistamine products and subsequent dosage with antihistaminic tablets or capsules such as chlortrimenton or benedryl. Whether "foreign protein" dermatitis is due to an allergy or whether it is due to some toxin manufactured and elaborated by the individual dog is a disputed point.

Most cases of eczema start with reddening of the skin in certain parts. The areas most affected seem to be the region along the spine and at the base of the tail. In house dogs this may have its inception from enlarged and plugged anal glands. The glands when full and not naturally expressed are a source of irritation. The dog will rub his hind parts on the grass in order to alleviate the itching sensation. Fleas, lice, and ticks may be inciting factors, causing the dog to rub and roll in the grass in an attempt to scratch the itchy parts.

In hunting dogs, it is believed that the vegetative cover through which the dogs hunt causes the dermatitis. In this class of dogs the skin becomes irritated and inflamed in the armpits, the inner surfaces of the thighs, and along the belly. Some hunting dogs are bedded down in straw or hay, and such dogs invariably show a general reddening of the skin and a tendency to scratch.

As a general rule, the difference between moist and dry eczema lies in the degree to which the dog scratches the skin with his feet or chews it with his teeth. The inflammation ranges from a simple reddening of the skin to the development of papules, vesicles, and pustules with a discharge. Crusts and scabs like dandruff may form, and if the condition is not treated, it will become chronic and then next to impossible to treat with any success. In such cases the skin becomes thickened and may be pigmented. The hair follicles become infected, and the lesions are constantly inflamed and exuding pus.

When inflammation occurs between the toes and on the pads of the feet, it closely resembles "athletes foot" in the human. Such inflammation generally causes the hair in the region to turn a reddish brown. The ears, when they are affected, emit a peculiar moldy odor and exude a brownish black substance. It is thought that most cases of canker of the ear are due to a primary invasion of the ear canal by a vegetative fungus. If there is a pustular discharge, it is due to the secondary pus-forming bacteria that gain a foothold after the resistance of the parts is lowered by the fungi.

Some breeds of dogs are more susceptible to skin ailments than are others. However, all breeds of dogs are likely to show some degree of dermatitis if they are exposed to causative factors.

Most cases of dermatitis are seen in the summer time, which probably accounts for their being referred to as "summer itch" or "hot spots." The warm moist days of summer seem to promote the growth and development of both fleas and fungi. When the fleas bite the dog, the resulting irritation causes the dog to scratch or bite to alleviate the itch. The area thus becomes moist and makes a perfect place for fungi spores to propagate. That the fungi are the cause of the trouble seems evident, because most cases respond when treated externally with a good fungicide. Moreover, the use of a powder containing both an insecticide and a fungicide tends to prevent skin irritation. Simply dusting the dog once or twice a week with a good powder of the type mentioned is sound procedure in the practice of preventive medicine.

(Editor's note: I have had some success with hydrogen peroxide in treating mild skin troubles. Saturate a cotton pad with a mixture of 2 parts 3% hydrogen peroxide to 1 part boiled water. Apply, but do NOT rub, to affected skin. Let dry naturally and when *completely* dry apply an antiseptic talcum powder like Johnson & Johnson's Medicated Powder. When this treatment was suggested to my veterinarian, he confirmed that he had had success with it. If the skin irritation is not noticeably better after two of these treatments, once daily, the case should be referred to a veterinarian.)

RINGWORM

Ringworm is a communicable disease of the skin of dogs, readily transmissible to man and to other dogs and animals. The disease is caused by specific fungi, which are somewhat similar to ordinary molds. The lesions caused by ringworm usually first appear on the face, head, or legs of the dog, but they may occur on any part of the surface of his body.

The disease in dogs is characterized by small, circular areas of dirty gray or brownish-yellow crusts or scabs partially devoid of hair, the size of a dime. As the disease progresses, the lesions increase both in size and in number and merge to form larger patches covered with crusts containing broken off hair. A raw, bleeding surface may appear when crusts are broken or removed by scratching or rubbing to relieve itching. In some cases, however, little or no itching is manifested. Microscopic examination and culture tests are necessary for accurate diagnosis.

If treatment of affected dogs is started early, the progress of the disease can be immediately arrested. Treatment consists of clipping the hair from around the infected spots, removing the scabs and painting the spots with tincture of iodine, five percent salicylic acid solution, or other fungicide two or three times weekly until recovery takes place. In applying these remedies it is well to cover the periphery of the circular lesion as well as its center, since the spots tend to expand outward from their centers. Scabs, hair, and debris removed from the dog during his treatments should be burned to destroy the causative organisms and to prevent reinfection. Precautions in the handling of animals affected with ringworm should be observed to preclude transmission to man and other animals. Isolation of affected dogs is not necessary if the treatment is thorough.

COAT CARE

Skin troubles can often be checked and materially alleviated by proper grooming. Every dog is entitled to the minimum of weekly attention to coat, skin and ears; ideally, a daily stint with brush and comb is highly recommended. Frequent examination may catch skin disease in its early stages and provide a better chance for a quick cure.

The outer or "guard" hairs of a dog's coat should glint in the sunlight. There should be no mats or dead hair in the coat. Wax in the outer ear should be kept at a minimum.

It is helpful to stand the dog on a flat, rigid surface off the floor at a height convenient to the groomer. Start at the head and ears brushing briskly *with* the lay of short hair, *against* the lay of long hair at first then with it. After brushing, use a fine comb with short teeth on fine, short hair and a coarse comb with long teeth on coarse or long hair. If mats cannot be readily removed with brush or comb, use barber's thinning shears and cut into the matted area several times until mat pulls free easily. Some mats can be removed with the fingers if one has the patience to separate the hair a bit at a time.

After brushing and combing, run your palms over the dog's coat from head to tail. Natural oils in your skin will impart sheen to your dog's coat.

The ears of some dogs secrete and exude great amounts of wax. Frequent examination will determine when your dog's ears need cleaning. A thin coating of clean, clear wax is not harmful. But a heavy accumulation of dirty, dark wax needs removal by cotton pads soaked in diluted hydrogen peroxide (3% cut in half with boiled water), or alcohol or plain boiled water if wax is not too thick.

There are sprays, "dry" bath preparations and other commercial products for maintaining your dog's coat health. Test them first, and if they are successful, you may find them beneficial time-savers in managing your dog's coat.

First Aid

JOHN STEINBECK, the Nobel Prize winning author, in *Travels with Charley in Search of America* bemoans the lack of a good, comprehensive book of home dog medicine. Charley is the aged Poodle that accompanies his illustrious author-owner on a motor tour of the U.S.A.

As in human medicine, most treatment and dosing of dogs are better left in the experienced, trained hands and mind of a professional—in this case, the veterinarian. However, there are times and situations when professional aid is not immediately available and an owner's prompt action may save a life or avoid permanent injury. To this purpose, the following suggestions are given.

The First Aid Kit

For instruments keep on hand a pair of tweezers, a pair of pliers, straight scissors, a rectal thermometer, a teaspoon, a tablespoon, and swabs for cotton.

For dressings, buy a container of cotton balls, a roll of cotton and a roll of 2″ gauze. Strips of clean, old sheets may come in handy.

For medicines, stock ammonia, aspirin, brandy, 3% hydrogen peroxide, bicarbonate of soda, milk of bismuth, mineral oil, salt, tea, vaseline, kaopectate, baby oil and baby talcum powder.

Handling the Dog for Treatment

Approach any injured or sick dog calmly with reassuring voice and gentle, steady hands. If the dog is in pain, slip a gauze or sheet strip noose over its muzzle tying the ends first under the throat and then back of the neck. Make sure the dog's lips are not caught between his teeth, but make noose around muzzle *tight*.

If the dog needs to be moved, grasp the loose skin on the back of the neck with one hand and support chest with the other hand. If the dog is too large to move in this manner, slide him on a large towel, blanket or folded sheet which may serve as a stretcher for two to carry.

If a pill or liquid is to be administered, back the dog in a corner in a sitting position. For a pill, pry back of jaws apart with thumb and forefinger of one hand and with the same fingers of your other hand place pill as far back in dog's throat as possible; close and hold jaws, rubbing throat to cause swallowing. If dog does not gulp, hold one hand over nostrils briefly; he will gulp for air and swallow pill. For liquids, lift the back of the upper lip and tip spoon into the natural pocket formed in the rear of the lower lip; it may be necessary to pull this pocket out with forefinger. Do not give liquids by pouring directly down the dog's throat; this might choke him or make the fluid go down the wrong way.

After treatment keep dog quiet, preferably in his bed or a room where he cannot injure himself or objects.

Bites and Wounds

Clip hair from area. Wash gently with pure soap and water or hydrogen peroxide. If profuse bleeding continues, apply sheet strip or gauze tourniquet between wound and heart but nearest the wound. Release tourniquet briefly at ten-minute intervals. Cold water compresses may stop milder bleeding.

For insect bites and stings, try to remove stinger with tweezers or a dab of cotton, and apply a few drops of ammonia. If dog is in pain, give aspirin at one grain per 10 pounds. (An aspirin tablet is usually 5 grains.)

Burns

Clip hair from area. Apply strong, lukewarm tea (for its tannic acid content) on a sheet strip compress. Vaseline may be used for slight burns. Give aspirin as recommended if dog is in pain. Keep him warm if he seems to be in shock.

Constipation

Give mineral oil: one-quarter teaspoon up to 10 pounds; half teaspoon from 10 to 25 pounds; full teaspoon from 25 to 75 pounds; three-quarters tablespoon over 75 pounds.

Diarrhea

Give kaopectate in same doses by size as indicated for mineral oil above, but repeat within four and eight hours.

Fighting

Do not try forcibly to separate dogs. If available throw a pail of cold water on them. A sharp rap on the rump of each combatant with a strap or stick may help. A heavy towel or blanket dropped over the head of the aggressor, or a newspaper twisted into a torch, lighted and held near them, may discourage the fighters. If a lighted newspaper is used, be careful that sparks do not fall or blow on dogs.

Fits

Try to get the dog into a room where he cannot injure himself. If possible, cover him with a towel or blanket. When the fit ends, give aspirin one grain for every 10 pounds.

Nervousness

Remove cause or remove the dog from the site of the cause. Give the recommended dose of aspirin. Aspirin acts as a tranquilizer.

Poisoning

If container of the poison is handy, use recommended antidote printed thereon. Otherwise, make a strong solution of household salt in water and force as much as possible into the dog's throat using the lip pocket method. Minutes count with several poisons; if veterinarian cannot be reached immediately, try to get dog to an MD or registered nurse.

Shock

If dog has chewed electric cord, protect hand with rubber glove or thick dry towel and pull cord from socket. If dog has collapsed, hold ammonia under its nose or apply artificial respiration as follows: place dog on side with its head low, press on abdomen and rib cage, releasing pressure at one- or two-second intervals. Keep dog warm.

Stomach Upsets

For mild stomach disorders, milk of bismuth in same doses as recommended for mineral oil under *Constipation* will be effective. For more severe cases brandy in the same doses but diluted with an equal volume of water may be helpful.

Swallowing Foreign Objects

If object is still in mouth or throat, reach in and remove it. If swallowed, give strong salt solution as for *Poisoning*. Some objects that are small, smooth or soft may not give trouble.

Porcupines and Skunks

Using tweezers or pliers, twist quills one full turn and pull out. Apply hydrogen peroxide to bleeding wounds. For skunk spray, wash dog in tomato juice.

WARNING! Get your dog to a veterinarian *soonest* for severe bites, wounds, burns, poisoning, fits and shock.

Internal Canine Diseases
and Their Management

THE word *management* is employed in this chapter heading rather than *treatment,* since the treatment of disease in the dog is the function of the veterinarian, and the best counsel it is possible to give the solicitous owner of a sick dog is to submit the case to the best veterinarian available and to follow his instructions implicitly. In general, it may be said, the earlier in any disease the veterinarian is consulted, the more rapid is the sick animal's recovery and the lower the outlay of money for the services of the veterinarian and for the medicine he prescribes.

Herein are presented some hints for the prevention of the various canine maladies and for their recognition when they occur. In kennel husbandry, disease is a minor problem, and, if preventive methods are employed, it is one that need not be anticipated.

DISTEMPER

Distemper, the traditional bugbear of keeping dogs, the veritable scourge of dog-kind, has at long last been well conquered. Compared with some years ago when "over distemper" was one of the best recommendations for the purchase of a dog, the incidence of distemper in well-bred and adequately cared for dogs is now minimal.

The difference between then and now is that we now have available preventive sera, vaccines, and viruses, which may be employed to forestall distemper before it ever appears. There are valid differences of opinion about which of these measures is best to use and at what age of the dog they are variously indicated. About the choice of preventive measures and the technique of administering them, the reader is advised to consult his veterinarian and to accept his advice. There can be no doubt, however, that any person with a valued or loved young dog should have him immunized.

For many years most veterinarians used the so-called "three-shot" method of serum, vaccine and virus, spaced two weeks apart after the puppy was three or four months old, for permanent immunization. For temporary immunization lasting up to a year, some veterinarians used only vaccine; this was repeated annually if the owner wished, though since a dog was considered most susceptible to distemper in the first year of his life, the annual injection was often discontinued. Under both these methods, serum was used at two-week intervals from weaning to the age when permanent or annual immunization was given.

Until 1950 living virus, produced by the methods then known to and used by laboratories, was considered too dangerous to inject without the preparation of the dog for it by prior use of serum or vaccine (killed virus). Then, researchers in distemper developed an attenuated or weakened live virus by injecting strong virus into egg embryos and other intermediate hosts. The weakened virus is now often used for permanent, one-shot distemper immunization of puppies as young as eight weeks.

Today certain researchers believe that the temporary immunity given by the bitch to her young depends on her own degree of immunity. If she has none, her puppies have none; if she has maximum immunity, her puppies may be immune up to the age of 12 weeks or more. By testing the degree of the bitch's immunity early in her pregnancy, these researchers believe they can determine the proper age at which her puppies should receive their shots.

The veterinarian is best qualified to determine the method of distemper immunization and the age to give it.

Canine distemper is an acute, highly contagious, febrile disease caused by a filterable virus. It is characterized by a catarrhal inflammation of all the mucous membranes of the body, frequently accompanied by nervous symptoms and pustular eruptions of the skin. Its human counterpart is influenza, which, though not identical with distemper, is very similar to it in many respects. Distemper is so serious and complicated a disease as to require expert attention; when a dog is suspected of having it, a veterinarian should be consulted immediately. It is the purpose of this discussion of the malady rather to describe it that its recognition may be possible than to suggest medication for it or means of treating it.

Distemper is known in all countries and all parts of the United States in all seasons of the year, but it is most prevalent during the winter months and in the cold, damp weather of early spring and late autumn. No breed of dogs is immune. Puppies of low constitutional vigor, pampered, overfed, unexercised dogs, and those kept in overheated, unventilated quarters contract the infection more readily and suffer more from it than hardy animals, properly fed and living in a more natural environment. Devitalizing influences which decrease the resistance of the dog, such as rickets, parasitic infestations, unsanitary quarters, and especially an insufficient or unbalanced diet, are factors predisposing to distemper.

While puppies as young as ten days or two weeks have been known to have true cases of distemper, and very old dogs in rare instances, the usual subjects of distemper are between two months (after weaning) and full maturity at about eighteen months. The teething period of four to six months is highly critical. It is believed that some degree of temporary protection from distemper is passed on to a nursing litter through the milk of the mother.

As was first demonstrated by Carré in 1905 and finally established by Laidlaw and Duncan in their work for the Field Distemper Fund in 1926 to 1928, the primary causative agent of distemper is a filterable virus. The clinical course of the disease may be divided into two parts, produced respectively by the primary Carré filterable virus and by a secondary invasion of bacterial organisms which produce serious complicating conditions usually associated with the disease. It is seldom true that uncomplicated Carré distemper would cause more than a fever with malaise and indisposition if the secondary bacterial invasion could be avoided. The primary disease but prepares the ground for the secondary invasion which produces the havoc and all too often kills the patient.

Although it is often impossible to ascertain the source of infection in outbreaks of distemper, it is known that the infection may spread from affected to susceptible dogs by either direct or indirect contact. The disease, while highly infectious throughout its course, is especially easy to communicate in its earliest stages, even before clinical symptoms are manifested. The virus is readily destroyed by heat and by most of the common disinfectants in a few hours, but it resists drying and low temperatures for several days, and has been known to survive freezing for months.

The period of incubation (the time between exposure to infection and the development of the first symptoms) is variable. It has been reported to be as short as three days and as long as two weeks. The usual period is approximately one week. The usual course of the disease is about four weeks, but seriously complicated cases may prolong themselves to twelve weeks.

The early symptoms of distemper, as a rule, are so mild and subtle as to escape the notice of any but the most acute observer. These first symptoms may be a rise in temperature, a watery discharge from the eyes and nose, an impaired appetite, a throat-clearing cough, and a general sluggishness. In about a week's time the symptoms become well marked, with a discharge of mucus or pus from the eyes and nose, and complications of a more or less serious nature, such as broncho-pneumonia, hemorrhagic inflammation of the gastro-intestinal tract, and disturbances of the brain and spinal cord, which may cause convulsions. In the early stages of distemper the body temperature may suddenly rise from the normal 101°F. to 103°. Shivering, dryness of the nostrils, a slight dry cough, increased thirst, a drowsy look, reluctance to eat, and a desire to sleep may follow. Later, diarrhea (frequently streaked with blood or wholly of blood), pneumonia, convulsions, paralysis, or chorea (a persistent twitching condition) may develop. An inflammation of the membranes of the eye may ensue; this may impair or destroy the sight through ulceration or opacity of the cornea. Extreme weakness and great loss of body weight occur in advanced stages.

All, any, or none of these symptoms may be noticeable. It is believed that many dogs experience distemper in so mild a form as to escape the owner's observation. Because of its protean and obscure nature and its strong similarity to other catarrhal affections, the diagnosis of distemper, especially in its early stages, is difficult. In young dogs that are known to have been exposed to the disease, a rise of body temperature, together with shivering, sneezing, loss of appetite, eye and nasal discharge, sluggishness, and diarrhea (all or any of these symptoms), are indicative of trouble.

There is little specific that can be done for a dog with primary distemper. The treatment is largely concerned with alleviating the symptoms. No drug or combination of drugs is known at this time that has any specific action on the disease. Distemper runs a definite course, no matter what is done to try to cure it.

Homologous anti-distemper serum, administered subcutaneously or intravenously by the veterinarian, is of value in lessening the severity of the attack. The veterinarian may see fit to treat the secondary pneumonia with penicillin or one of the sulpha drugs, or to allay the secondary intestinal infection with medication. It is best to permit him to manage the case in his own way. The dog is more prone to respond to care in his own home and with his own people, if suitable quarters and adequate nursing are available to him. Otherwise, he is best off in a veterinary hospital.

The dog affected with distemper should be provided with clean, dry, warm but not hot, well ventilated quarters. It should be given moderate quantities of nourishing, easily digested food—milk, soft boiled eggs, cottage cheese, and scraped lean beef. The sick dog should not be disturbed by children or other dogs. Discharges from eyes and nose should be wiped away. The eyes may be bathed with boric acid solution, and irritation of the nose allayed with greasy substances such as petrolatum. The dog should not be permitted to get wet or chilled, and he should have such medication as the veterinarian prescribes and no other.

When signs of improvement are apparent, the dog must not be given an undue amount of food at one meal, although he may be fed at frequent intervals. The convalescing dog should be permitted to exercise only very moderately until complete recovery is assured.

In the control of distemper, affected animals should be promptly isolated from susceptible dogs. After the disease has run its course, whether it end in recovery or death, the premises where the patient has been kept during the illness should be thoroughly cleaned and disinfected, as should all combs, brushes, or other utensils used on the dog, before other susceptible dogs are brought in. After an apparent recovery has been made in the patient, the germs are present for about four weeks and can be transmitted to susceptible dogs.

CHOREA OR ST. VITUS DANCE

A frequent sequela of distemper is chorea, which is characterized by a more or less pronounced and frequent twitching of a muscle or muscles. There is no known remedy for the condition. It does not impair the usefulness of a good dog for breeding, and having a litter of puppies often betters or cures chorea in the bitch. Chorea is considered a form of unsoundness and is penalized in the show ring. The condition generally becomes worse.

ECLAMPSIA OR WHELPING TETANY

Convulsions of bitches before, during, or shortly after their whelping are called eclampsia. It seldom occurs to a bitch receiving a sufficient amount of calcium and vitamin D in her diet during her pregnancy. The symptoms vary in their severity for nervousness and mild convulsions to severe attacks which may terminate in coma and death. The demands of the nursing litter for calcium frequently depletes the supply in the bitch's system.

Eclampsia can be controlled by the hypodermic administration of calcium gluconate. Its recurrence is prevented by the addition to the bitch's ration of readily utilized calcium and vitamin D.

RICKETS, OR RACHITIS

The failure of the bones of puppies to calcify normally is termed rickets, or more technically rachitis. Perhaps more otherwise excellent puppies are killed or ruined by rickets than by any other disease. It is essentially a disease of puppies, but the malformation of the skeleton produced by rickets persists through the life of the dog.

The symptoms of rickets include lethargy, arched neck, crouched stance, knobby and deformed joints, bowed legs, and flabby muscles. The changes characteristic of defective calcification in the puppy are most marked in the growth of the long bones of the leg, and at the cartilaginous junction of the ribs. In the more advanced stages of rickets the entire bone becomes soft and easily deformed or broken. The development of the teeth is also retarded.

Rickets results from a deficiency in the diet of calcium, phosphorus, or vitamin D. It may be prevented by the inclusion of sufficient amounts of those substances in the puppy's diet. It may also be cured, if not too far advanced, by the same means, although distortions in the skeleton that have already occurred are seldom rectified. The requirements of vitamin D to be artificially supplied are greater for puppies raised indoors and with limited exposure to sunlight or to sunlight filtered through window glass.

(It is possible to give a dog too much vitamin D, but very unlikely without deliberate intent.)

Adult dogs that have had rickets in puppyhood and whose recovery is complete may be bred from without fear of their transmission to their puppies of the malformations of their skeletons produced by the disease. The same imbalance or absence from their diet that produced rickets in the parent may produce it in the progeny, but the disease in such case is reproduced and not inherited.

The requirements of adult dogs for calcium, phosphorus, and vitamin D are much less than for puppies and young dogs, but a condition called osteomalacia, or late rickets, is sometimes seen in grown dogs as the result of the same kind of nutritional deficiency that causes rickets in puppies. In such cases a softening of the bones leads to lameness and deformity. The remedy is the same as in the rickets of puppyhood, namely the addition of calcium, phosphorus, and vitamin D to the diet. It is especially essential that bitches during pregnancy and lactation have included in their diets ample amounts of these elements, both for their own nutrition and for the adequate skeletal formations of their fetuses and the development of their puppies.

BLACKTONGUE

Blacktongue (the canine analogue of pellagra in the human) is no longer to be feared in dogs fed upon an adequate diet. For many years, it was a recognized scourge among dogs, and its cause and treatment were unknown. It is now known to be caused solely by the insufficiency in the ration of vitamin B complex and specifically by an insufficiency of nicotinic acid. (Nicotinic acid is vitamin B_2, formerly known as vitamin G.)

Blacktongue may require a considerable time for its full develop-

105

ment. It usually begins with a degree of lethargy, a lack of appetite for the kind of food the dog has been receiving, constipation, often with spells of vomiting, and particularly with a foul odor from the mouth. As the disease develops, the mucous membranes of the mouth, gums, and tongue grow red and become inflamed, with purple splotches of greater or lesser extent, especially upon the front part of the tongue, and with ulcers and pustules on the lips and the lining of the cheeks. Constipation may give way to diarrhea as the disease develops. Blacktongue is an insidious malady, since its development is so gradual.

This disease is unlikely to occur except among dogs whose owners are so unenlightened, careless, or stingy as to feed their dogs exclusively on a diet of cornmeal mush, salt pork, cowpeas, sweet potatoes, or other foodstuffs that are known to be responsible for the development of pellagra in mankind. Blacktongue is not infectious or contagious, although the same deficiency in the diet of dogs may produce the malady in all the inmates throughout a kennel.

Correct treatment involves no medication as such, but consists wholly in the alteration of the diet to include foods which are good sources of the vitamin B complex, including nicotinic acid; such food as the muscles of beef, mutton, or horse, dried yeast, wheat germ, milk, eggs, and especially fresh liver. As an emergency treatment, the hypodermic injection of nicotinic acid may be indicated. Local treatments of the mouth, its cleansing and disinfection, are usually included, although they will avail nothing without the alteration in the diet.

LEPTOSPIROSIS OR CANINE TYPHUS

Leptospirosis, often referred to as canine typhus, is believed to be identical with Weil's disease (infectious jaundice) in the human species. It is not to be confused with non-infectious jaundice in the dog, which is a mere obstruction in the bile duct which occurs in some liver and gastric disorders. Leptospirosis is a comparatively rare disease as yet, but its incidence is growing and it is becoming more widespread.

It is caused by either of two spirocheates, *Leptospira canicola* or *Leptospira icterohenorrhagiae*. These causative organisms are found in the feces or urine of infected rats, and the disease is transmitted to dogs by their ingestion of food fouled by those rodents. It is therefore wise in rat infested houses to keep all dog food in covered metal containers to which it is impossible for rats to gain access. It is also possible for an ill dog to transmit the infection to a well one, and, it is believed, to man. Such cases, however, are rare.

Symptoms of leptospirosis include a variable temperature, vomiting, loss of appetite, gastroenteritis, diarrhea, jaundice and depression. Analysis of blood and urine may be helpful toward diagnosis. The disease is one for immediate reference to the veterinarian whenever suspected.

Prognosis is not entirely favorable, especially if the disease is neglected in its earlier stages. Taken in its incipience, treatment with penicillin has produced excellent results, as has antileptospiral serum and vaccine.

Control measures include the extermination of rats in areas where the disease is known to exist, and the cleaning and disinfection of premises where infected dogs have been kept.

INFECTIOUS HEPATITIS

This is a virus disease attacking the liver. Apparently it is not the same virus that causes hepatitis in humans. Symptoms include an unusual thirst, loss of appetite, vomiting, diarrhea, pain causing the dog to moan, anemia and fever. The afflicted dog may try to hide.

The disease runs a fast course and is often fatal. A dog recovering from it may carry the virus in his urine for a long period, thus infecting other dogs months later.

Serum and vaccine are available to offer protection. A combination for distemper and hepatitis is now offered.

TURNED-IN OR TURNED-OUT EYELIDS

When the eyelid is inverted, or turned-in, it is technically termed entropion. When the eyelid is turned-out, it is referred to as extropion. Both conditions seem to be found in certain strains of dogs and are classified as being heritable. Both conditions may be corrected by competent surgery. It is possible to operate on such cases and have complete recovery without scar formation. However, cognizance should be taken of either defect in a dog to be used for breeding purposes.

CONJUNCTIVITIS OR INFLAMMATION OF THE EYE

Certain irritants, injuries or infections, and many febrile diseases, such as distemper, produce conjunctivitis, an inflammation of the membranes lining the lids of the dog's eyes. At first there is a slight reddening of the membranes and a watery discharge. As the condition progresses, the conjunctivae become more inflamed looking and the color darkens. The discharge changes consistency and color, becoming muco-purulent in character and yellow in color. The eyelids may be pasted shut and granulation of the lids may follow.

When eye infection persists for an extended period of time, the cornea sometimes becomes involved. Ulcers may develop, eventually penetrating the eyeball. When this happens, the condition becomes very painful and, even worse, often leads to the loss of vision.

Home treatment, to be used only until professional care may be had, consists of regular cleaning of the eye with a 2% boric acid solution and the application of one of the antibiotic eye ointments.

When anything happens to the dog's eye, it is always best to seek professional help and advice.

RABIES

This disease, caused by a virus, is transmissible to all warm blooded animals, and the dog seems to be the number one disseminator of the virus. However, outbreaks of rabies have been traced to wild animals—the wolf, coyote, or fox biting a dog which in turn bites people, other dogs, or other species of animals.

The virus, which is found in the saliva of the rabid animal, enters the body only through broken skin. This usually is brought about by biting and breaking the skin, or through licking an open cut on the skin. The disease manifests itself clinically in two distinct forms. One is called the "furious type" and the other the "dumb type." Both types are produced by the same strain of virus.

The disease works rather peculiarly on the dog's disposition and character. The kindly old dog may suddenly become ferocious; just the reverse may also occur, the mean, vicious dog becoming gentle and biddable. At first the infected dog wants to be near his master, wants to lick his hand or his boots; his appetite undergoes a sudden change, becoming voracious, and the animal will eat anything—stones, bits of wood, even metal. Soon there develops a sense of wanderlust, and the dog seems to wish to get as far away as possible from his owner.

In all rabid animals there is an accentuation of the defense mechanisms. In other words, the dog will bite, the cat will hiss and claw, the horse will bite and kick, and the cow will attack anything that moves.

An animal afflicted with rabies cannot swallow because there is usually a paralysis of the muscles of deglutinition. The animal, famished for a drink, tries to bite the water or whatever fluid he may be attempting to drink. The constant champing of the jaws causes the saliva to become mixed and churned with air, making it appear whipped and foamy. In the old days when a dog "frothed at the mouth," he was considered "mad." There is no doubt but what some uninfected dogs have been suspected of being rabid and shot to death simply because they exhibited these symptoms.

One of the early signs of rabies in the dog is the dropping of the lower jaw. This is a sign of rabies of the so-called "dumb type." The animal has a "faraway" look in his eyes, and his voice or bark has an odd pitch. Manifesting these symptoms, the dog is often taken to the clinic by the owner, who is sure the dog has a bone in the throat. The hind legs, and eventually the whole hindquarters, subsequently become paralyzed, and death ensues.

Many commonwealths have passed laws requiring that all dogs be vaccinated against rabies, and usually, a vaccination certificate must be presented before a dog license may be issued. The general enforcement of this law alone would go a long way toward the eradication of rabies.

Some will ask why a dog must be impounded as a biter when he has taken a little "nip" at someone and merely broken the skin—if this must be done, they cannot understand the "good" of the vaccination. But the vaccination does not give the dog the right to bite. Statistics show that rabies vaccination is effective in about 88% of the cases. All health authorities wish it were 100% effective, thus eliminating a good deal of worry from their minds. Because the vaccination is not 100% effective, we cannot take a chance on the vaccine alone. The animal must be impounded and under the daily supervision of a qualified observer, generally for a period of fourteen days. It is pretty well recognized that if the bite was provocated by rabies, the biting animal will develop clinical symptoms in that length of time; otherwise, he will be released as "clinically normal."

THE SPAYING OF BITCHES

The spaying operation, technically known as an ovariectomy, is the subject of a good deal of controversy. It is an operation that has its good and its bad points.

Spayed bitches cannot be entered in the show ring, and of course can never reproduce their kind. However, under certain circumstances, the operation is recommended by veterinarians. If the operation is to be performed, the bitch should preferably be six to eight months of age. At this age, she has pretty well reached the adolescent period; time enough has been allowed for the endocrine balance to become established and the secondary sex organs to develop.

Mechanical difficulties sometimes arise in the urinary systems of bitches that have been operated on at three or four months of age. In a very small percentage of the cases, loss of control of the sphincter muscles of the bladder is observed. But this can readily be corrected by an injection of the female hormone stilbestrol.

There are many erroneous ideas as to what may happen to the female if she is spayed. Some people argue that the disposition will be changed, that the timid dog may become ferocious, and, strangely enough, that the aggressive animal will become docile. Some breeders say that the spayed bitch will become fat, lazy, and lethargic. According to the records that have been kept on bitches following the spaying operation, such is not the case. It is unjust to accuse the spaying operation when really the dog's owner is at fault—he just feeds the dog too much.

110

THE CASTRATION OF DOGS

This operation consists of the complete removal of the testes. Ordinarily the operation is not encouraged. Circumstances may attenuate the judgment, however. Castration may be necessary to correct certain pathological conditions such as a tumor, chronic prostatitis, and types of perineal troubles. Promiscuous wetting is sometimes an excuse for desexing.

It must be remembered that as with the spayed bitch, the castrated dog is barred from the show ring.

ANAL GLANDS

On either side of the anus of the dog is situated an anal gland, which secretes a lubricant that better enables the dog to expel the contents of the rectum. These glands are subject to being clogged, and in them accumulates a fetid mass. This accumulation is not, strictly speaking, a disease—unless it becomes infected and purulent. Almost all dogs have it, and most of them are neglected without serious consequences. However, they are better if they are relieved. Their spirits improve, their eyes brighten, and even their coats gradually grow more lively if the putrid mass is occasionally squeezed out of the anus.

This is accomplished by seizing the tail with the left hand, encircling its base with the thumb and forefinger of the right hand, and pressing the anus firmly between thumb and finger. The process results in momentary pain to the dog and often causes him to flinch, which may be disregarded. A semi-liquid of vile odor is extruded from the anus. The operation should be repeated at intervals of from one week to one month, depending on the rapidity of glandular accumulation. No harm results from the frequency of such relief, although there may be no apparent results if the anal glands are kept free of their accumulations.

If this process of squeezing out of the glands is neglected, the glands sometimes become infected and surgery becomes necessary. This is seldom the case, but, if needful at all, it must be entrusted to a skillful veterinary surgeon.

METRITIS

Metritis is the acute or chronic inflammation of the uterus of the bitch and may result from any one of a number of things. Perhaps the most common factor, especially in eight- to twelve-year-old bitches, is pseudocyesis, or false pregnancy. Metritis often follows whelping; it may be the result of a retained placenta, or of infection of the uterus following the manual or instrument removal of a puppy.

The term pyometria is generally restricted to cases where the uterus is greatly enlarged and filled with pus. In most such cases surgery must be resorted to in order to effect a cure.

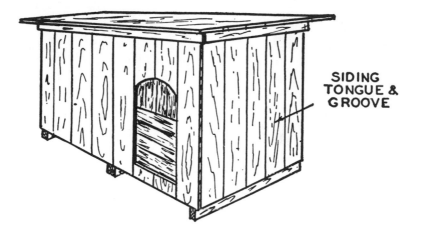

SIDING
TONGUE &
GROOVE

ASSEMBLED VIEW

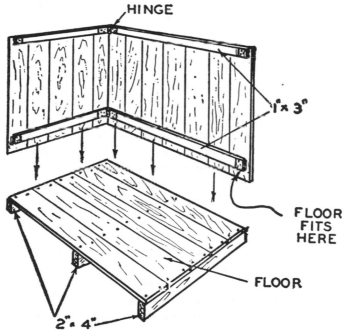

HINGE

1" x 3"

FLOOR
FITS
HERE

FLOOR

2" x 4"

Housing for Dogs

EVERY owner will have, and will have to solve, his own problems about providing his dog or dogs with quarters best suited to the dog's convenience. The special circumstances of each particular owner will determine what kind of home he will provide for his dogs. Here it is impossible to provide more than a few generalities upon the subject.

Little more need be said than that fit quarters for dogs must be secure, clean, dry, and warm. Consideration must be given to convenience in the care of kennel inmates by owners of a large number of dogs, but by the time one's activities enlarge to such proportions one will have formulated one's own concept of how best to house one's dogs. Here, advice will be predicated upon the maintenance of not more than three or four adult dogs with accommodations for an occasional litter of puppies.

First, let it be noted that dogs are not sensitive to aesthetic considerations in the place they are kept; they have no appreciation of the beauty of their surroundings. They do like soft beds of sufficient thickness to protect them from the coldness of the floors. These beds should be secluded and covered to conserve body heat. A box or crate of adequate size to permit the dog to lie full length in it will suffice. The cushion may be a burlap bag stuffed with shredded paper, *not straw, hay, or grass*. Paper is recommended, for its use will reduce the possibility of the dog's developing skin trouble.

114

Most dogs are allergic to fungi found on vegetative matter such as straw, hay, and grass. Wood shavings and excelsior may be used with impunity.

The kennel should be light, except for a retiring place; if sunshine is available at least part of the day, so much the better. Boxes in a shed or garage with secure wire runs to which the dogs have ready access suffice very well, are very inexpensive, and are easy to plan and to arrange. The runs should be made of wire fencing strong enough that the dogs are unable to tear it with their teeth and high enough that the dogs are unable to jump or climb over it. In-turning flanges of wire netting at the tops of the fences tend to obviate jumping. Boards, rocks, or cement buried around the fences forestall burrowing to freedom.

These pens need not be large, if the dogs are given frequent respites from their captivity and an opportunity to obtain needed exercise. However, they should be large enough to relieve them of the aspect of cages. Concrete floors for such pens are admittedly easy to keep clean and sanitary. However, they have no resilience, and the feet of dogs confined for long periods on concrete floors are prone to spread and their shoulders to loosen. A further objection to concrete is that it grows hot in the summer sunshine and is very cold in winter. If it is used for flooring at all, a low platform of wood, large enough to enable the dogs to sprawl out on it full length, should be provided in each pen.

A well drained soil is to be preferred to concrete, if it is available; but it must be dug out to the depth of three inches and renewed occasionally, if it is used. Otherwise, the accumulation of urine will make it sour and offensive. Agricultural limestone, applied monthly and liberally, will "sweeten" the soil.

Gates, hinges, latches, and other hardware must be trustworthy. The purpose of such quarters is to confine the dogs and to keep them from running at large; unless they serve such a purpose they are useless. One wants to know when one puts a dog in his kennel, the dog will be there when one returns. An improvised kennel of old chicken wire will not suffice for one never knows whether it will hold one's dogs or not.

Frequently two friendly bitches may be housed together, or a dog housed with a bitch. Unless one is sure of male friendships, it is seldom safe to house two adult male dogs together. It is better, if possible, to provide a separate kennel for each mature dog. But, if the dogs can be housed side by side with only a wire fence between them, they can have companionship without rancor. Night barking can be controlled by confining the dogs indoors or by shutting them up in their boxes.

Adult dogs require artificial heat in only the coldest of climates, if they are provided with tight boxes placed under shelter. Puppies need heat in cold weather up until weaning time, and even thereafter if they are not permitted to sleep together. Snuggled together in a tight box with shredded paper, they can withstand much cold without discomfort. All dogs in winter without artificial heat should have an increase of their rations—especially as pertains to fat content.

Whatever artificial heat is provided for dogs should be safe, foolproof, and dog-proof. Caution should be exercised that electric wiring is not exposed, that stoves cannot be tipped over, and that it is impossible for sparks from them to ignite the premises. Many fires in kennels, the results of defective heating apparatus or careless handling of it, have brought about the deaths of the inmates. It is because of them that this seemingly unnecessary warning is given.

No better place for a dog to live can be found than the home of its owner, sharing even his bed if permitted. So is the dog happiest. There is a limit, however, to the number of dogs that can be tolerated in the house. The keeper of a small kennel can be expected to alternate his favorite dogs in his own house, thus giving them a respite to confinement in a kennel. Provision must be made for a place of exercise and relief at frequent intervals for dogs kept in the house. An enclosed dooryard will serve such a purpose, or the dog may be exercised on a lead with as much benefit to the owner as to the dog.

That the quarters of the dog shall be dry is even more important than that they shall be warm. A damp, drafty kennel is the cause of much kennel disease and indisposition. It is harmless to permit a dog to go out into inclement weather of his own choice, if he is provided with a sheltered bed to which he may retire to dry himself.

By cleanness, sanitation is meant—freedom from vermin and bacteria. A little coat of dust or a degree of disorder does not discommode the dog or impair his welfare, but the best dog keepers are orderly persons. They at least do not permit bedding and old

116

bones to accumulate in a dog's bed, and they take the trouble to spray with antiseptic or wash with soap and water their dog's house at frequent intervals. The feces in the kennel runs should be picked up and destroyed at least once, and better twice, daily. Persistent filth in kennels can be counted on as a source of illness sooner or later. This warning appears superfluous, but it isn't; the number of ailing dogs kept in dirty, unsanitary kennels is amazing. It is one of the axioms of keeping dogs that their quarters must be sanitary or disease is sure to ensue.

GOOD DOG KEEPING PRACTICES

Pride of ownership is greatly enhanced when the owner takes care to maintain his dog in the best possible condition at all times. And meticulous grooming not only will make the dog look better but also will make him feel better. As part of the regular, daily routine, the grooming of the dog will prove neither arduous nor time consuming; it will also obviate the necessity for indulging in a rigorous program designed to correct the unkempt state in which too many owners permit their dogs to appear. Certainly, spending a few minutes each day will be well worth while, for the result will be a healthier, happier, and more desirable canine companion.

THAT DOGGY ODOR

Many persons are disgusted to the point of refusal to keep a dog by what they fancy is a "doggy odor." Of course, almost everything has a characteristic odor—everyone is familiar with the smell of the rose. No one would want the dog to smell like a rose, and, conversely, the world wouldn't like it very well if the rose smelled doggy. The dog must emit a certain amount of characteristic odor or he wouldn't be a dog. That seems to be his God-given grant. However, when the odor becomes too strong and obnoxious, then it is time to look for the reason. In most cases it is the result of clogged anal glands. If this be the case, all one must do to rid the pet of his odor is to express the contents of these glands and apply to the anal region a little soap and water.

If the odor is one of putrefaction, look to his mouth for the trouble. The teeth may need scaling, or a diseased root of some one or two teeth that need to be treated may be the source of the odor. In some dogs there is a fold or a crease in the lower lip near the lower canine tooth, and this may need attention. This spot is favored by fungi that cause considerable damage to the part. The smell here is somewhat akin to the odor of human feet that have been attacked by the fungus of athlete's foot.

The odor may be coming from the coat if the dog is heavily infested with fleas or lice. Too, dogs seem to enjoy the odor of dead fish and often roll on a foul smelling fish that has been cast up on the beach. The dog with a bad case of otitis can fairly "drive you out of the room" with this peculiar odor. Obviously, the way to rid the dog of odor is to find from whence it comes and then take steps to eliminate it. Some dogs have a tendency toward excessive flatulence (gas). These animals should have a complete change of diet and with the reducing of the carbohydrate content, a teaspoon of granular charcoal should be added to each feeding.

BATHING THE DOG

There is little to say about giving a bath to a dog, except that he shall be placed in a tub of warm (not hot) water and thoroughly scrubbed. He may, like a spoiled child, object to the ordeal, but if handled gently and firmly he will submit to what he knows to be inevitable.

The water must be only tepid, so as not to shock or chill the dog. A bland, unmedicated soap is best, for such soaps do not irritate the skin or dry out the hair. Even better than soap is one of the powdered detergents marketed especially for this purpose. They rinse away better and more easily than soap and do not leave the coat gummy or sticky.

It is best to begin with the face, which should be thoroughly and briskly washed with a cloth. Care should be taken that the cleaning solvent does not get into the dog's eyes, not because of the likelihood of causing permanent harm, but because such an experience is unpleasant to the dog and prone to prejudice him against future baths. The interior of the ear canals should be thoroughly cleansed until they not only look clean but also until no unpleasant odor comes from them. The head may then be rinsed and dried before proceeding to the body. Especial attention should be given to the drying of the ears, inside and outside. Many ear infections arise from failure to dry the canals completely.

With the head bathed and the surplus water removed from that part, the body must be soaked thoroughly with water, either with a hose or by dipping the water from the bath and pouring it over the dog's back until he is totally wetted. Thereafter, the soap or detergent should be applied and rubbed until it lathers freely. A stiff brush is useful in penetrating the coat and cleansing the skin. It is not sufficient to wash only the back and sides—the belly, neck, legs, feet, and tail must all be scrubbed thoroughly.

If the dog is very dirty, it may be well to rinse him lightly and repeat the soaping process and scrub again. Thereafter, the dog must be rinsed with warm (tepid) water until all suds and soil come away. If a bath spray is available, the rinsing is an easy matter. If the dog must be rinsed in standing water, it will be needful to renew it two or three times.

When he is thoroughly rinsed, it is well to remove such surplus water as may be squeezed with the hand, after which he is enveloped with a turkish towel, lifted from the tub, and rubbed until he is dry. This will probably require two or three dry towels. In the process of drying the dog, it is well to return again and again to the interior of the ears.

THE DOG'S TEETH

The dog, like the human being, has two successive sets of teeth, the so-called milk teeth or baby teeth, which are shed and replaced later by the permanent teeth. The temporary teeth, which begin to emerge when the puppy is two and a half to three weeks of age, offer no difficulty. The full set of milk teeth (consisting usually of six incisors and two canines in each jaw, with four molars in the upper jaw and six molars in the lower jaw) is completed usually just before weaning time. Except for some obvious malformation, the milk teeth may be ignored and forgotten about.

At about the fourth month the baby teeth are shed and gradually replaced by the permanent teeth. This shedding and replacement process may consume some three or four months. This is about the most critical period of the dog's life—his adolescence. Some constitutionally vigorous dogs go through their teething easily, with no seeming awareness that the change is taking place. Others, less vigorous, may suffer from soreness of the gums, go off in flesh, and require pampering. While they are teething, puppies should be particularly protected from exposure to infectious diseases and should be fed on nutritious foods, especially meat and milk.

The permanent teeth normally consist of 42—six incisors and two canines (fangs) in each jaw, with twelve molars in the upper jaw and fourteen in the lower jaw. Occasionally the front molars fail to emerge; this deficiency is considered by most judges to be only a minor fault, if the absence is noticed at all.

Dentition is a heritable factor in the dog, and some dogs have soft, brittle and defective permanent teeth, no matter how excellent the diet and the care given them. The teeth of those dogs which are predisposed to have excellent sound ones, however, can be ruined by an inferior diet prior to and during the period of their eruption. At this time, for the teeth to develop properly, a dog must have an adequate supply of calcium phosphate and vitamin D, besides all the protein he can consume.

Often the permanent teeth emerge before the shedding of the milk teeth, in which case the dog may have parts of both sets at the same time. The milk teeth will eventually drop out, but as long as they remain they may deflect or displace the second teeth in the process of their growth. The incisors are the teeth in which a malformation may result from the late dropping of the baby teeth. When it is realized just how important a correct "bite" may be deemed in the show ring, the hazards of permitting the baby teeth to deflect the permanent set will be understood.

The baby teeth in such a case must be dislodged and removed. The roots of the baby teeth are resorbed in the gums, and the teeth can usually be extracted by firm pressure of thumb and finger, although it may be necessary to employ forceps or to take the puppy to the veterinarian.

The permanent teeth of the puppy are usually somewhat overshot, by which is meant that the upper incisors protrude over and do not play upon the lower incisors. Maturity may be trusted to remedy this apparent defect unless it is too pronounced.

An undershot mouth in a puppy, on the other hand, tends to grow worse as the dog matures. Whether or not it has been caused by the displacement of the permanent teeth by the persistence of

120

the milk teeth, it can sometimes be remedied (or at least bettered) by frequent hard pressure of the thumb on the lower jaw, forcing the lower teeth backward to meet the upper ones. Braces on dog teeth have seldom proved efficacious, but pressure and massage are worth trying on the bad mouth of an otherwise excellent puppy.

High and persistent fevers, especially from the fourth to the ninth month, sometimes result in discolored, pitted, and defective teeth, commonly called "distemper teeth." They often result from maladies other than distemper. There is little that can be done for them. They are unpleasant to see and are subject to penalty in the show ring, but are serviceable to the dog. Distemper teeth are not in themselves heritable, but the predisposition for their development appears to be. At least, at the teething age, the offspring from distemper toothed ancestors seem to be especially prone to fevers which impair their dentition.

Older dogs, especially those fed largely upon carbohydrates, tend to accumulate more or less tartar upon their teeth. The tartar generally starts at the gum line on the molars and extends gradually to the cusp. To rectify this condition, the dog's teeth should be scaled by a veterinarian.

The cleanliness of a dog's mouth may be brought about and the formation of tartar discouraged by the scouring of the teeth with a moist cloth dipped in a mixture of equal parts of table salt and baking soda.

A large bone given the dog to chew on or play with tends to prevent tartar from forming on the teeth. If tartar is present, the chewing and gnawing on the bone will help to remove the deposit mechanically. A bone given to puppies will act as a teething ring and aid in the cutting of the permanent teeth. So will beef hide strips you can buy in pet shops.

CARE OF THE NAILS

The nails of the dog should be kept shortened and blunted right down to the quick—never into the quick. If this is not done, the toes may spread and the foot may splay into a veritable pancake. Some dogs have naturally flat feet, which they have inherited. No pretense is made that the shortening of the nails of such a foot will obviate the fault entirely and make the foot beautiful or serviceable.

It will only improve the appearance and make the best of an obvious fault. Short nails do, however, emphasize the excellence of a good foot.

Some dogs keep their nails short by digging and friction. Their nails require little attention, but it is a rare dog whose foot cannot be bettered by artificially shortening the nails.

Nail clippers are available, made especially for the purpose. After using them, the sides of the nail should be filed away as much as is possible without touching the quick. Carefully done, it causes the dog no discomfort. But, once the quick of a dog's nail has been injured, he may forever afterward resent and fight having his feet treated or even having them examined.

The obvious horn of the nail can be removed, after which the quick will recede to permit the removal of more horn the following week. This process may be kept up until the nail is as short and blunt as it can be made, after which nails will need attention only at intervals of six weeks or two months.

Some persons clip the nails right back to the toes in one fell swoop, disregarding injury to the quick and pain of the dog. The nails bleed and the dog limps for a day or two, but infection seldom develops. Such a procedure should not be undertaken without a general anesthetic. If an anesthetic is used, this forthright method does not prejudice the dog against having his feet handled.

NAIL TRIMMING
ILLUSTRATED

The method here illustrated is to take a sharp file and stroke the nail downwards in the direction of the arrow, as in Figure 24, until it assumes the shape in Figure 25, the shaded portion being the part removed, a three-cornered file should then be used on the underside just missing the quick, as in Figure 26, and the operation is then complete, the dog running about quickly wears the nail to the proper shape.

Care for
the Old Dog

First, how old is old, in a dog? Some breeds live longer than others, as a general rule. The only regularity about dog ages at death is their irregularity breed to breed and dog to dog.

The dog owner can best determine senility in his canine friend by the dog's appearance and behavior. Old dogs "slow down" much as humans do. The stairs are a little steeper, the breath a little shorter, the eye dimmer, the hearing usually a little harder.

As prevention is always better than cure, a dog's life may be happily and healthfully extended if certain precautionary steps are taken. As the aging process becomes quite evident, the owner should become more considerate of his dog's weaknesses, procrastinations and lapses. A softer, drier, warmer bed may be advisable; a foam rubber mattress will be appreciated. If a kennel dog has been able to endure record-breaking hot or cold, torrential or desert-dry days, he may in his old age appreciate spending his nights at least in a warm, comfy human house. And if the weather outside is frightful during the day, he should—for minimum comfort and safety—be brought inside before pneumonia sets in.

The old dog should NOT be required or expected to chase a ball, or a pheasant, or one of his species of different sex. The old bitch should not continue motherhood.

If many teeth are gone or going, foods should be softer. The diet should be blander—delete sweet or spicy or heavy tidbits—and there should be less of it, usually. The older dog needs less fat, less carbohydrate and less minerals unless disease and convalescence dictate otherwise. DON'T PERMIT AN OLD DOG TO GET FAT! It's cruel. The special diet known as PD or KD may be in order, if the dog has dietary troubles or a disease concomitant with old age. The veterinarian should be asked about PD or KD diets. Vitamin B-12 and other vitamin reinforcements may help.

The dog diseases of old age parallel many of the human illnesses. Senior male dogs suffer from prostate trouble, kidney disease and cancer. Senior bitches suffer from metritis and cancer. Both sexes suffer blindness, deafness and paralysis. Dogs suffer from heart disease; I know one old dog that is living an especially happy old age through the courtesy of digitalis. If the symptoms of any disease manifest themselves in an old dog the veterinarian MUST be consulted.

Many dog owners are selfish about old dogs. In their reluctance to lose faithful friends, they try to keep their canine companions alive in terminal illnesses, such as galloping cancer. If the veterinarian holds little or no promise for recovery of a pet from an illness associated with old age, or if the pet suffers, the kindest act the owner can perform is to request euthanasia. In this sad event, the kindest step the owner may take in *his* interest is to acquire a puppy or young dog of the same breed immediately. Puppies have a wonderful way of absorbing grief!

Glossary of Dog Terms

Achilles tendon: The large tendon attaching the muscle of the calf in the second thigh to the bone below the hock; the hamstring.

A.K.C.: The American Kennel Club.

Albino: An animal having a congenital deficiency of pigment in the skin, hair, and eyes.

American Kennel Club: A federation of member show-giving and specialty clubs which maintains a stud book, and formulates and enforces rules under which dog shows and other canine activities in the United States are conducted. Its address is 51 Madison Ave., New York, N. Y. 10010.

Angulation: The angles of the bony structure at the joints, particularly of the shoulder with the upper arm (front angulation), or the angles at the stifle and the hock (rear angulation).

Anus: The posterior opening of the alimentary canal through which the feces are discharged.

Apple head: A rounded or domed skull.

Balance: A nice adjustment of the parts one to another; no part too big or too small for the whole organism; symmetry.

Barrel: The ribs and body.

Bitch: The female of the dog species.

Blaze: A white line or marking extending from the top of the skull (often from the occiput), between the eyes, and over the muzzle.

Brisket: The breast or lower part of the chest in front of and between the forelegs, sometimes including the part extending back some distance behind the forelegs.

Burr: The visible, irregular inside formation of the ear.

Butterfly nose: A nose spotted or speckled with flesh color.

Canine: (Noun) Any animal of the family *Canidae*, including dogs, wolves, jackals, and foxes.

(Adjective) Of or pertaining to such animals; having the nature and qualities of a dog.

Canine tooth: The long tooth next behind the incisors in each side of each jaw; the fang.

Castrate: (Verb) Surgically to remove the gonads of either sex, usually said of the testes of the male.

Character: A combination of points of appearance, behavior, and disposition

125

contributing to the whole dog and distinctive of the individual dog or of its particular breed.

Cheeky: Having rounded muscular padding on sides of the skull.

Chiseled: (Said of the muzzle) modeled or delicately cut away in front of the eyes to conform to breed type.

Chops: The mouth, jaws, lips, and cushion.

Close-coupled: Short in the loins.

Cobby: Stout, stocky, short-bodied; compactly made; like a cob (horse).

Coupling: The part of the body joining the hindquarters to the parts of the body in front; the loin; the flank.

Cowhocks: Hocks turned inward and converging like the presumed hocks of a cow.

Croup: The rear of the back above the hind limbs; the line from the pelvis to the set-on of the tail.

Cryptorchid: A male animal in which the testicles are not externally apparent, having failed to descend normally, not to be confused with a castrated dog.

Dentition: The number, kind, form, and arrangement of the teeth.

Dewclaws: Additional toes on the inside of the leg above the foot; the ones on the rear legs usually removed in puppyhood in most breeds.

Dewlap: The pendulous fold of skin under the neck.

Distemper teeth: The discolored and pitted teeth which result from some febrile disease.

Down in (or on) pastern: With forelegs more or less bent at the pastern joint.

Dry: Free from surplus skin or flesh about mouth, lips, or throat.

Dudley nose: A brown or flesh-colored nose, usually accompanied by eye-rims of the same shade and light eyes.

Ewe-neck: A thin sheep-like neck, having insufficient, faulty, or concave arch.

Expression: The combination of various features of the head and face, particularly the size, shape, placement and color of eyes, to produce a certain impression, the outlook.

Femur: The heavy bone of the true thigh.

Fetlock or Fetlock joint: The joint between the pastern and the lower arm; sometimes called the "knee," although it does not correspond to the human knee.

Fiddle front: A crooked front with bandy legs, out at elbow, converging at pastern joints, and turned out pasterns and feet, with or without bent bones of forearms.

Flews: The chops; pendulous lateral parts of the upper lips.

Forearm: The part of the front leg between the elbow and pastern.

Front: The entire aspect of a dog, except the head, when seen from the front; the forehand.

Guard hairs: The longer, smoother, stiffer hairs which grow through the undercoat and normally conceal it.

Hackney action: The high lifting of the front feet, like that of a Hackney horse, a waste of effort.

Hare-foot: A long, narrow, and close-toed foot, like that of the hare or rabbit.

Haw: The third eyelid, or nictitating membrane, especially when inflamed.

Height: The vertical distance from withers at top of shoulder blades to floor.

Hock: The lower joint in the hind leg, corresponding to the human ankle; sometimes, incorrectly, the part of the hind leg, from the hock joint to the foot.

Humerus: The bone of the upper arm.

Incisors: The teeth adapted for cutting; specifically, the six small front teeth in each jaw between the canines or fangs.

126

Knuckling over: Projecting or bulging forward of the front legs at the pastern joint; incorrectly called knuckle knees.

Leather: Pendant ears.

Lippy: With lips longer or fuller than desirable in the breed under consideration.

Loaded: Padded with superfluous muscle (said of such shoulders).

Loins: That part on either side of the spinal column between the hipbone and the false ribs.

Molar tooth: A rear, cheek tooth adapted for grinding food.

Monorchid: A male animal having but one testicle in the scrotum; monorchids may be potent and fertile.

Muzzle: The part of the face in front of the eyes.

Nictitating membrane: A thin membrane at the inner angle of the eye or beneath the lower lid, capable of being drawn across the eyeball. This membrane is frequently surgically excised in some breeds to improve the expression.

Occiput or occiputal protuberance: The bony knob at the top of the skull between the ears.

Occlusion: The bringing together of the opposing surfaces of the two jaws; the relation between those surfaces when in contact.

Olfactory: Of or pertaining to the sense of smell.

Out at elbow: With elbows turned outward from body due to faulty joint and front formation, usually accompanied by pigeon-toes; loose-fronted.

Out at shoulder: With shoulder blades loosely attached to the body, leaving the shoulders jutting out in relief and increasing the breadth of the front.

Overshot: Having the lower jaw so short that the upper and lower incisors fail to meet; pig-jawed.

Pace: A gait in which the legs move in lateral pairs, the animal supported alternatively by the right and left legs.

Pad: The cushion-like, tough sole of the foot.

Pastern: That part of the foreleg between the fetlock or pastern joint and the foot; sometimes incorrectly used for pastern joint or fetlock.

Period of gestation: The duration of pregnancy, about 63 days in the dog.

Puppy: Technically, a dog under a year in age.

Quarters: The two hind legs taken together.

Roach-back: An arched or convex spine, the curvature rising gently behind the withers and carrying over the loins; wheel-back.

Roman nose: The convex curved top line of the muzzle.

Scapula: The shoulder blade.

Scissors bite: A bite in which the incisors of the upper jaw just overlap and play upon those of the lower jaw.

Slab sides: Flat sides with insufficient spring of ribs.

Snipey: Snipe-nosed, said of a muzzle too sharply pointed, narrow, or weak.

Spay: To render a bitch sterile by the surgical removal of her ovaries; to castrate a bitch.

Specialty club: An organization to sponsor and forward the interests of a single breed.

Specialty show: A dog show confined to a single breed.

Spring: The roundness of ribs.

Stifle or stifle joint: The joint next above the hock, and near the flank, in the hind leg; the joint corresponding to the knee in man.

Stop: The depression or step between the forehead and the muzzle between the eyes.

Straight hocks: Hocks lacking bend or angulation.

127

Straight shoulders: Shoulder formation with blades too upright, with angle greater than 90° with bone of upper arm.

Substance: Strength of skeleton, and weight of solid musculature.

Sway-back: A spine with sagging, concave curvature from withers to pelvis.

Thorax: The part of the body between the neck and the abdomen, and supported by the ribs and sternum.

Throaty: Possessing a superfluous amount of skin under the throat.

Undercoat: A growth of short, fine hair, or pile, partly or entirely concealed by the coarser top coat which grows through it.

Undershot: Having the lower incisor teeth projecting beyond the upper ones when the mouth is closed; the opposite to overshot; prognathous; underhung.

Upper arm: The part of the dog between the elbow and point of shoulder.

Weaving: Crossing the front legs one over the other in action.

Withers: The part between the shoulder bones at the base of the neck; the point from which the height of a dog is usually measured.

(End of Part II. Please see Contents page for total number of pages in book.)